The Politics of Disenfranchisement

The Politics of Disenfranchisement

★

Why Is It So Hard to Vote in America?

Richard K. Scher

M.E.Sharpe
Armonk, New York
London, England

For Aida

Library of Congress Cataloging-in-Publication Data

Scher, Richard K.
The politics of disenfranchisement : why is it so hard to vote in America?
/ by Richard K. Scher.
    p. cm.
Includes index.
ISBN 978–0-7656–2735–3 (cloth : alk. paper)—ISBN 978-0-7656-2736-0 (pbk. : alk. paper)
1. Voting—United States. 2. Political participation—United States. I. Title.

JK1976S355 2010
324.60973—dc22   2010019784

Printed in the United States of America

The paper used in this publication meets the minimum requirements of
American National Standard for Information Sciences
Permanence of Paper for Printed Library Materials,
ANSI Z 39.48-1984.

∞

IBT (c)   10   9   8   7   6   5   4   3   2   1
IBT (p)   10   9   8   7   6   5   4   3   2   1

Contents

Preface

Why This Book?

Like many other book projects, this one began as something else.

During the aftermath of the 2000 presidential election in Florida, my telephones rang incessantly. It was always reporters and commentators and pundits, from all parts of the United States and around the world, wanting to know what had happened, and why, and what would happen. I stopped counting at 137 interviews, and that was a mere two weeks after the election, several days before Thanksgiving. The phone calls did not end until after the Electoral College met to hand the presidency to George W. Bush.

The subtext of virtually every interview was a variant on: how could Florida make such a mess of things? Didn't people in Florida know how to count? What's going on down there? I thought, while all of this post hoc activity was occupying and indeed consuming me, I would write a book on the Florida fiasco.

But as more dust settled and time passed, I was able to step back and think about what was fundamental and what was sideshow in the whole business; I realized that what happened in Florida was really just the tip of a vast iceberg. In fact, with few exceptions it could have occurred in other states as well (as the 2004 presidential election in Ohio and the 2008 Minnesota U.S. Senate race demonstrated). I began to see that our electoral system was seriously flawed, even sick. We were singularly unprepared to deal with elections whose results were nanoscopically close. More fundamentally, I realized that much of what lay at the heart of the disputes over the Florida results was caused by the clumsy, antediluvian, unnecessarily complicated, nontransparent, often arbitrary, and generally unfair ways we vote in this country, from the question of who is a legitimate voter to how ballots are cast to their tallying and recounting.

It also rapidly became clear that there were serious and nasty racial components to the difficulties: black voters were disenfranchised at much greater rates and numbers than whites, and black ballots were disqualified and tossed out—or not even counted—at rates and numbers greater than for whites. Further investigations showed that other peoples of color also were experiencing difficulties voting, including Hispanics, Asians, and others. Whites generally had fewer problems than these other population groups (unless they were also part of disenfranchised groups, to be discussed in chapter 3), but poor whites living in rural areas or on the wrong side of the tracks had more trouble than their suburban middle-class counterparts.

I began to gather materials on how we vote in America, and I was thunderstruck by how much of what we do in our electoral system was designed to make voting difficult, if not impossible, for significant portions of the population. It seemed that we were in the business of disenfranchising people rather than encouraging them to vote (as our elementary school teachers had repeatedly urged, because it is our civic duty and privilege). Nor did we do much to facilitate their ability to do so; indeed, we often did the opposite.

So I abandoned the idea of writing a book on the Florida presidential election of 2000 in favor of a more fundamental, broadly based book that asks, "Why is it so hard to vote in America?" This question seemed to capture what I wanted to write about: Americans put so many structural and procedural barriers in front of potential voters that many are discouraged from even trying to cast a ballot, and too many of those who want to do so cannot. Further, as a polity we bend over backward, through laws, rules, administrative decisions, customs, and practices, to ensure that certain population groups either cannot vote or can do so only with the greatest difficulty, hence, a pervasive theme in the book is that of "disenfranchisement as public policy."

To be frank, even as a professional political scientist I had not paid much attention to the mechanics of voting, much less the policies involved—or their consequences. I learned that I am not alone in that omission. It just seemed that voting was something we did when elections rolled around, and we scheduled election-day activity around having to find time to head to the polls. True, at times the process of voting did seem inconvenient. In the 1976 presidential election I waited more than four hours on line to vote, as the old-style, lever-operated voting machines in my precinct had broken down and only one was usable. I voted well after 10 P.M., having been informed by others waiting who had portable radios that Jimmy Carter had already won. But like many others, I ascribed these difficulties to bad luck, chance, and the cost of doing my civic duty. It never occurred to me that I was witnessing and actually participating in a deep systemic weakness in the mechanics of our electoral system.

On the other hand, I was deeply interested in the *right* to vote. As a college student I was an active sympathizer of Dr. Martin Luther King, Jr., the Southern Christian Leadership Conference, the Student Nonviolent Coordinating Committee, the Congress of Racial Equality (CORE), and all of the other courageous participants in the civil rights movement who demanded the right to vote as well as other civil rights. But then, in March 1965, President Lyndon Johnson signed the Voting Rights Act into law. Didn't this solve the problem? Couldn't everybody now vote, regardless of race or color or ethnicity or religion?

The answer, of course, was a definite "No!" As a young political scientist, I began to orient my scholarship toward Florida and Southern politics, and those efforts convinced me that while the Voting Rights Act had solved some problems for Southern blacks and poor whites, it did not resolve them all. V.O. Key, the dean of students of Southern politics, had shown how deeply ingrained in the political system racism was, and how intransigent white politicians and just regular Southern white folks could be on the issue of black enfranchisement. Other scholars and writers—Earl and Merle Black, Alexander Lamis, Steven Lawson, the participants in the biennial Citadel Symposia on Southern Politics, Robert Sherrill, Chet Fuller, Harry Golden, Willie Morris, and many others—seemed to underscore the same conclusion that I had reached: the Voting Rights Act was not a complete solution to Southern black disenfranchisement. More blacks and poor whites could vote in the South than ever before, but there were ongoing reports about Southern county officials who were dragging their feet. In spite of federal monitors and section 5 of the Voting Rights Act, too many potential voters in the region were still being denied the franchise.

As the 1970s wore on, it became obvious that populations in other parts of the country were also having trouble registering and voting. Puerto Ricans in New York City, Hispanics in other parts of the country, Asian Americans out West, Native Americans in Alaska and elsewhere—none of these groups were included under the Voting Rights Act, and in too many instances they were being denied the right to vote. In 1982, when the Voting Rights Act came up for renewal, it was expanded to a significant degree to cover some of these disenfranchised populations. It also made a modest beginning toward an attack on the ongoing gerrymandering of districts where African Americans, other groups of color, and political minorities resided—gerrymandering carried out to such a degree that from a functional standpoint, these groups' votes didn't count; indeed, they were rendered meaningless.

During the late 1980s and 1990s, much of the "action" on voting rights switched to federal courts, with judges and justices seeking to determine which population groups could be covered by the Voting Rights Act (that is, given federal protection); what coverage meant; whether there was an affirmative duty to help minority groups elect their "candidate(s) of choice" through the redrawing of legislative districts, and, if so, how far that duty extended; how section 5 was to be used; and many other important questions. Decisions of the U.S. Supreme Court such as *Mobile v. Bolden, Thornburg v. Gingles, Davis v. Bandemer, Shaw v. Reno, Miller v. Johnson,* and others clarified some questions, but muddied others. And then, of course, the 2000 presidential election exploded onto the political and legal scene, demonstrating, among other things, how voters in Florida (especially but not only African Americans), and to a lesser degree in some other states, could be manipulated by state and local officials and denied the franchise, in spite of Voting Rights Act protections.

But all of this was at the macro level. Events at the micro level dramatized and brought into relief the systemic barriers that were placed in front of individuals and groups wanting to vote. What happened is too well known to require more than a mention here: individual blacks seeking to register were intimidated, harassed, tortured, terrorized, and in too many instances murdered for seeking to exercise a right that was legitimately theirs. The Birmingham Civil Rights Memorial, a project of the Southern Poverty Law Center, pays tribute to those who gave their lives in the pursuit of voting rights. (The memorial can be viewed online at www. splcenter.org/crm/memorial.jsp.) But there were many others who were not killed but were beaten or economically and psychologically attacked just because they wanted to vote.

Even after white Southerners stopped intimidating and killing their black neighbors who sought to vote, blacks and other peoples of color continued to have problems casting ballots. The new millennium brought reports in 2000, 2004, and 2008 of minority voters whose names somehow, without any justification, appeared on lists of felons (as in Florida), or who found when arriving at their polling stations (as in Cleveland, Ohio) that there were not enough voting machines to accommodate them, so that they could not cast ballots. In 2008 in Mississippi and Louisiana, thousands found that they had been illegally purged from voter lists. During the run-up to the presidential election, the U.S. Supreme Court had to order the Ohio Republican Party to stop challenging (that is, harassing) black voters who showed up for early voting, because of minor discrepancies between the rendering of their names on ID cards and master lists.

All of this will be discussed in subsequent chapters. The point is that, as more of these incidents became media stories, and the more that organizations such as People for the American Way, the American Civil Liberties Union, the United States Commission on Civil Rights, the Brennan Center for Justice, and the Lawyers' Committee for Civil Rights Under Law documented ongoing difficulties that African Americans and others faced in trying to vote, the more I became convinced that a broad-based examination of how we vote in America was needed. It seemed that our electoral system was as much geared to keeping some people away from the polls as welcoming others.

Indeed, the more I learned about barriers to voting, the more professionally interested and curious I became. The issue was not just the *right* to vote, central as that is; of equal importance were the mechanics of voting, the rules and laws and customs and attitudes and state and local administrative decisions that determined which people could vote, how they did so, how their ballots were treated, and whether or not they would be counted. Much of this seemed grossly arbitrary, capricious, and unreasonable, and always unfair. How could this happen in America? Our elementary school teachers drummed into our heads the importance of voting; then why do we take pains to make sure that only some Americans can do so? The idea of the universal franchise in this country now seemed to me not just a lie, but a hypocrisy. So much for equal protection of the laws. So much for the right to vote. So much for too much of the promise that American democracy holds out to those who live here and those who immigrate here, especially if they are people of color or are otherwise somehow marginalized.

What forces are operating behind the constraints we put on the reach of the franchise? The short answer, to be expanded in subsequent chapters, is that elections are too important to be left to the voters. The difference between winning and losing, from the presidency down to the most obscure local office, can be (but is not always) substantial. Important political and policy questions may depend on who wins and who loses an election: Will we go to war? Who is going to be the next Supreme Court nominee? Will environmental regulations be tightened or loosened? Will police response times and other public services be better for one side of town than for the other? And money—sometimes considerable sums of money—may be at stake in an election outcome. Who will decide which companies administer recently privatized state Medicaid contracts? How will the Department of Agriculture direct farm subsidies? Will a security company be hired to serve as our surrogate army in some distant land? Which developer will get a zoning variance for a shopping center? Who will get to award the contract to construct a new civic center or build a bridge?

When the consequences of winning or losing elections can be substantial, the most interested parties don't want a level playing field. They want it tilted in their favor. And so they seek to intervene in how elections are conducted, from registering voters, to determining the location and opening hours of polling stations, to defining the proper identification of voters, to overseeing how ballots are cast and counted. None of this can be left to chance, or some vague, neutral, "good government process" described by our civics teachers. To the extent possible, interested parties want to rig the election rules in their own favor. And they want consistency and predictability as much as control of the rules; they want to be able to anticipate, with some degree of certainty, what the outcome will be. One of the best and easiest ways to tilt the election playing field in favorable directions and to promote predictability and consistency is to limit the universe of voters. Thus in our election system, structures and rules become as much concerned with disenfranchisement as with enfranchisement.

The way in which this takes place forms the subject matter of this book. It does so from a worm's-eye perspective. It posits an individual voter who sets out to vote, and discovers that he may very well not be able to, because officials at his polling place refuse his credentials, whether disapproving of his appearance or his demeanor or for no apparent reason at all, regardless of his race, ethnicity, nationality, or any of the other labels of identity we use. Or it might happen that he can vote but his intent is undermined, because his ballot is not recorded correctly or tallied accurately. Or his ballot may be tossed out because of a technicality or a recount or a court decision. Or—and this may be the cruelest cut of all—he may have done everything correctly and his vote might be counted accurately, but it has no impact on the outcome because of deep structural flaws in our electoral system that render some individuals' votes irrelevant and inconsequential, whereas those of others count fully.

What is especially troubling is that, in most of the above instances, the voter may never know that his franchise has been corrupted and his vote snatched from him. Why? Because nothing in our electoral system is accountable to him, or, for that matter, to anyone else. It operates out of public view, and he has no way of finding out how his vote was treated. But since he doesn't know this, he blithely—and blindly—awaits the next election, assuming in good faith that his ballot will help determine the outcome. The facts may well prove otherwise.

This book has a very definite view of our election system. This view derives from the consequences of our efforts to disenfranchise as much as enfranchise people. It is that we as Americans cannot legitimately claim to hold fully democratic elections, although that is what we may believe, and what we boast in July Fourth speeches and promote internationally when we preach to other countries about how they should run their elections. Unless we make major changes in our electoral system, we might as well give up on the self-congratulation. Our belief that we have truly democratic elections needs to be qualified, because in fact, the franchise is limited and its extent is bounded, sometimes severely so. Our elections are democratic only in a narrow, formalistic sense.

Not everyone will be receptive to this provocative argument. It certainly is not what we learned in school, although our teachers are hardly to blame for that; as we will see in the first chapter, myths about our election system are hard to dispel. Some readers may be uncomfortable with the argument, point of view, and conclusions of this book. Others may disagree vehemently. A few might be offended, or find it unpatriotic. Many will be mystified because, like me, they never gave any thought to the mechanics of voting—they either took the trouble to go to the polls, or they didn't. But if this volume raises the voting consciousness of even a few people, it will have been well worth the effort put into it. In my own case, when I compare my thoughts on voting today to those of just a few years ago, it is as if I had entered a new universe. I invite others to join me in it.

With Appreciation

The section at the end of the preface to many books, in which authors thank those who influenced or helped them, can be a minefield. Inevitably there are hurt feelings because someone was not mentioned who should have been. Or, if the list is long, one has the feeling that the author has turned it into an Academy Award acceptance speech, casting the acknowledgment net unnecessarily widely, or in some cases expressing thanks through gritted teeth, more out of a sense of obligation than heartfelt appreciation.

The present work owes a debt of gratitude to many people, including students in my classes at the University of Florida, Central European University in Budapest, Debrecen University in Hungary, Bogazici University in Istanbul, and the German students and faculty who attended my lectures on elections and voting reform in their country. Probably most of them got more of an earful about voting rights than they bargained for or wanted, but their suggestions, comments, and questions were always stimulating and helpful.

Instead of thanking a long list of people by name, let me just say that they know who they are because I have told them so privately and personally. No two helped in the same way. But there are three individuals whose assistance has been so important that they must be publicly identified and thanked.

My editor at M.E. Sharpe, Patricia Kolb, has been a continuing source of inspiration to me for more than a decade. I am grateful for her patience and her unflagging confidence in me.

Without doubt, M. Margaret Conway (or as she prefers, "Peggy"), Emerita Distinguished Professor of Political Science at the University of Florida, made this book happen. At a lunch a few years ago she gave me all the reasons why I should write it. Peggy has an extraordinary ability to force colleagues to sharpen and focus their thinking. She cuts through intellectual bloviating and temporizing sharply and convincingly, but always with a gentle and supportive touch. At the conclusion of writing virtually every paragraph of this book I would ask myself, "What would Peggy think?" I can only hope that most of them measure up to her high standards.

But Aida is the driving force behind this book, the person who, in sharing her life with me, gave me the strength and dedication to see it through, especially in those dark hours of doubt and uncertainty that confront every author. And this is aside from the acuity of her insight; like Peggy Conway, Aida can see through intellectual chicanery and sophistry with almost superhuman clarity. At the end of the day, her opinion on the content of this book is more important than anyone else's, as far as I am concerned. More than any other person I have ever known, Aida makes life joyful and worthwhile. And she always shows and teaches me new things, and shows and teaches me old things in new ways. My gratitude to her is profound.

The Politics of Disenfranchisement

1

Trying to Vote in America

Why is it so hard to vote in America?

This deceptively simple question constitutes the heart of this book. It is in part an investigation of the barriers that prospective voters in the United States must overcome in order to exercise their franchise, cast a vote, and have it recorded and counted. But the book will also look more deeply at these matters, and ask why these barriers exist in the first place. After all, it is not enough to point out what has become all too well known, namely, that voting in America is often a struggle for the individual citizen. The real question is, why have we structured our voting procedures and mechanics so that this happens? Surely it is not just an accident, a matter of accumulated bad voting practices over time. Rather, it is much more likely, as Jonathan Kozol has eloquently and movingly written in another context, to be the result of conscious human decisions—or sometimes nondecisions. What, then, does the difficulty of exercising the franchise say about attitudes toward voting in America? What are its implications for our democratic elections, or indeed, our democratic system of governance?

It is no secret that problems have arisen in American elections since the founding of the nation, including during the twenty-first century, to the extent that too often their legitimacy, fairness, and accuracy have been called into question. We know that eligible voters are not always able to cast ballots, or have them counted even if they do vote. For this situation to exist in a modern, mature democracy is both anomalous and intolerable. We know how to structure election systems that expand rather than restrict the franchise. We know how to fashion election procedures so that voting is a non-burdensome activity. And we can construct voting and counting machines such that the results of elections are not matters of doubt and controversy, or their legitimacy in question. Other democracies do so all the time.

Yet our policy and practice is not to do this. This book asks why.

Let's be clear at the outset about what this book is and is not. It is an investigation of what is wrong with the American voting system. But unlike many—even most—critiques of American voting, it does not inquire from a top-down, bird's-eye view. Instead, it looks at voting from the perspective of the individual voter—from a street-level view, in other words. Although my approach is certainly systemic (and systematic), my task is to deconstruct the steps individual prospective voters have to take, and hurdles they have to overcome, in order to successfully exercise the franchise and have their vote recorded and counted accurately.

The word "prospective" is crucial in the preceding sentence. There are numerous studies—long shelves in libraries, in fact—that explore the reasons why Americans vote, or do not. This book is not one of them. I start from the premise that there are people out there who want to vote, for whatever reasons, and head out of the house or take time from a job to do so. The question then becomes, will they be able to? Why or why not? And, equally importantly, does their vote really count? Or matter?

This is also not a book about election systems. I am not concerned, in this text, with whether the way in which most elections take place in this country is "the best" (the plurality, first-past-the-post system is the most commonly used, although other systems are used as well, especially in some local contests), or whether it should be replaced with something else (instant runoffs, for example, or approval or cumulative voting, or one of a dozen or more other types). My concern in this book is with the individual voter: whether or not he will be able to cast a ballot regardless of the type of ballot offered to him or the kind of election system he confronts.

Nor is this book an "encyclopedia" of the structures, rules, laws, and processes of voting machinery in fifty different states. Rather, its purpose is to synthesize the experience of voters throughout the nation who sought to vote but could not, and to see what is common among the barriers and hurdles that the different states erect to keep people away from the polls, or, if they are allowed to vote, to ignore, reject, or miscount their ballots.

Finally, this book is not an examination of the legal issues in voting rights. I am not a lawyer and am not competent to make such an analysis. Nonetheless, the politics of legal issues permeate this book. Indeed, it is a reasonable argument that the political forces that interpret and implement the legal issues of voting rights are just as important as what happens in courtrooms, and that will be our touchstone in this text.

The Political Context

There is a powerful ethos—even mythology—about voting in this country that holds that there are few if any problems or barriers associated with casting ballots. With few exceptions, anybody eighteen and over who is a citizen can vote: you register, you show up at your polling place on election day, you vote, the ballot is recorded and counted, and you go about your business. The whole process is said to be mechanical, neutral, and value-free. It doesn't matter who you are or where you live or what is your race or color or nationality or religion or social class. If you don't want to register, or if you choose not to vote, it's because you're too lazy, or don't care, or don't recognize your civic duty. In other words, it's your problem, not your fellow citizens' and certainly not the state's. And besides, over 120 million

Americans managed to vote in the 2004 presidential election, nearly 70 million in 2006, and more than 133 million in 2008; how hard can voting really be? Our voting system, according to the mythology, works for most people.

So the myth is repeated endlessly from parents' laps to grade school, onward through the life cycle, and perpetuated more or less intact. True, one occasionally hears or reads voices suggesting that there are limitations on the franchise, but the general view seems to be that if you are not eligible to vote, or cannot, or don't, something is wrong with you. Perhaps you belong to one of the many groups of marginalized Americans (maybe you can't speak English, for example, or you have a serious disease or disability) who somehow don't have the "capability" or "qualities" or "wherewithal" or "prerequisites" or "credentials" required to be a voter. Maybe you've been a crook and have had your voting rights taken away. In other words, the exclusionary policies of the franchise are often rationalized by blaming the disenfranchised, by believing that somehow they don't "measure up." And, to be blunt, it is likely that many Americans think there is nothing wrong with this—that it is just the way things are. Voting is not like walking into a restaurant or buying a ticket to a movie—something just about anybody can do. You have to meet some preexisting but not always articulated or specified standard, or you have to jump through a series of basically arbitrary hoops before you can be awarded the franchise.

It is long past time to bury the myths. The extent of disenfranchisement, and particularly the way in which the franchise is differentially and unequally awarded across the range of the U.S. population (disenfranchisement disproportionately affects African Americans and other peoples of color) fatally undermines our voting mythology.

But the matter of "trying to vote in America" extends beyond the question of who has the franchise and who does not. In fact, even those persons who have the franchise face considerable hurdles—for some, impenetrable structural barriers—to its free exercise. We will discuss in detail these barriers in subsequent chapters; all we need note here is that they range from qualifying and registering to vote, through the actual act of casting a ballot, to concerns over whether it is accurately recorded and tallied, to the very fundamental question of whether the ballot cast has any significance or meaning.

As readers will learn, the list of stumbling blocks and impediments goes on and on, but the point is clear. It is difficult beyond belief to vote in America. The whole process is stacked against many of those wishing to exercise the franchise, and it completely ignores the substantial obligation that the state has to the voter. Voting in America is much more a matter of faith and belief that the system "works right" than that it is sound, reliable, fair, and accurate. The evidence I present in this book will suggest that these words—and similar ones like "transparent" and "accountable"—apply to our system of voting only minimally, and too often not at all.

Indeed, in spite of repeated efforts at "reform," recent studies continue to document just how difficult it is to vote in the United States: those of the Century Foundation (2005) and Cooperative Congressional Election Survey conducted by MIT (2009) come to mind.[1] It is the premise of this book that most of the "reform" efforts are doomed to failure and that problems will persist because of the fundamental structure of elections and voting in this country.

The Intellectual Context

This book is not solely a study of barriers to voting. It will additionally address two major theoretical questions, one based on constitutional issues and one rooted in mainstream American democratic theory.

First, the existence of a range of voting rules and procedures across the states raises a Fourteenth Amendment question. If voting is a right, and if one person's vote is worth the same as another's irregardless of location, then does not the equal protection clause demand far more uniformity in voting procedures, across the board, than currently exists? The U.S. Supreme Court in *Bush v. Gore* (2000) raised the possibility that variations in election practices might trample on the Fourteenth Amendment. It backed away from pushing the point, but it remains very much problematic—a 900-pound gorilla that sooner or later has to be confronted.

I am neither a lawyer nor a published constitutional scholar. As a political scientist, however, I am qualified to outline the political ramifications of a possible Fourteenth Amendment issue on how we vote in America. Indeed, I believe I have a scholarly obligation to provoke such a discussion. This will be done in the concluding chapter.

Second, much of mainstream American democratic theory since its origins rests on the view that a politically inert, passive, nonparticipatory citizenry is neither noteworthy nor harmful to democracy. Beginning in the late nineteenth century, scholars such as Woodrow Wilson and Arthur Bentley, and continuing through giants of American political science like Lawrence Chamberlain, David Truman, Harold Lasswell, Robert Dahl, Gabriel Almond, Sidney Verba, and Heinz Eulau, among many others, have advanced variations on this theme. These theorists argue in different ways, and with different data sets, that elite rule, in which the mass public merely votes occasionally to confirm the position of one or another set of elites, preserves stability and continuity in democracy. It is fair to say that in one way or another, all are far more elitist than populist in their views of politics. Limiting the franchise and making voting onerous are neither a problem nor a liability in their writings, but are in fact functional steps for us to take because they ensure that nonelite "outsiders," not to mention extremists or the lunatic fringe, cannot vote, let alone be elected.

This book takes serious issue with these views. Its theoretical reference point is rooted in the work of such authors as V.O. Key, Floyd Hunter, C. Wright Mills, Grant McConnell, William Domhoff, and Howard Zinn, among others, who question whether the political and social stability brought on by apathy and low rates of participation caused in part by hurdles to voting is indeed healthy. It takes as its starting point Carole Pateman's sardonic comment about Giovanni Sartori: "political apathy is not, as one writer dismissively claimed, 'nobody's fault' . . . but . . . is a socially structured and maintained phenomenon." As Jonathan Kozol more recently put it in another context, the existence of social pathologies, including inequality and discrimination, is not a matter of inevitability or a result of "naturally occurring" conditions, but one created by the deliberate decisions—or nondecisions—of human beings.

This book will address the question of whether the difficulty hundreds of thousands of citizens face in voting is "nobody's fault." If it is a systemic (if not systematic) characteristic of our electoral system, what does this say about how we really regard the right to vote? Indeed, what does it say about the nature of American democracy?

The Politics of Disenfranchisement and Other Works

Although *The Politics of Disenfranchisement* is a unique book, it rests on the shoulders of two distinguished intellectual and political traditions in this country. The first might be called "progressive populism." It has its roots in the Jefferson/Jackson political tradition celebrating everyday Americans and their struggle to participate in the American dream. This tradition was carried on in the late nineteenth and early twentieth centuries by such figures as William Jennings Bryan and Upton Sinclair, and still later by John Dos Passos, Dorothy Parker, John Steinbeck, the artist Diego Rivera, and the musician Aaron Copeland, among a host of others. None were social scientists, of course, but they provided an intellectual and artistic, as well as political, foundation for understanding the struggle of the dispossessed, marginalized, poverty-stricken characters depicted in their art against huge social, economic, and political forces allied against them, forces that they could only dimly imagine but whose impact on their lives they knew all too well.

By mid-twentieth century a well-conceived social science literature had developed that systematically and empirically examined what the artists and writers had imagined; writers would include such political scientists and sociologists as Key, Mills, and Hunter. Social science writings continued in this vein, on a more theoretical level, with Peter Bachrach and his collaboration with Morton Baratz, Noam Chomsky, and others. At the journalistic level, the progressive/populist tradition has most recently been given expression by (among others) I.F. Stone, Jim Hightower, Studs Terkel, and Barbara Ehrenreich, and by such periodicals as the *Nation, Mother Jones,* and the *Village Voice.* Emerging blogs and online "magazines" (the *American Prospect* comes to mind, among others) have pursued similar themes.

The second tradition on which this book rests can be called "the struggle for full and equal rights." It reaches back to the Bill of Rights, ratified in 1791, and extends through the Thirteenth, Fourteenth, and Fifteenth Amendments of the post–Civil War era, each of which was concerned with providing civil and voting rights for former slaves. These efforts moved forward with the ratification in 1920 of the Nineteenth Amendment, which afforded unqualified suffrage to women. In that same year, the American Civil Liberties Union was founded, whose many reports and documents have informed the present project. But the most powerful intellectual foundation for this book is unquestionably Dr. Martin Luther King, Jr.'s 1963 "Letter from a Birmingham Jail." In this extraordinarily profound statement, King successfully melds the themes of full civil rights and voting rights for all Americans, not solely African Americans. He understood better than most that if these rights are not granted and fully realized, then the promise of American democracy becomes a hollow shell, a chimera, a lie, for all Americans; to deprive even one person of his civil and voting rights is to undermine and cheapen those of everyone else. And yet, King saw, Americans spend as much time running away from this profound idea, especially but not only as it applies to the poor and marginalized, as embracing it. It is King's remarkable insight into American democracy's heart of darkness that permeates and energizes this whole study.

Why the Hurdles, Difficulties, and Impediments?

Why do the hurdles, difficulties, and impediments placed in front of the prospective voter exist, and persist? Why perpetuate practices that demean the value and meaning of the vote? Why not get rid of them, and make voting easy and meaningful? After all, if we really believe in popular participation and democratic governance, our goal should be to maximize ready access to the polls, and ensure that voters can exercise their franchise swiftly, conveniently, and accurately.

There are many reasons why voting is not made easy. But first, let us get rid of a major red herring that proponents of the "lets-not-make-voting-easy" school of thought advance: preventing vote fraud. This became a major issue in the late stages of the 2008 presidential campaign, as Republicans in particular sought to purge voter lists or demand strict verification of signatures or impose draconian requirements at the polls (including in some cases documentation of citizenship) as part of an effort to suppress voting under the guise of preventing vote fraud.[2]

The argument, in various forms, runs something like this: if the franchise were truly universal and access to the polls truly easy, the "system" would quickly degenerate into a cesspool of corruption and fraud. Cheating would be easy, unqualified people would overwhelm the polls, there would be no way to keep the process orderly, vote counts could easily be manipulated, and the results would lack credibility because no one would know what proportion of the votes were genuine and "legitimate."

The fatal flaw in this point of view is that it describes the present situation, not one in which the franchise is universal. Why would anyone seriously believe that limiting access to the polls prevents or stops corruption? On the contrary, limiting access and manipulating voters (and the vote outcome) go hand in hand. Whether it was Tammany Hall or Mayor Richard Daley *pere,* racist Southern voting officials, late-nineteenth-century Progressives, the contemporary GOP with its vise-grip on state voting machinery in any number of states, or some other group or organization that limited access to the polls or determined which votes were to be counted, the results were always the same: voting officials have conducted elections with outcomes lacking legitimacy.

No, it is not universal voting that promotes corruption in elections. Corruption results from the desire of those in charge of the voting apparatus to influence or determine the outcome of elections. As I noted in the Preface, many parties interested in the outcome of elections believe elections are too important to be left to the whims and caprices of the public; they prefer to gain control of who votes and how, and tilt the playing field favorably for themselves. They want to do this ante facto if possible, but if not then post facto; even if that requires stealing the election by miscounting or suppressing votes, then so be it. In any case, they will work to be sure that as they engage in fraud it will be essentially—even assuredly—free of any burden of public accountability and transparency. How many state and local voting officials, how many officials of private interests involved in elections in this country, have gone to jail because of election fraud? The answer is few, if any.

In any case, it is the intervention of special interests, including partisan politics, into the free and open conduct of elections that promotes corruption and causes illegitimate outcomes. Indeed, one can, and must, make the opposite argument: the more access there is to the polls, the more universal the franchise, the less likely are the results to be manipulated or corrupted, and the more likely they are to be perceived as legitimate. The reason is apparent: with fewer constraints on voters, officials and agencies will have no place to hide, no valid way to defend their manipulations or their failure to treat all votes equally.

There is another important point to be made here as well. As I noted, a long tradition of scholarship in American politics holds that a politically inert population, and an electoral system that limits the extent of the franchise, is healthy for democracy because it promotes stability, consistency, and predictability. As further noted, this book takes serious issue with this political position. It is difficult to see how limiting the franchise, that is, keeping some population groups and individuals from voting, promotes democracy, at least if democracy means something like "government of the people, by the people, and for the people." If some people are left out, deliberately so, the cause of democracy is hardly advanced, indeed, the contrary would be true.

It is true, however, that limiting the franchise promotes stability and continuity. Marginalized, even demonized groups, such as felons, noncitizens, and the homeless, are not permitted into the political arena because they are viewed as weird or unacceptable or—most importantly—unpredictable. Those who are allowed in are predictable. And the truth of the matter is that Democrats, Republicans, and Independents who do participate, in spite of campaign and other rhetoric, share more political values than not. The result is a politics of sameness, bland, with minor differences in style and rhetoric but little of substance. But leaving others on the sidelines, others who may have very different political values, and not allowing them into the political game is hardly the sign of a robust democracy. Indeed, the latter is characterized by vigorous debate and high-energy dynamics that are inclusive rather than exclusive. The scholars and writers and pundits who point to our quiescent politics with limited participation and a bounded franchise as a sign of a healthy democracy evidently have never envisioned what one would be like.

So the argument that limiting the franchise undermines corruption, prevents vote fraud, and is an indicator of a viable democracy is sheer sophistry.[3] But what does account for the perpetuation of practices that keep people from the free and ready exercise of their franchise?

Failure to Recognize That Voting Is a Right

In spite of the 1965 Voting Rights Act, Americans still have not grasped that voting is a right. True, it is not a constitutionally guaranteed right, like a First Amendment right. But just because it is legally and not constitutionally based does not mean it is any less of a right.

Rather, it is likely that many—even most—Americans think voting is a privilege, something the prospective voter has to earn, to prove worthy of in order to be able to vote. They probably regard voting as more on the order of getting a driver's license than, say, exercising rights of free speech or the right of assembly. Even knowledgeable people fall into this trap. It is not unusual, for example, on TV news programs to hear correspondents talking about the "privilege" of voting, rather than the "right" to vote. They should know better.

Is there any evidence that Americans think of voting more as a privilege than a right? The discussion in the previous section on the range of structural problems that serve as hurdles to be overcome by prospective voters constitutes valid evidence. Whether it was the poll tax in the nineteenth century or literacy tests or character testimonials—directed primarily but not exclusively at blacks—or more recently, complicated registration procedures and draconian voter ID requirements, the effect is that of making potential voters jump through hoops and leap over barriers before they can vote. If Americans truly thought of voting as a right, there would be few if any obstructions to voting. It would be afforded those of sufficient age as a matter of course, not something people had to earn or demonstrate or achieve.

There are many problems with thinking of voting as a privilege instead of a right. But the most important is that it gives public officials—legislators, voting supervisors, secretaries of state, even judges—license to convey, or withhold, the ballot. Too often discretion is left to officials to determine if the voter has satisfactorily met some arbitrary, unspecified "standard" so that he or she can vote. As a result, determining who gets the franchise and who doesn't potentially wallows in the muck of arbitrary, capricious, and unreasonable decision making. There is usually no recourse for the voter who is turned down, and no accountability for the official making the decision. If voting were regarded as a right and not a privilege, public officials would not have so much discretionary authority. Indeed, the burden would be on those officials to show why a prospective voter should not have the franchise, rather than on the voter to show that he/she has satisfactorily met the standard in order to cast a ballot. It is critical to remember that the 1965 legislation was called the Voting *Rights* Act, not the Voting *Privilege* Act.

Structural Problems

There are numerous structural and administrative hurdles placed in front of potential voters that limit their ability to cast ballots. Without doubt, the single most important one is archaic registration rules. Indeed, scholars of voting have for decades pointed to difficult, often arbitrary and capricious, registration rules as the single most important factor that keeps people away from the polls.

Later we will look at where voter registration requirements came from, and why they so profoundly limit access to the polls. For the moment, let us note that it does not have to be this way. In many modern democracies voter registration is easy, often automatic as soon as the person reaches the right age. All he or she need do is show up at the polls to vote. In the United States, the process is hard. Registration forms are often long, complicated, and difficult to navigate. It is easy to make a mistake in filling them out, which could have the effect of disqualifying the potential voter.

While literacy tests have long been outlawed, it is a reasonable argument that most registration forms constitute their reincarnation. And even though residence requirements are a thing of the past, in most states there are substantial time periods between the last day of voter registration and the election date (or even the onset of early voting), which in effect constitutes a form of residence requirement; very few states allow same-day voter registration. Moreover, increasingly in the United States, even if the voter shows up with a valid registration card, he or she still is not guaranteed the opportunity to vote. The voter often has to prove his or her identity first, not always an easy task.

The truth is, the structural problems—and there are many more besides those just mentioned, which I will detail in subsequent chapters—are too great for many potential American voters to negotiate successfully. Their effect is to limit the franchise sharply.

Partisan Politics

As in so many other areas of American public and even private life, partisan politics has intruded on the right to vote. It is possible to see the history of voting rights in America from the nineteenth century to the present as a clash between the Democratic and Republican parties. The struggle at times has reached titanic, even epic, proportions, as the dramatic conclusion to the 2000 presidential election in Florida demonstrated. It has frequently been nasty, and sometimes sordid. At its heart, it has been a clash between the parties about who should be allowed to vote, ranging from the individual level to which groups—national, ethnic, religious, racial, social class—were to be afforded the franchise and which kept from the polls, by force and violence if necessary. And it has been a struggle to determine whether all votes were to be counted, and counted equally, as well as by whom, when, and under what conditions.

As Piven and Cloward, as well as a host of other scholars, have detailed,[4] when immigrant groups arrived on American shores, they were often met and introduced to America by representatives of one or the other political parties. But the process of greeting and assisting immigrants by political parties was neither random nor willy-nilly. While there were exceptions, Republicans tended to favor groups from northern Europe and the British Isles (except for Ireland). Democrats accommodated the Irish, and also heavily Catholic groups from central, eastern, and southern Europe, Russians, and Jews. Later they took in non-Cuban Hispanics. Neither wanted the Chinese or other Asians on the West Coast. Neither wanted African Americans.

Indeed, even as the complex processes of socialization, if not assimilation, took place, the political parties carefully monitored their group composition. They were assiduous in protecting those groups whose votes they could manipulate and/or count on, and in finding ways to keep all the others, especially members of the other party, away from the polls. They did not have to worry about voter registration or some of the other formalisms of modern voting. Voter registration as a serious matter did not begin until the late nineteenth century, and noncitizens had no trouble voting until the practice was outlawed during the 1920s. Even so, neither voter registration nor citizenship requirements proved a burden to either political party. Indeed, they became additional instruments for them to use in allowing some groups to vote but not others.

It was power politics, pure and simple: our groups can vote, yours can't. A tremendous amount of time, energy, and resources were spent over the course of decades keeping out "undesirable" voters—that is, those in the other camp(s). By limiting the franchise, of course, the parties were seeking to optimize their electoral chances. Years later, the eminent political scientist E.E. Schattschneider theorized about and described this situation perfectly when he talked about the need for contending political interests to define and limit the scope of conflict by writing rules and procedures favoring them, and disadvantaging the other side(s).[5] This is exactly what our major political parties have done for over 100 years and continue to do today.

The power and validity of Schattschneider's observations can be demonstrated with examples. In the post-Reconstruction South, the Democratic Party was the primary instrument for writing, institutionalizing, and enforcing Jim Crow laws and other practices that kept former slaves and their descendents from voting. Racial discrimination, prejudice, and hatred were behind Jim Crow, of course, but they were not the whole story. As V.O. Key and many others have detailed,[6] it was a matter of practical politics as well. As Democratic "Redeemers" and Bourbons seized control of state politics following the end of Reconstruction, they quickly realized they were an electoral minority. If blacks—and poor whites—had ready access to the polls, they could be voted out of office because, to the extent that post–Civil War Southern blacks had any political affiliation at all, they were Republicans. If blacks and poor whites formed political alliances—as the late-nineteenth-century Populist movement sought to create—the position of Democrats would become tenuous and precarious indeed.

To ensure that this did not happen, ruling whites engaged in practices aimed at disenfranchising blacks, and to some extent poor whites (the latter were also manipulated into active hostility against blacks). Poll taxes, literacy tests, and other tactics of disenfranchisement were established; if they did not work well enough, terror and violence reinforced them. Thus, the goal of Southern Democrats, at least until 1965 as Earl Black has shown,[7] was to maintain their position of power by keeping blacks away from the polls. After that, white Southern Democrats began to convert to Republicanism, as the national Democratic Party took up the cause of civil and voting rights. The partisan politics of disenfranchisement began to shift.

More recently it has been the Republican Party at national and state levels that has actively sought restrictions on the franchise. I will detail these matters later in the book, but for now we can point out that efforts to stop third-party voter registration (including third-party registration by ACORN and the nonpartisan League of Women Voters) in states such as Ohio and Florida have their roots in the Republican Party. And the recent draconian measures requiring voter ID, as well as demonstration of citizenship requirements in Indiana, Florida, Georgia, Arizona, and elsewhere, have similarly been the product of Republican political power, mainly in state legislatures and governors' offices, but also in the Bush administration's Department of Justice, Office of Civil Rights. Voter purges in Georgia, Michigan, Louisiana, and Mississippi, during the 2008 presidential election—the latter two of which potentially affected thousands of black voters in those states (20,000 and 11,000 voters purged, respectively)—can be traced to the Republican Party and GOP secretaries of state.[8] So can challenges to voters during early voting periods in a number of states as well as other mechanisms of voter suppression.

These examples should make the point clear. Partisan politics play a major role in determining which individuals and groups of voters have ready access to the polls and which do not.

Administrative Discretion

On Florida's primary day in late summer 2008, a young man showed up to vote at his polling place wearing an Obama T-shirt; Barack Obama was not on the ballot that day. The man lived in a small town in a rural part of the panhandle, solid

Republican/McCain country. He was not allowed to vote even though he was apparently correctly registered and had at hand the necessary photo ID.[9]

According to reports, this voter was denied a ballot because his shirt violated the "50 foot rule." In Florida, no campaign signs or advertisements are permitted within fifty feet of the entrance to a polling place. The T-shirt did not meet the legal definition of a political advertisement, as an endorsement, or just an image on a T-shirt, is not necessarily an advertisement. In addition, articles of clothing are exempt. However, local administrators decided that it constituted a violation of the 50-foot rule and denied the voter the chance to cast a ballot.

The impact of administrative discretion will be a frequent and recurring theme in this book. There is substantial evidence on the effect of administrative discretion in depriving voters of their right to cast ballots.[10] Local voting officials have an extraordinary range and depth of discretion at all phases of the voting process: handling snail-mail and electronic requests for voter registration materials; evaluating completed registration forms; expediting (or not) requests for absentee ballots; counting returned absentee ballots; determining the location of polling places; designing ballots; determining whether or not voters showing up at the polls produce the required documentation, including voter ID;[11] judging whether a voter's eccentric behavior or articles of clothing disqualify him/her from voting;[12] deciding whether or not to offer provisional ballots to voters whose credentials were questioned; deciding what to do with provisional ballots, including whether or not to count them; how to deal with requests for assistance to voters, including those from language minorities and those with physical disabilities; how to handle breakdowns of voting equipment; how to accommodate—or not—voters who make mistakes or spoil their ballots; how to deal with voters standing on line even after the polling hours officially end; how to expedite local counting of ballots (if done on-site) or facilitate their secure transit to county offices for official counting; and so on.

At each and every step of the voting process local voting officials have broad authority to make decisions about who gets to vote and how ballots are handled. It should be emphasized that most carry out their tasks diligently, honestly, and in a consistent fashion. But in a sense this is not the point; democratic elections demand nothing less.

The problem arises when these standards are not met, or when local officials overstep their bounds or make unreasonable, arbitrary, or capricious decisions based on personal or partisan political views, biases and prejudices, or something else. Local supervisors of elections, in their training sessions and manuals, try to anticipate as many peculiar circumstances as possible, but there is no way to foretell all of them; human behavior being what it is, something out of the ordinary or exceptional will always arise. When local polling officials, reacting to circumstances, make one or more decisions preventing a potential voter from getting a ballot or having it treated like everyone else's, then questions of both equity and fairness have to be raised.

Occasions may arise when there is a valid reason to block access to the ballot box, for example, if the official can demonstrate that the voter already cast a ballot earlier, or elsewhere. But unfortunately, there are too many cases on record in which local voting officials regard themselves as gatekeepers to the ballot box rather than facilitators of voting. The assumption of the gatekeeping role results in the acquisition of a great deal of discretionary power by local voting officials. For example, it changes the burden of proof in disputes over who can vote. Instead of the burden being on local officials to show why a potential voter should not be allowed to vote, the burden is on the voter to show why she should be permitted to do so. This is a misplaced, and unfair, burden. Even if it amounts to denying the rights of only one voter on Election Day, this is one too many.

Making matters worse is the fact that there is almost no accountability for local officials who exercise their discretion and prevent voters from casting ballots. True, voters who feel they have been unfairly prevented from voting can file complaints; some 11,000 did in Florida in 2000. But in no case did the complaints do any good. By the time they were processed, the election was long over and the results certified. In no case was a complainant in that election allowed to revote and his vote counted. This is the usual case with voters who try to file complaints against officials whom they believe treated them illegally or unfairly. Moreover, the Bush administration's Department of Justice, which handled many of the complaints, was so partisan and politicized that it allowed only a handful of complaints to stand, while the others were tossed away as invalid. In no instance was a local voting official censured, or fired, or brought to trial because of discretionary decisions he or she had made on Election Day.

Racism and Xenophobia

The continuing existence of racism in America is too well known and documented to require more than a passing comment here. Indeed, much of the rest of the book will offer evidence that peoples of color—not solely African Americans—are at much greater risk of being denied their voting rights than white Americans, especially Anglo-Saxon Americans. While numerous explanations are offered to justify this situation—"they didn't register correctly," "their registration names and those on other 'approved' lists don't match," "they 'didn't do it/something right' "—they are virtually always bogus. The truth is, there are still too many forces at play in America that seek to minimize political participation among African Americans and other peoples of color, and try to delegitimize what participation exists.[13]

The same is true of xenophobia. Although we are a nation of immigrants, in fact there are powerful forces at play in this nation that are openly hostile to new arrivals, especially those from Latin America, Africa, and the Middle East. Evidence for the power of these forces can be seen in the extraordinary levels of vituperation and hostility expressed at immigrants, especially illegal aliens, during the Bush administration's attempt to revise U.S. immigration policy early in its second term. It was difficult for advocates of a change in the traditional policy, one that was designed to provide a mechanism whereby even illegal aliens could become residents and eventually citizens, to be heard over the cacophony of bitterness and anger directed toward those who found themselves in a no-man's land, literally people without a country and no place to go.

Is there a difference between racism and xenophobia? Does it matter? For the purpose of voting rights, it doesn't. Rather, both are manifestations of a long and hurtful tradition in America of marginalizing, even demonizing, those who are somehow "different," who are somehow defined as outside "mainstream" America. Often this is just because they look different: the Chinese come to mind in this regard, or those with visible physical impairments and disabilities. Others may have different, usually dark, skin color: African Americans are the archetypal example, but this group can also include people with relatively dark or olive skin from the Mediterranean regions of Europe and North Africa, or some Native Americans. Others are marginalized because of religion: for a time it was Catholics, then it was Jews; most recently it is Muslims, who are often and unfairly identified as, or associated with, terrorists. All of these groups have had difficulty securing and maintaining their voting rights at one time or another.

It is an unfortunate fact of American life, but if one seeks to explain why it is so hard for some groups to vote in America, especially compared to white Americans, one has to point squarely at the ongoing, devastating, and destructive impact of racism and xenophobia.

Economic Pillars

The major pillars of the U.S. economy also serve as a force to limit the franchise and keep the process of voting arduous for all but the most committed (or, perhaps, "deserving"). Yet they do not do so by direct political action. Bank of America or Exxon-Mobil or Procter & Gamble or American Express or Cargill or other giant conglomerates, corporations, and centers of vast capital are not visible in the halls of Congress or state legislatures actively working to disenfranchise potential voters. Their interest in political arenas is far more concerned with tax and import/export policies; environmental, health-care, and safety regulations; and maintaining various forms of corporate welfare, than with the mechanics of voting. Most recently, of course, major sectors of the U.S. economy, including banking, real estate, financial services, and auto manufacturing, have been looking to the federal government for bailout money just to stay alive.

Some important economic pillars have been involved with voting. Labor unions in particular have conducted voter registration drives and get-out-the-vote (GOTV) campaigns as part of their political arsenal. So have some corporations. But, truth be told, most of these activities are limited in nature. Unions, for example, recruit new voters who are likely to support their candidates; their GOTV campaigns are mainly confined to members and their fellow travelers. We look in vain for robust, broadly based efforts by corporations and unions to dramatically expand the pool of voters in America, or to push ways to expedite voting and make it easier and more accessible to new voters, or those already active.

The reason they don't do more is obvious. To return to a point made in the Preface, the pillars of the American economy want regularity, consistency, and predictability in elections. They don't want hordes of new voters coming to the polls, especially if they are poor, marginalized, less-educated groups (including those for whom English is a foreign language). There is a genuine fear on their part that these new kinds of voters might not ascribe to the centrality and importance of big business, big labor, big agriculture, big financial services, big banking and insurance, big medical care, big oil and gas, big media, and all the other major sectors of the U.S. economy. They may not, for example, support favorable tax policies or other forms of corporate welfare.

So while the pillars of the U.S. economy might give lip service to the importance of "free elections" and proclaim that "voting is your civic duty," because they engage in huge efforts and spend vast sums of money to improve their public images, widespread participation in elections is not what they really want. They want to make sure that whether this Republican candidate or that Democratic candidate wins, their own economic position remains secure. They understand that neither of the major parties is interested in putting them out of business, even as they might disagree slightly at the margins on tax issues, import/export policies, environmental regulations, and the like. They do not want a Hugo Chávez or Juan Evo Morales elected, who might threaten them, and they certainly do not want supporters and sympathizers of that type of politician having access to ballots. So they do not seek to expand the universe of American voters.

How do they operate, if they are not active lobbyists against increased enfranchisement or electoral reform resulting in greater access to ballots? For one thing, as just noted, they operate by doing nothing to foster either of these. More fundamentally, the pillars of the U.S. economy influence our political attitudes and values—what is known as our political culture—by helping to define the limits of acceptability. They do this through the kinds of images and values they evoke in their public relations campaigns, through public statements by their executives and leaders (including appearances before congressional committees or administrative agencies), by the positions they take in civil lawsuits, and the like. Examples include promotion of patriotic (even chauvinistic) themes in advertising campaigns ("Buy American"), promoting nationalism ("Keep America Strong by Keeping American Business Strong"), and opposing policies (such as NAFTA) that they claim might weaken America's position in the global economic universe. But their efforts to define the limits of acceptability might also extend to opposition to certain policy changes—such as universal health care operated by the federal government, or relaxed immigration rules, or hikes in the minimum wage, or increased safety/health measures for workers and employees. Deviations from the content of these pronouncements and positions are unacceptable to them and, presumably not in the best interests (or so they would have us believe) of most Americans.

Thus their impact on the electoral system, including who gets to vote and how, is indirect. U.S. corporations and other pillars of the U.S. economy help define the value system within which the mechanics of our elections are created and maintained, with an emphasis on how far the limits of acceptability extend. But to say their influence on our electoral system is indirect is not to diminish its importance. One shudders to imagine the level of discomfort such giants as Citi-Bank, Halliburton, or the United Auto Workers would feel if massive numbers of new voters suddenly started determining the outcome of elections, and how they would respond.

Political Leadership

Ensuring the existence and vitality of political rights requires ongoing and careful vigilance. It is a cliché, but also a truism, that once rights are taken away, they may well prove difficult, and sometimes impossible, to replace.

This is especially true of voting rights. Unlike constitutional rights, especially those covered by the First Amendment, voting rights appear not to occupy a prominent place on the radar screens of most people. Because voting rights are taken for granted and frequently regarded as a privilege to be earned, the public generally affords them scant attention, especially if it is not election season.

But it is precisely for this reason that voting rights are so fragile, and those of certain groups can successfully be attacked, virtually with impunity. It is not the case that state and local voting officials work to protect the voting rights of all eligible voters and groups; too often, as the experience of the November 2008 general election reveals, partisan politics intervene to the extent that voting rights for some groups are threatened, as they were for African Americans in Ohio, Louisiana, Mississippi, and a few other places. Nor do federal courts consistently uphold and strengthen the voting rights of all citizens. In many instances in recent years they have done the opposite, perhaps culminating in the June 2008 Supreme Court decision allowing Indiana's draconian voter ID law to stand.[14]

Keeping voting rights at the forefront of public consciousness and demanding constant surveillance would seem in recent years to have become the responsibility of private groups and organizations. One thinks in this connection of the American Civil Liberties Union (ACLU), People for the American Way, the NAACP, the Brennan Center for Justice at New York University, Lawyers Committee for Civil Rights Under Law, Project VoteSmart, and the League of Women Voters, to name just a few. None of these has any formal constitutional or legal standing; rather, their task has been to investigate possible violations of voting rights and bring them to the attention of responsible public officials, including the courts. The latter, of course, may or may not respond positively, or at all.

From time to time, however, presidents and governors have pushed voting rights as part of their agendas. One thinks of President Lyndon B. Johnson—shortly after the mayhem on the Edmund Pettus Bridge in Selma, Alabama, March 1965, as blacks sought their voting rights—invoking and endorsing the anthem of the civil rights movement, "We Shall Overcome," as he addressed Congress, seeking voting rights legislation. Later that summer, LBJ signed the Voting Rights Act into law, regarded by many as the most significant piece of civil rights legislation ever passed in this country.

But presidential leadership has not always advanced the cause of voting rights. President Ronald Reagan, opposed to extending the Voting Rights Act, had to be persuaded to sign it as amended in 1982. During the administration of George W. Bush, the Department of Justice, including the Office of Civil Rights, became highly politically charged, to the extent that senior officials motivated solely by narrow partisan interests overruled the objections of career staff attorneys who claimed that Georgia's new voter ID law was too strict and potentially unconstitutional. Previously Georgians could have shown any of seventeen forms of ID at the polls and received a ballot, but under the new law only a specially digitized card issued by the state, costing $20 and expiring in five years, would be acceptable. This was but one example of partisanship trumping voting rights in that administration. Throughout the whole sorry episode, Mr. Bush's silence on the potential impact of the proposed change on the voting rights of the poor, elderly, and peoples of color in Georgia was deafening.

Voting rights were also not enhanced when in 2000 the Republican governor of Florida, Jeb Bush (who was also his brother George's state election co-chair) authorized and used a list of some 57,700 alleged felons to disqualify otherwise registered voters from voting. The list was appallingly flawed and biased against African American voters, especially males. It turned out that many people on the list were not felons at all, and a large number who were felons had had their rights restored and thus should have been entitled to vote. Governor Bush may or may not have been aware of the flaws in the list, but nonetheless he supported its use throughout the state, with the result that thousands of eligible African American voters never cast ballots.

And during the 2004 presidential election another political executive, Ohio's Republican secretary of state, Kenneth Blackwell, failed to provide sufficient numbers of voting machines in inner-city, largely black precincts of Cleveland. The result was that many registered voters never got to cast ballots. Blackwell also achieved notoriety in subsequent years by pursuing and punishing a number of private organizations and community activists engaging in voter registration drives, and imposing such strict registration requirements (including at one point specifying the weight of paper that had to be used for forms) that it became virtually impossible for any but a few agencies to meet them.[15]

Thus, at least some of the blame for backtracking on voting rights is the result of failure of leadership by political executives. Facts require the observation that most of the activity, behavior, and language that has resulted in reduction or narrowing of voting rights has taken place under Republican administrations. Why this is true is a topic for another book, but it is no accident that the targets of most of their efforts have been Democratic-leaning groups of voters, particularly young people and African Americans.

But more generally, these instances show how important political leadership is to the health and vitality of voting rights. When it has been present, as with Presidents Lyndon Johnson and Bill Clinton, and such governors as William Winter of Mississippi, Jimmy Carter of Georgia, and Reubin Askew of Florida, voting rights were at the top of political agendas, and the opportunity to vote grew for many previously disenfranchised individuals and groups. But when political leadership is lacking or even hostile, voting rights rapidly erode.

The Public, Democracy, and the Nature of Our Elections

In the end, the vitality of American voting rights depends on what the public wants, or specifically, how much democracy the public wishes to promote here at home. If the public insists that the franchise be spread deeply and widely, it is because it has a healthy trust in a robust democracy and the belief that people should be empowered. But if its view is that democracy means granting power to just some people and excluding others from its exercise, so will voting rights be curtailed.

We have lived through periods exemplifying each of these views (although in truth there have been more of the latter than of the former). It took "mainstream" America an unfortunately long time to come to grips with what the civil rights movement was all about and why it was important. But once public opinion moved behind it, voting rights for blacks—and poor whites—were expanded rapidly. It happened because for at least a brief time, Americans wanted to implement Lincoln's peerless definition of democracy: "government of the people, by the people, and for the people."

But we have lived through very different periods as well. One thinks of the 1920s, a time of great xenophobia in the United States, when a variety of rights, including voting rights, were attacked. Or the McCarthy era of the 1950s, when a variety of civil and political rights were under assault. In the first decade of the new millennium, even during the 2008 presidential election, one finds efforts, again largely spearheaded by Republican groups and agents, to block new registrants from voting, purge them from voting lists, or disqualify them at polls so that they cannot cast ballots. This kind of effort stems from a limited view of democracy, perhaps best summed up as "government of some people, by some people, for some people."

Americans may never decide with finality what kind of democracy, and what kind of voting rights, they really want. What is certain, however, is that as public views shift on this fundamental issue, the consequences for voting rights are immediate and sometimes wrenching. When it comes to voting rights, change is not always for the better.

There is another way to consider the issues of how much democracy the public wants and how broadly it wishes voting rights to extend: What should our elections be like? More specifically, are they to be public enterprises or essentially private ones? The question of public versus private may surprise some readers, because there is probably a presumption among Americans that, of course our elections are public! They are established by laws written by legislatures and managed by state and county officials, both public agencies and agents. Their administration and results are subject to public scrutiny. They are accountable to the residents of the jurisdiction in which they are held, and if irregularities are alleged, can be challenged by another set of public agencies, the courts.

But one thesis of this book is that American elections are not nearly as public as is generally thought. While they are not established or conducted by private groups, there exists a considerable range of private groups that can have substantial impact on how elections are carried out. It is true that some private organizations advocate expansion of voting rights. One thinks in this connection of "good government" groups such as the League of Women Voters and Common Cause, or civil liberties organizations, such as the ACLU or the Lawyers Committee for Civil Rights Under Law.

However, if we expand the notion of "private" to include narrow, special, and especially partisan interests, then matters grow darker. There are private groups that have worked to limit the franchise. In recent years these have included some very conservative, right-wing, secular groups, but also religious, especially evangelical, associations. As we saw earlier, the history of American elections can be read as efforts by one or the other major political party to seize control and thwart efforts by the other party to register voters or permit them to vote.

The reason this is a serious matter is that when the parties and their private allies control the election machinery, elections themselves become privatized in the sense that they are literally captured by the narrow, parochial, special interests they represent. Other interests not in tune with these are left out or pushed aside. Transparency, public accountability, responsiveness to public needs, fairness—indeed, voting rights themselves—are threatened and potentially lost. One leading student of voting rights noted that the protracted and intensive efforts by Republican Party officials during the 2008 presidential campaign to limit access to the polls by purging or disenfranchising voters was done "without any public scrutiny at all."[16] It was a blatant example of an effort by the GOP and its allies inside and outside of government in many states to privatize the presidential election.

The same can be said of the actual conduct of the election—where voting is done and when the polls are open,[17] how votes are cast and counted, how recounts and appeals are to be carried out. To the extent the public is shut out of the process and the process is dominated by partisan interests, we can say that the public element in our elections is undermined, even lost, and they become privatized. On the other hand, if elections are not dominated by one or the other political party and its constellation of private associations, and instead, a range of interests and groups is brought into the design and administration of elections and the whole process made fully transparent, accountable, and open to public scrutiny, so will the public components of our elections be enhanced. And so, too, will voting rights be strengthened.

The tension between the public-private nature of our elections will be noted throughout this book. Indeed, most of the text illustrates just how "private"—in the sense developed here—our elections really are. We shall return explicitly to this issue in the concluding chapter.

A Note on the 2008 General Election

In the days immediately following the 2008 general election there was a good deal of political commentary in the print and electronic media assessing that it had gone reasonably smoothly, especially considering that turnout rose 9 million over 2004, to over 133 million voters. It is not clear why so many pundits and analysts reached the conclusion they did. Perhaps they were relieved that it did not turn into the Florida fiasco of 2000, or the 2004 Ohio turmoil that caused consternation and anger well beyond the borders of the Buckeye State.

In fact, the 2008 general election was anything but smooth. What gave it a reasonably pacific appearance on the surface was that it was not close at the presidential level in any state except Missouri. Barack Obama swamped his opponent John McCain throughout the land, and the Missouri results made absolutely no difference to the final outcome. So the election did not come down to a single closely fought, controversial state outcome as in 2000 and 2004.

At the Senate level, some contests were very close, and the results not known for some time after Election Day. Alaskans were slow to count provisional ballots, and it took more than two weeks to discover that Democrat Mark Begich won by a few thousand votes over incumbent, and convicted felon, Ted Stevens. Minnesota has in place a well-defined recount procedure that had to be employed to determine the nano-close race between Al Franken and incumbent Norm Carlson; it took until the summer of 2009 to resolve that contest. Georgia required a run-off between incumbent Saxby Chambliss and Democrat Jim Martin because neither reached the requisite 50 percent plus 1 mark.

Because of the way in which the close Senate contests were being resolved, could it not be argued, as so many did, that in fact the 2008 election was smooth, and produced fair, legitimate results? Perhaps. The problem is that this conclusion only works for what occurred subsequent to November 4. As it happened, the period leading up to Election Day was fraught with major difficulties. Indeed, it would have to be said that in many parts of the country there was a collective holding of the breath while events unfolded on Election Day as public officials, voting officials, lawyers from voting rights groups, civil rights organizations, much of the media, and even the public waited to see if an avalanche of disasters took place while people voted and ballots were counted.

The story of the 2008 election and its election troubles is recent history, and I encourage those wanting more information and documentation about what happened to avail themselves of a library or the Internet. What is important to point out is that the forces discussed earlier that serve to disenfranchise voters were in full force prior to November 4, 2008. Early on in the campaign, partisan politics were manifested in powerful ways to block access to the polls for some people. The Republican Party began crying "voter fraud" from the campaign's beginning, and desperately tried to make an issue of ACORN and other voter registration groups, arguing that they were registering voters fraudulently. Actual documented cases of fraud were virtually nonexistent, however, and where errors had been made, they were corrected administratively. The *New York Times* reported on October 8 that in at least six "swing" states, voters were being illegally purged from voter lists.[18] As early voting began in many states, Republicans again sought to force draconian methods for verifying voter ID, including matching of signatures with approved lists and demanding certain types of photo identification for new voters. Indeed, matters became so egregiously partisan and unfair that the U.S. Supreme Court—even with the addition of Bush-appointed justices John Roberts and Samuel Alito—overturned a federal appeals court decision and put a stop to GOP demands in Ohio.[19] There were disputes in other states about the standards that Republicans insisted on for new voters (because there were millions of them in the 2008 elections) that may not have reached the Supreme Court, but were no less intense than the Ohio battle.

But matters did not stop there. As Election Day drew near, there were fears that local jurisdictions would not have enough election machines, or ballots, to accommodate the flood of voters that was expected. Early voters and absentee ballots undoubtedly helped relieve some of the pressure (the former reached record numbers), but there were numerous documented reports from around the nation of voters waiting on lines three, four, and more hours before casting a ballot.

Once voting began on Election Day, reports of trouble began almost immediately. Some difficulties were clearly silly, resulting from human error: in Virginia, one polling place did not open on time because a poll worker overslept; in Florida, one precinct could not open because someone had changed the locks on the door.[20] Other matters were more serious. There were numerous documented reports of voters arriving at their polling stations only to find that they had been purged from voter lists, for which they had no prior warning. In jurisdictions continuing to use touch-screen technology there were numerous reports of breakdowns, including machines that cast votes for candidates other than the voters' choices. Even the more reliable optical scanning equipment became dysfunctional in some places because of electrical failures, jammed machines, inoperable or dirty scanners, and so forth.

The evidence is that while the 2008 general election may have gone smoothly at the macro level—at least compared to 2000 and 2004—at the micro level, where it matters most because that is the level of the individual voter, it did not.

Indeed, we can conclude that the experience of the 2008 general election is further documentation of just how difficult it is to vote in America. In too many instances, voters were either disenfranchised or threatened with disenfranchisement. In those instances where they could vote, in many locations the process was unnecessarily time- and energy-consuming, as well as emotionally taxing.

Indeed, the 2008 general election provides grist for the mill of this book. In the ensuing pages we shall examine in detail what has just been outlined: trying to vote in America is a task of monumental proportions, and much of our policy as a nation is aimed at making sure as few people vote as possible, rather than ensuring that more of them can.

Before proceeding, let us dismiss as bogus one argument heard following the 2008 election: because so many more people showed up to vote than four years prior, is that not evidence that voting really is not really that hard? Not if one considers how much time, effort, and money had to be put in play—mainly but not wholly on behalf of Democrats—in order to ensure that several million new voters could actually cast ballots. If we go back to before the beginning of the primary season in January 2008, we see Herculean efforts to bring new people to the polls. Nothing wrong with that, but why is it not a matter of course that new voters are automatically added to voter rolls, and old voters encouraged to show up to cast a ballot? Why did we have to expend so many resources to make sure people, especially new voters, could vote?

Indeed, the question just suggested—Is it really all that hard to vote?—is the wrong one. A better question is, why are so many people prevented from voting? We are not concerned in this book with people who choose not to vote or don't want to. Our focus is on those who want to vote, who may set out to do so and find that they cannot. Perhaps one or more kinks in the election system disenfranchise them. Perhaps their vote is not recorded or counted accurately. Or perhaps their vote turns out to be meaningless. Thus, our concern in this book is not with those who succeed in voting, but those who do not or cannot. For them, the system does not work. There are millions of such people. And for a sizable portion of this group—we will see who they are in later chapters—disenfranchisement is permanent.

If voters were welcomed to the polls, and if casting ballots were truly regarded as a natural part of civic life in this country open to as many people as possible, voting—even for new voters—would be easy. Instead, we erect barriers to voting. This book explains what they are, shows along the way how to tear them down, and in the end asks if the will is present in this country to do so.

The Plan of the Book

After this initial chapter, the book consists of three major sections:

Part I: Disenfranchisement as Public Policy includes two chapters, one historical and one contemporary, on the way in which Americans have designed public policy to keep certain groups from voting.

Part II: The Mechanics of Voting is also composed of two chapters. The first discusses how one becomes a voter; the second deals with how ballots are actually cast, including the technology of voting.

In Part III: Trying to Vote in America, the first chapter deals with how our voting systems are gamed to disenfranchise some groups or render their votes meaningless. The final chapter, the Conclusion, asks about the obligation of the state to voters, and whether we as a public truly have the will to expand and strengthen voting rights and make them less susceptible to the pressures of narrowly partisan, essentially private, interests.

Notes

1. Century Foundation, *Voting in 2004: A Report to the Nation on America's Election Process* (New York: TCF, 2005); Ian Urbina, "Hurdles to Voting Persisted in 2008," *New York Times,* National Edition, March 11, 2009, p. A14. See also Stephen Ansolabehere, "Guide to the 2008 Cooperative Congressional Election Survey, Rough Draft," February 2009. Viewed online at http://web.mit.edu/polisci/portl/cces/material/CCES_Guide_2008_Rough_Draft_v2.pdf, accessed March 16, 2009.

2. Ian Urbina, "States' Actions to Block Voters Appear Illegal," www.nytimes.com/2008/10/09/us/politics/09voting.html?ei=5070&emc=eta1; Abbe Boudreau and Scott Bronstein, "Some Voters Purged from Voter Rolls," www.cnn.com/2008/POLITICS/10/26/voter.suppression/index.html. Both accessed October 27, 2008.

3. We will return to the issue of vote fraud in Chapter 4, when we look at recent requirements about voter IDs.

4. Frances Fox Piven and Richard A. Cloward, *Why Americans Still Don't Vote,* rev. and updated ed. (Boston: Beacon Press, 2000). For classic discussions of the role of political parties in meeting and socializing immigrants to America, see (among others) Lee S. Greene, ed., "City Bosses and Political Machines," *Annals of the American Academy of Political and Social Science,* vol. 353 (May 1964); Charles N. Glaub and A. Theodore Brown, *A History of Urban America* (New York: Macmillan, 1967); Allen M. Wakestein, ed., *The Urbanization of America: an Historical Anthology* (Boston: Houghton-Mifflin, 1970); and Bruce M. Stave, ed., *Urban Bosses, Machines, and Progressive Reformers* (Lexington, MA: D.C. Heath, 1972).

5. E.E. Schattschneider, *The Semisovereign People* (Hinsdale, IL: Dryden Press, 1975).

6. V.O. Key, Jr., *Southern Politics in State and Nation* (New York: Vintage, 1949); C. Vann Woodward, *The Strange Career of Jim Crow* (New York: Oxford University Press, 1966); J. Morgan Kousser, *The Shaping of Southern Politics* (New Haven: Yale University Press, 1974).

7. Earl Black, *Southern Governors and Civil Rights* (Cambridge: Harvard University Press, 1976).

8. Allen Sayre, "NAACP Challenges Louisiana Vote Purge," www.washingtonpost.com/wp-dyn/content/article/2007/08/31/AR2007083100501.html, accessed November 21, 2008; Rick Hanson, Election Law Blog, "Voter Purge in Mississippi," March 6, 2008, www.washingtonpost.com/wp-dyn/content/article/2007/08/31/AR2007083100501.html, accessed November 21, 2008.

9. The author was made aware of this incident at the opening of the "Oh Freedom Over Me" multimedia exhibit mounted by the Bay County Public Library, Panama City, Florida, October 3–4, 2008. The author was the invited keynote speaker and panel participant at the occasion, and the matter was mentioned to him there by one of the librarians.

10. Nonsystematic but credible data can be found in publications of such organizations and agencies as the United States Commission on Civil Rights, the Brennan Center for Justice at New York University Law School, Project VoteSmart, and others. Citations of these literatures will be given in ensuing chapters. However, an excellent recent volume documents, through careful historical, legal, and administrative analysis, the impact that local voting officials and practices have had on voting rights. See Alec C. Ewald, *The Way We Vote: The Local Dimension of American Suffrage* (Nashville, TN: Vanderbilt University Press, 2009).

11. Readers are reminded that in 2000 in Florida, there were documented reports from Palm Beach County that some African American voters were asked for two forms of ID, even though the law only required one. There were no reports that white voters there were asked for two IDs.

12. The young man with the Obama T-shirt is not the only documented case of a voter being turned away on account of "unsuitable" attire. Voters who appeared drunk have also been denied ballots, although there are no extant laws on the books that make public drunkenness a reason to disqualify a voter. Nor is eccentric behavior, such as might accompany nervous tics or idle chatter, catatonic or epileptic fits, grounds for disqualification, although voters have been denied ballots because they struck polling officials as acting strangely.

13. Readers interested in or concerned about this issue are urged to consult an insightful recent book by Frances Fox Piven, Lorraine C. Minnite, and Margaret Groark, *Keeping Down the Black Vote: Race and the Demobilization of American Voters* (New York: The New Press, 2009).

14. *Crawford v. Marion County Election Board,* April 28, 2008.

15. Blackwell was not the only state official to move to prevent private groups from registering voters. In Florida, the Republican-dominated legislature passed laws following the 2004 election to keep private groups from engaging in voter registration. They were so punitive and draconian that the League of Women Voters, which has been registering voters since its origin, ceased all efforts in the state to continue the practice. Later, the rules were suspended pending the outcome of litigation, but there is no question that the imposition of these rules had a chilling effect until 2007–2008, when the Obama campaign and Democratic Party actively recruited and registered new voters in the Sunshine State.

16. "Some Voters Purged from Voter Rolls," www.cnn.com/2008/POLITICS/10/26/voter. suppression/index.html, accessed October 27, 2008.

17. The Republican-dominated Florida legislature in 2005 limited the hours and days of "early voting" out of purely partisan interests. Governor Charlie Crist, in late October 2008, ordered that early voting hours be extended, contravening the legislation.

18. Ian Urbina, "States' Action to Block Voters Appears Illegal"; see also Myrna Perez, "Voter Purges," a report of the Brennan Center for Justice, New York University School of Law, September 30, 2008, found at www.brennancenter.org/content/resource/voter_purges/, accessed November 21, 2008. This is a comprehensive study of voter purges in twelve states.

19. "High Court Rejects GOP in Ohio Voting Dispute," MSNBC, October 17, 2008, www.msnbc.msn.com/id/27238980/; "US. Supreme Court Upholds Ohio Voters' Rights," *Election Protection,* October 17, 2008, http://8660urvote.articulatedman.com/newsroom/ press-releases?id=0023. Both accessed on November 19, 2008.

20. "Supreme Court Sides with Ohio Secretary of State," *Election Protection,* October 17, 2008, www.8660urvote.org/state/news?id=0052, accessed July 7, 2009.

Part I

Disenfranchisement
as Public Policy

The Great American Tradition

Part I of this book consists of two chapters dealing with the American tradition of voter disenfranchisement. Some readers may be startled to learn that in fact the expansion of the franchise, and access to the polls, has been a long, slow, arduous, nonlinear, and incomplete process in the United States. But the conclusion from the historical and contemporary data we shall examine is incontrovertible: voting in the United States for most of our history was a privilege denied significant portions of the population, and even now is a right not universally enjoyed here.

2

Let Everyone Vote?
Not on Your Life!

An underlying theme of this book is that of "disenfranchisement as public policy." This requires a bit of an explanation. In this book, "policy" refers to more than just what government does: "policy is the rational attempt to attain objectives," as one recent author put it.[1] Other analysts suggest that "policy" is actually limited to the public sector.[2] Such a view seems unnecessarily narrow. As used here, policy does indeed refer to the actions of public bodies that seek to limit the franchise, whether by law or by administrative rules and procedures. But it also refers to more informal activity—customs, traditions, attitudes, beliefs, and behaviors (many of which are probably reflexive and unconscious) that have the effect of disenfranchising individuals or groups.

Examples abound that illustrate the point. Disenfranchisement of former slaves occurred widely throughout the South following the demise of Reconstruction. It was carried out through institutionalization of Jim Crow laws by state legislatures, but it also resulted from local practices and community prejudices. In the North, the Irish, and later Italians and other eastern and southern Europeans, were repeatedly victimized, harassed, and kept from voting, sometimes by law but more often by thuggery and intimidation.

Thus, a "great tradition" of the United States has been to implement policies of disenfranchisement. Whether that policy resulted from the specific acts of public bodies or was simply the result of local attitudes, beliefs, traditions, and customs is not very important. What is essential is the effect of those policies: in the United States a great deal of effort has gone into keeping some voters away from the polls, rather than welcoming them to cast ballots.

This chapter will look closely at the "great American tradition" of disenfranchisement. After a brief overview of the extent of disenfranchisement at the origins of the nation, we will examine the most egregious case: that of African Americans. We will also look at the struggle of women to gain the franchise and then turn our attention to Chinese immigrants. In the next chapter we explore the disenfranchisement of a variety of other groups. The goal of these two chapters is to show readers that in fact our policy of limiting the franchise goes very deep into the American past and, arguably, into the very soul of our nation.

The Franchise at the Nation's Origin

Even before 1776, when the thirteen colonies declared themselves an independent nation, the franchise was highly restricted.[3] In general, four types of limitations were imposed on potential voters: property or taxpaying requirements, residency, gender, and race. Failure to meet the requisite standard automatically disqualified anyone seeking to vote.

In this early period, property or taxpaying requirements were the most common test for voter eligibility. As early as 1715, Connecticut imposed the restriction of a "Freehold estate worth 40 shillings per year or 40 pounds personal estate."[4] Other colonies followed suit, such that by the time of the Revolution, twelve of the thirteen nascent states had some form of property requirement for voting. Only Vermont had none.[5]

South Carolina and Virginia had probably the most restrictive property requirements: in both states prospective voters had to possess a freehold of at least fifty acres. In South Carolina that property had to be in the possession of the freeholder at least six months before the election, and in Virginia the land had to have on it a dwelling "at least 12 feet square."[6]

Likewise, all but three states (Connecticut, New Hampshire, and Rhode Island) imposed residency requirements on prospective voters. Massachusetts had no such requirement for voting for Senate, but had a one-year residency requirement "in town" for the House. Maryland waived the residency requirement if the individual held a fifty-acre freehold, otherwise the residency requirement was one year. Three states—Delaware, Pennsylvania, and South Carolina—required two years of residence before voting was possible.[7]

Gender restrictions were also imposed early in our history. Five states—Connecticut, Delaware, Georgia, New Jersey, and Rhode Island—made no stipulations about gender as a prerequisite for voting. But only in New Jersey could women actually vote—that is, if they owned property. By 1807 even this limited extension of the franchise was removed, and women were no longer permitted to vote there.[8] Four states (Maryland, North Carolina, Pennsylvania, and Vermont) specified that voters had to be "freemen," which of course eliminated the possibility that slaves could vote. Georgia, Massachusetts, New Hampshire, New York, South Carolina, and Virginia all specified that voters had to be males.

Only three states—Georgia, South Carolina, and Virginia—required that voters be white. During the early years of independence, Alexander Keyssar tells us, African Americans could actually vote in a few states, including New Jersey, Maryland, and Connecticut.[9] In the Southern states blacks could not vote, and elsewhere they could vote only with difficulty, if at all. Again, custom and local practice, if not law, disenfranchised blacks.

With the coming of the nineteenth century, suffrage requirements began to change in the young United States. Some requirements were relaxed or removed, while others were stiffened. The first to disappear were property and taxation requirements.[10] This, of course, was in keeping with expanding notions of democracy during the first third of the nineteenth century as the nation grew westward and new states and territories were inhabited. It was more immediately a result of the democratic impulse of the Jacksonian era, in which the rights of everyday citizens (white males, at least) were recognized. In 1790, ten of the thirteen states had some kind of property requirement for voting; by 1855, when there were thirty-one states, only three still had a property requirement (Rhode Island, New York, and South Carolina), but Rhode Island exempted native-born citizens, New York's rule applied only to blacks, and South Carolina offered a residency alternative.[11]

But on issues of race and citizenship, suffrage requirements were made stricter in the first half of the nineteenth century. By 1855, of the thirty-one states admitted to the Union, twenty-four specified that only whites (males) could vote. A number of other states offered no racial requirement, such as Georgia. But it was clear that in most of these "no requirement" states, African Americans could not vote, if not because of legal or constitutional language then because of local practices, customs, and beliefs. Indiana, Kentucky, and Texas offered language excluding "Negroes," "Mulattos," and "Indians" from voting. New York permitted "men of color" to vote if they met property and taxation requirements, and Tennessee did likewise if the individual was "a competent witness in a court of justice against a white man."[12]

It was during this period also that citizenship requirements were imposed in order to vote. In the early days of the Republic, citizenship was not necessarily a prerequisite to voting if the individual met other requirements (such as property ownership or residency). Some states very early on required state or U.S. citizenship to vote: South Carolina in 1810 was the first. But by the 1830s, many states began to require citizenship as a prerequisite to voting, and by the 1850s all of them did.

The reason for the rapid expansion of citizenship requirements is readily understandable. First, it meant that Native Americans could not be voters, since in most instances it was impossible for them to become citizens. Likewise, before the Emancipation Proclamation, slaves could not be citizens, and even in some Northern states free slaves and blacks who had never been slaves had difficulty qualifying for citizenship. Citizenship requirements were a way of ensuring that these political and social outsiders were kept from the polls. The 1840s also saw the onset of massive immigration to the United States, particularly (but not exclusively) from Ireland. Citizenship requirements were a way to keep immigrants from voting, especially the Irish, who were widely scorned and discriminated against.

Thus, the early years of the United States were a period in which public policy was aimed at limiting the franchise to a select few. True, as the nineteenth century wore on, some early requirements such as property ownership and taxation were eliminated; so too were religious tests. But even as these roadblocks to voting were being eliminated, others took their place—in the form of residency and citizenship requirements, and racial barriers. Gender barriers remained solidly in place.

Indeed, a reading of the history of this period indicates that far more effort went into shutting people out of the franchise than affording it to them.

Disenfranchising African Americans

Prior to the Emancipation Proclamation of 1863, most African Americans were slaves. True, by 1790 there were about 60,000 freedmen in the states, many in the South. By the dawn of the nineteenth century all of the Northern states provided some mechanism for emancipation. As a result, the number of freedmen rose rapidly, until there were about a half-million on the eve of the Civil War. Nonetheless, following the Revolutionary War the number of slaves had grown rapidly in the United States, reaching about 4 million in 1860, almost all in the South and border states. As Eric Foner points out, by that date the "South had become the largest, most powerful slave society the modern world has known."[13]

It is difficult for modern readers to grasp the significance and consequences of the slave society in the United States, so distant does it seem from the present. Perhaps it would help to note that in a slave society, slaves were not considered human. They were property, chattel—no different from clothes, a table, or a horse. Most importantly, because slaves were not considered human, they had no rights whatsoever. Perhaps this is the most difficult concept for the modern reader to grasp; we are, after all, accustomed to the idea that even the most depraved felons or prisoners of war have certain basic rights that cannot be (but unfortunately sometimes are) ignored. Slaves did not rise even to this level. Only to the extent that their owners treated them decently or afforded them limited privileges did they have the opportunity to live as nonslaves might. But this seldom happened, and even though it was in the economic self-interest of slave owners to keep their slaves reasonably healthy, most treated their slaves abominably. As Foner observes,

> Slaves, of course, experienced the institutions of politics and the law quite differently from white Americans. Before the law, slaves were property who had virtually no legal rights. They could be bought, sold, leased, and seized to satisfy an owner's debt, their family ties had no legal standing, and they could not leave the plantation or hold meetings without the permission of their owner. Masters had almost complete discretion in inflicting punishment, and rare was the slave who went through his or her life without experiencing a whipping. The entire system of southern justice, from the state militia and courts to slave patrols in each locality, was committed to enforcing the master's control over his human property, and no aspect of their lives, no matter how intimate, was beyond the reach of his interference.[14]

It is well recognized that the existence of a slave society caused considerable discomfort and mental anguish throughout the United States, including in the South. Such major Enlightenment intellectuals as Thomas Jefferson and James Madison were deeply troubled by the presence of slaves, yet neither made any effort to free theirs. The slave society was an early example of "green handcuffs" in the South:

the existence of a plantation economy that depended totally for its success on an abundance of slaves meant that it was not possible to dump the system, even if the will had been present to do so.

The framers of the Constitution in 1787 were indeed troubled by the existence of the slave system, and of course there was deep division between slave and nonslave states over what to do about it. As is so often the case in the politics of document-drafting, the framers wrote around the issue. Neither "slaves" nor "slavery" is mentioned in the Constitution. Slaves were referred to as "other persons" in the document, as sanitary a euphemism as the writers could conjure. But the Constitution, as Foner notes, underscored and even strengthened the institution of slavery: "The Constitution allowed the slave trade from Africa to continue for twenty more years, required states to return to their owners fugitives from bondage, and provided that three-fifths of the slave population be counted in allocating electoral votes and Congressmen among the states."[15]

This latter point underscores the fundamental inhumanity of the eighteenth-century American view of slaves and slavery: they counted, for the purpose of enumeration, only as 60 percent of a person. Nowadays even convicted felons are counted as whole individuals for census purposes. Not so for slaves in the Constitution. Perhaps nothing underscores the capacity of the slave society to deny the basic humanity of slaves as the Constitution's failure to enumerate them as full, bona fide human beings.

Under these circumstances, it was not possible for slaves to vote; indeed, to award the franchise to them would have afforded them a measure of humanity, and that was inconceivable. Because they were property, they were no more entitled to the franchise than chickens, or a wagon, or cotton bolls.

Thus, it is of interest that as early as 1763 Virginia felt compelled to establish a law preventing blacks from voting; Georgia followed in 1777. Undoubtedly these measures were a result of the presence of black freedmen in the states; no one wanted them to vote either.

But the effect of these and other early race-exclusionary laws (South Carolina, 1790; Delaware, 1792; Kentucky, 1799)[16] was to change dramatically the nature of disenfranchisement policy. No longer was it merely confined to slaves. In fact, race became a major focus of who could vote and who could not. It would be wrong to say that these early measures merely institutionalized racism in disenfranchisement policy; matters were much deeper and more pernicious, because these measures reflected early racial attitudes and views that were based on the supposed biological and moral inferiority of the black race. Even where blacks were not slaves, they were not to be considered in any way equal to whites. Indeed, they had to be kept apart from whites, and were to be afforded none of the rights and privileges that whites, even the poorest and most derelict of whites, could claim.

Thus, it was the development of American racial attitudes and views, not just the existence of slavery, that gave rise to policies of disenfranchisement of blacks. Institutionalized racism started very early in this nation's history, and one sees it very clearly in the creation of race-based legislation aimed at excluding blacks, slaves or not, from voting.

These kinds of measures were not limited to the South. Ohio in 1803 and New Jersey in 1807 were the first Northern states to adopt laws keeping blacks from voting. Laws like these spread like wildfire, with state after state adopting them (including those such as Wisconsin, which had very few black residents). California was the last, in 1850. As Keyssar notes, by 1855, of the thirty-one states in the Union, twenty-five (81 percent) had adopted some kind of race-exclusionary language for the franchise, either by statute or constitutional provision.[17] Thus, as the Civil War loomed, public policy in the United States created a largely impermeable barrier between blacks—slaves or not—and the franchise.

At the conclusion of the Civil War in 1865 and the onset of Reconstruction, the position of ex-slaves in the South was precarious. True, they were no longer slaves, hence no longer someone's chattel or property. But even this improvement of political rights was circumscribed. The Emancipation Proclamation did not necessarily apply to all slaves; the Thirteenth Amendment (1865) was required to assure that slavery and involuntary servitude were finally abolished.

However, socially and economically blacks remained pariahs and occupied the lowest rung of the ladder. Nowhere in the South did former slaves become social equals to whites, nor were they welcomed into white culture. In the North, blacks remained objects of discrimination, unable to hold any but the most menial jobs and forced to live in the meanest, often ghettoized areas. The development of the tenant-lien system of agriculture in the South assured that blacks would live lives of abject poverty and economic dependency, unable to free themselves from increasing mountains of debt to the landowners from whom they leased plots. One way out would have been for former slaves to purchase land, but in many places they were not legally able to do so, even if they could afford it. But more importantly, they would remain subject to white economic pressure and control.[18] In a sense, blacks traded political slavery for social and economic slavery; it was hard to say which was worse.[19]

But there was a strange feature of the Reconstruction period created entirely by forces exogenous to the South: former slaves (at least males) could vote, run for, and even be elected (or be appointed) to public office. None of this came immediately upon the stillness settling over the Appomattox courthouse. Rather, it required the ratification of the Fourteenth Amendment (1868), the Fifteenth Amendment (1870), and action by Radical Republicans in the U.S. Congress to force the admission of former slaves into the political arena. It is important to point out that while blacks did vote and hold public office (including in state legislatures, the lieutenant governorships in Louisiana and South Carolina, and seats in Congress), in a number of instances they were appointed by Union military officers charged with implementing Reconstruction policies. More generally, it was white Northern support, especially among former abolitionists and Radical Republicans, the on-site presence of Northern carpetbagger politicians, and the Northern army-of-occupation, that gave former slaves whatever political authority and position they held. Nowhere, South or North, were blacks able to create an independent base of political power. This was especially true in the South, where they were completely dependent on outside political forces to vote or hold political office.[20]

Such an artificial situation could not last forever, and it did not. In fact, by 1876 it started to come apart. In that year the Republican Party, headed by its presidential nominee, Rutherford B. Hayes, stole the election from Democrat Samuel Tilden (who won the popular vote) primarily with disputed ballots in Louisiana and (where else?) Florida. As part of the bargain to pull off the heist, Hays began to remove the army-of-occupation from the South. The immediate effect was to eliminate one of the major supports that African Americans needed to maintain their artificial political position.

But disenfranchisement of the former slaves did not begin immediately. Even before the army-of-occupation left, Bourbon Redeemers (the heirs of the old ruling class in the South) had begun to reassert themselves and inveigle their way back into positions of power in Southern politics. Once the army left, there was nothing to stop them from seizing control completely. But they moved slowly. They saw that too swift a power grab, and too rapid an assault on black political rights, would cause questions up North; a worst-case scenario was that the army would return, and that was what they most wanted to avoid.[21]

But even as they temporized, they were aided by events in the North. As it happened, Northern enthusiasm for propping up Southern blacks began to wane; with a few exceptions, they were no longer the object of Radical Republicans' interest or pity. The attention of the nation began to shift to other matters.[22] The winds of imperialism were blowing in Washington, and policymakers began to look abroad, not South, to find America's destiny. Besides, if one of the bases of American imperialism was that foreign cultures (especially those of peoples of color) were inferior to those of whites, what was the use pretending that Southern blacks were equal to whites? Obviously such an incongruity, indeed inconsistency, could not stand. Northern white support for Southern blacks collapsed. They were now at the mercy of racist Southern politicians and public attitudes that placed blame for the Glorious Defeat, onto the backs of Southern blacks, and sought revenge for the burdens of Reconstruction. In this view, it was time to put those pariahs in their place. It was time for Jim Crow laws.

The Jim Crow Era

The Jim Crow era did not begin in 1890, but it was certainly well entrenched by then. Indeed, the basis for the Jim Crow era probably began in the mid-1870s, when, in two stunning decisions, the U.S. Supreme Court opened the doors for it to happen. In May 1870, as part of imposing a Reconstruction regime on the South, Congress passed the so-called "Enforcement Act," more commonly known as the "force bill." It was specifically designed to enforce the Fifteenth Amendment and contained severe penalties against those preventing otherwise qualified citizens (including former slaves) from voting.[23]

But in *U.S. v. Cruikshank*[24] and *U.S. v. Reese,*[25] the Supreme Court essentially gutted the Enforcement Act and, by extension, the Fifteenth Amendment, and significantly limited the application of the Fourteenth Amendment. In *Cruikshank,* the Court held that indictments against whites in Louisiana who had rioted to prevent blacks from voting, and who had in the process murdered more than 100, were illegal because the Fourteenth Amendment prevented state action against private citizens; thus, the amendment (and therefore the Constitution) offered blacks no protection against the wrath of private agents, including the Ku Klux Klan and its fellow travelers. In *Reese,* indictments against local voting officials who had declined to count the votes of blacks in Kentucky were dismissed on the grounds that the indictments did not specifically point to a racial intent to discriminate. "The Fifteenth Amendment does not confer the right of suffrage upon any one," Chief Justice Morrison R. Waite stated in writing for the majority.[26] It merely prevented the state from keeping otherwise qualified voters away from the polls on racial grounds, something that was not demonstrated in the facts of the case.

The effect of these decisions was to eliminate federal supervision of black voting in the South. Taken together, they placed enforcement of civil and voting rights in the hands of states, not the federal government. Indeed, they pushed the federal government out of the voting rights enforcement business altogether, as far as former slaves were concerned. Thus, the door was open for state officials to discriminate more or less as they pleased against African Americans seeking their civil and voting rights, with the recognition and knowledge that the federal government—including its army-of-occupation—would not intervene against them. Enter the era of Jim Crow.

As far as voting rights are specifically concerned, Jim Crow probably began in 1871, when Georgia passed a poll tax (in 1877 it was made cumulative, meaning that prospective voters had to pay back taxes before they could vote).[27] In theory, the poll tax was a revenue-raising device, but in fact it was a mechanism for keeping blacks (and poor whites) away from the polls. The tax, which spread widely to other Southern states, seems modest by today's standards—usually a dollar or two (unless it had to be paid cumulatively)—but in the sharecropper economy of the South (which operated on credit and barter, not cash) it was substantial. The poverty of the region was staggering, almost incomprehensible. In 1900, farms in Alabama were worth only $4.84 per acre, compared to the national average of $15.57; in Georgia the figure was $5.25 per acre, in Mississippi $6.30, and Texas $4.70.[28] But these figures are deceptive because they do not account for race. Farm values and incomes of ex-slaves were less than half those of whites. Given the crushing burden of poverty that Southerners bore, especially African American Southerners, it is easy to see why a dollar or two tax paid to vote (assuming they would be allowed to vote even after paying) was not realistic for most Southern blacks.

The constitutionality of the poll tax was not seriously challenged until 1937, in

Breedlove v. Suttles.[29] In another amazing display of judicial blindness, the U.S. Supreme Court argued that there was nothing in Georgia's poll tax law (and, by implication, those in other states) that was designed to disenfranchise, and that it was in fact a legitimate mechanism for raising revenues. "To make payment of poll taxes a prerequisite of voting is not to deny any privilege or immunity protected by the Fourteenth Amendment," the Court held, and it went on to point out, "Privilege [that word again] of voting is not derived from the United States, but is conferred by the state and, save as restrained by the Fifteenth and Nineteenth Amendments and other provisions of the Federal Constitution, the state may condition suffrage as it deems appropriate."

Obviously this kind of judicial language constituted a license for states to impose whatever kind of tax requirements on potential voters they wanted; as late as 1921 at least twenty-six states, including all of the Southern states, imposed a poll tax or other tax-paying requirement as a prerequisite to voting.[30] And these requirements were effective in disenfranchising voters; the Michigan study referenced above estimates that in Georgia the poll tax "reduced overall turnout by 16–28%," and, citing J. Morgan Kousser, among blacks by at least 50 percent.[31]

The poll tax was finally eliminated by the Voting Rights Act in 1965. But it was by no means the only Jim Crow mechanism designed to disenfranchise black voters. Literacy tests and character testimonials were also commonly used, and not only in the South. As late as 1924, some twenty-four states imposed literacy requirements on prospective voters, including all of the Southern states.[32] These could range from relatively modest requirements of demonstrating an ability to read, to requirements that prospective voters interpret sections of the state or federal constitution after reading them aloud to an election official. As it would often turn out, of course, it was far easier for whites to pass these "tests" than African Americans, even those who were well educated professionals. Local election officials would simply reject them out of hand, whereas interpretations offered by whites would be accepted. Literacy tests were also abolished by the Voting Rights Act in 1965.[33]

Character testimonials were not as common or widespread as literacy tests, but like the latter, they were differentially and racially applied. Prospective voters would be forced to provide at least one affidavit stating that they were of "good character." Those offering testimonials would usually have to be registered voters, which, in the South, overwhelmingly meant whites. Thus, a potential black voter would have to find and convince one or more registered white voters to vouch for his "character," something that was virtually impossible. The legal basis of character testimonials was never clear, nor was it always explicit; it was more frequently one of those local mores or customs used by voting officials to keep blacks from the polls. With the advent of the Voting Rights Act, especially its ability to force names onto registration lists, and the presence of federal monitors in covered areas, character testimonials were deservedly relegated to the scrap heap of history.

The all-white primary was another mechanism designed to disenfranchise blacks during the Jim Crow era. It was a product of the one-party system in the old South.[34] Following Reconstruction, the Republican Party throughout most of the South collapsed; except in a relatively few areas, it was more a figment of the imagination than a political force.[35] And after 1896, with the demise of the Southern Populist Party, the Democratic Party was the only political game in the region. As a result, electoral politics were centered in the Democratic primary; the winner of this contest would inevitably prevail in the general election, because the Republicans (and, after about 1910, the Populists) would not bother to contest, or if they did, would not put up much of a fight.

Texas Democrats had the bright idea of limiting eligibility to vote in the primary to whites. There were a number of cases brought to the U.S. Supreme Court protesting this policy, and they hinged on the issue of whether or not the primary was essentially a private function as opposed to a state one. In a 1935 case, *Grovey v. Townsend*,[36] the Court ruled that in fact the Texas primary system was fundamentally a private affair, even though it was mandated and regulated by state law.[37] This decision was reversed in the landmark case *Smith v. Allwright* (1944).[38] The Court held that the state was so involved in running primary elections that in fact it was a public function, and thus subject to the Fourteenth and Fifteenth Amendments.

Smith v. Allwright was arguably the first major victory for black enfranchisement since the Fifteenth Amendment had been ratified seventy-four years earlier. It did not, of course, address the issue of registering blacks to vote. In Texas, as in other states, blacks could register only with difficulty, if at all, although it is true that in some urban areas of the border South, blacks had less trouble registering, especially compared to the hard-shell Deep South. But *Smith* was important as a symbol; it signified to Southern blacks that the era of Jim Crow might eventually end.

But there were miles to go and many battles to be fought during the civil rights movement before anything like that could really be imagined. This was particularly true in view of the role brutality, lynchings, and violence against blacks played in keeping them from securing the franchise. Brutality had been a part of the African American experience since the very first slaves arrived on these shores; by its very nature, slavery is a brutalizing experience, designed to suck the humanity—the very soul—out of its victims (and for that matter, it does the same to its perpetrators). Even after slavery was officially abolished and the Civil War ended, it cannot be said that brutalization of former slaves ceased. It was not long after hostilities ended that America's premier terrorist organization, the Ku Klux Klan (founded in Pulaski, Tennessee, in December 1865) began its hooded rides across the South, targeting ex-slaves and, by the twentieth century, communists, Jews, and Catholics.[39]

It is important to note that the brutality that Southern blacks (and, occasionally, those elsewhere) faced was not purely physical. The beatings, maimings, murders, and lynchings are, of course, well known. The psychological aspect of the terror blacks faced could be equally devastating and demeaning. Those attempting to register to vote, or actually cast a ballot, often faced the most staggering consequences: they could be and were thrown off the land, fired from jobs, run out of town, and had their children kicked out of school;[40] this was apart from the distinct possibility of a nighttime visit from the Klan resulting in the burning of a cross, a house torched, shootings, kidnappings, beatings, and lynchings. All of this was very real to Southern blacks following the Civil War, and while the Klan actually died down late in the nineteenth century, its tactics were adopted by other terrorist entrepreneurs, including law enforcement personnel. By the 1920s, the Klan was back in business, and it remained a force until well into and even beyond the active phase of the civil rights movement.

The number of lynchings in the South between 1880 and 1950 is staggering. John Egerton, relying on Tuskegee Institute figures, places the number at 4,700, but he goes on to point out that there were assuredly many more.[41] More than 85 percent of these occurred in Southern or border South states. Some 1,500 blacks and 150 whites were lynched just between 1900 and 1930, and "it was exceedingly rare for anyone to be punished for taking part in a lynch mob."[42]

Not all of these horrifying acts occurred because blacks sought to secure their voting rights; many were a result of crimes they were alleged to have committed, accusations their white neighbors were all too willing to believe.[43] But other forms of violence all too often befell those who sought to register or vote. Isaac Nixon (1948), Alvin Jones (1950), Harry T. Moore (1951), and George Lee and Lamar Smith (1955), were all murdered for asserting their voting rights, and there were others. Most were beaten or shot; Moore and his wife were killed when their home in Brevard County, Florida, was bombed on Christmas Day.[44]

All of this, of course, was before the so-called "active" stage of the civil rights movement began. Once it started, its immediate effect was to initiate the period of "massive resistance" during which hard-core, intransigent whites in the South pushed back just as hard as Southern blacks pushed them.[45] The result was more than a decade of unprecedented violence against Southern blacks. Who can fail to be moved and horrified by the account of Annelle Ponder and Fannie Lou Hamer as they were assaulted and beaten—tortured, actually—for their involvement in voting rights in Winona, Mississippi, in the summer of 1963?[46] That same spring, Medgar Evers was gunned down in Jackson, Mississippi, for his work on voting rights. The following summer, so-called "Freedom Summer," was dedicated by the Student Nonviolent Coordinating Committee (SNCC) to securing voting rights in Mississippi; activists James Cheney, Andrew Goodman, and Michael Schwerner were murdered in Philadelphia, Mississippi, for their efforts, in a case that received international coverage. In March of the following spring, several hundred African Americans in Selma, Alabama, were gassed and savagely beaten as they prepared for a march to the state capitol building in Montgomery in pursuit of their voting rights.[47]

We could literally spend the rest of the book documenting brutality, intimidation, and violence directed against blacks seeking their voting rights, and not just in the South. But instead, we return to the theme outlined at the beginning of the chapter: namely, that it has historically been U.S. policy, and not simply that of a few Southern states, to disenfranchise blacks. We have seen that for centuries blacks were denied any form of civil rights, including voting rights. Even after the period of slavery ended, they were still denied, either as a matter of law, Supreme Court decisions, or state and local practice. Much of this happened, it must be said, with the approval—either tacit or explicit—of agents and agencies of the federal government.

But beyond these formalisms was the indifference and acquiescence of white Americans to the continued disenfranchisement of African Americans. From presidents (except for Harry Truman, Lyndon Johnson, and, toward the end of his life, John Kennedy) on down, Americans turned a cold shoulder to the civil and voting rights plight of their fellow citizens. Once Reconstruction ended, very few whites cared anymore, and those who did were shunned, ignored, or (in some cases) persecuted like blacks were.[48]

Nor have African Americans fully won their voting rights. As we shall see elsewhere, there are continuing instances—entirely too many—in which they have been denied the right to vote. Indeed, as Frances Fox Piven and her coauthors recently demonstrated, there are ongoing efforts in this country by government officials and others, including those responsible for voting rights, to demobilize black voters.[49]

This is not a discussion of where to place the responsibility for what happened. But it is appropriate to point out that the policy of black disenfranchisement in America is a result of decisions made and acquiesced to by whites.[50] African Americans did not create their own disenfranchisement, nor did they ask to be denied the right to vote. It was whites who created the policy of black disenfranchisement, by their actions and inaction, by their willingness to "go along" with and perpetuate traditional customs and beliefs of prejudice, intolerance, indifference, and bigotry. Few were the white voices that spoke out against this tradition. It is surely one of the most shameful strands in the long history of white political culture in America.

Women's Suffrage

Just as it is impossible to fix with certainty the date when the civil rights movement began, so is the origin of the women's suffrage movement uncertain. No one knows when the first woman wondered, to herself or out loud, why she did not have the right to vote even though at least some men did. A reasonable place to begin, however, would be with the publication in 1792 of Mary Wollstonecraft's *Vindication of the Rights of Women*.[51] Strictly speaking, the *Vindication* is not a text devoted to women's suffrage. It is generally regarded, however, as one of the first thoughtful, even philosophical, works on women's rights published in the West, as it advocates equality of the sexes.

The beginnings of the American version of the women's suffrage movement might be a little easier to affix. In 1840, a group of American women, headed by Lucretia Mott of Philadelphia, attended the World Anti-Slavery Convention in London. Mott was a prominent Quaker preacher and public intellectual, and founder in 1833 of the Female Anti-Slavery Society in Philadelphia.[52] Mott and her colleagues were not allowed to address the convention, however, solely on grounds of gender. Incensed, Mott and another participant, Elizabeth Cady Stanton, resolved that when they returned to the United States, they would convene a women's rights convention.[53]

It took until 1849, but Mott and Stanton did preside over a gathering in Seneca Falls, New York, on July 20. That historic meeting and its aftermath sounded the opening bell in a fight that would last more than fifty years, and would culminate in the 1920 ratification of the Nineteenth Amendment granting voting rights to women. Indeed, it was but four years after Seneca Falls at another women's rights convention held in Syracuse that Susan B. Anthony made her famous speech arguing that "the right women needed above every other . . . was the right of suffrage."[54]

In fact, issues of women's suffrage preceded Seneca Falls by quite a bit. As Keyssar points out, as early as the Revolutionary War there were some who held the view—albeit distinctly a minority one—that all "inhabitants" with a "stake in society" should be allowed to vote. This was generally interpreted to include women, particularly widows and other women who owned property. As early as 1776, New Jersey had a provision in its constitution reflecting the "stake in society" argument, and it was followed by a 1790 election law implementing it.[55] The effect was to grant the franchise to at least some women in the state.

No other state moved as far as New Jersey in this early period, and in fact, in 1807 New Jersey took the remarkable step of rescinding women's voting rights. Why it did so is not exactly clear. According to Keyssar, the state seemed not so much concerned that the effect of women's suffrage would break up the family or to allow unqualified and incompetent women to vote as it was determined to correct "defects" in the state constitution and to clarify "doubts" about what exactly constituted the "legitimate" electorate. But once that happened, "women everywhere in the nation were barred from the polls."[56]

The Reconstruction proposals for the Fourteenth and Fifteenth Amendments provided another opportunity for the women's suffrage movement to put its agenda before the public. It gained virtually no traction. While there were a number of issues considered, two were fundamental. First, there was a question of whether or not the language of either amendment included women's suffrage. The Fourteenth Amendment speaks, in Section 2, only of "male inhabitants," and later in the section, of "male citizens" as potential voters. But Section 1 seemed to offer some hope to women in its gender-neutral statement that "nor [shall any State] deny to any person within its jurisdiction the equal protection of the laws." It was the "any person" language that seemed to open the door, if only by a small crack, to women's suffrage. The problem for advocates of women's suffrage was that very few people outside the movement—and even a surprising number within it—accepted the view that "equal protection of the laws" included voting. But there was an even more fundamental constitutional problem: because voting was seen as a state function, it was not even clear, at that early date, that the Fourteenth

Amendment applied to it. Thus advocates of women's suffrage could hardly expect
Fourteenth Amendment protection.

The Fifteenth Amendment created just as many problems for the suffrage movement, in fact it split it almost irrevocably. The relevant portion of the text reads:

> Section 1. The right of citizens of the United States to vote shall not be denied or
> abridged by the United States or by any State on account of race, color, or previous
> condition of servitude.

The difficulty for advocates of women's suffrage was that once again there was
no agreement that women slaves were included in the intent of the amendment.
In fact, the preponderance of opinion was exactly the opposite—women were
excluded, and the amendment applied only to former male slaves.[57]

Indeed, it was at this point that the suffrage movement split into two parts.
One debated whether or not the movement should even support the Fourteenth
and Fifteenth Amendments. If they only applied to males, a number of suffrage
advocates argued against them, including Anthony and Stanton; they especially
vented their wrath on the Fourteenth. But the other side, including their ally Lucy
Stone, felt the amendments should be endorsed; they argued that once black males
were enfranchised, the next step would be women.[58] The split over this issue was
so profound that it lasted until 1890, when the two factions reconciled and formed
the National American Woman Suffrage Association, which did much of the heavy
lifting in preparation for adoption of the Nineteenth Amendment.[59]

But the amendments created another schism in the women's suffrage movement, one between blacks and whites. Involvement of African American women
in the suffrage movement prior to the Civil War was limited; Sojourner Truth was
undoubtedly the most prominent black women's suffrage activist at the time.[60] After
the Civil War there was an increase in the involvement of African American women,
although as Rosalyn Terborg-Penn notes, it was not always clear that white women
in the movement paid much attention to them. But the struggle over the Fifteenth
Amendment forced them to do so. Black women were generally more sympathetic
to it than their white sisters, but that was not the major point of contention. Rather,
it was by no means certain that the majority of white women in the movement were
sympathetic to black women's suffrage under any circumstances, no matter what
the Fifteenth Amendment said.[61] This is another example of race trumping other
considerations, in this instance gender, when it comes to voting rights.

But the Fourteenth and Fifteenth Amendments were not the only stumbling
blocks that the suffrage movement faced. In 1867 it suffered two major setbacks:
its efforts to lobby the New York State Constitutional Convention to include
women's suffrage, and its campaign to encourage Kansas to adopt a referendum
endorsing both black and women's voting rights both failed. Then, in 1874, the
U.S. Supreme Court decided that the U.S. Constitution did not guarantee the right
to vote to anyone, including women, but rather that this right is subject to the
constitutions and laws of individual states: "the Constitution of the United States

does not confer the right of suffrage upon any one, and . . . the constitutions and laws of the several States which commit that important trust to men alone are not necessarily void."[62]

As the last quarter of the nineteenth century loomed, it was clear that the disenfranchisement of women as public policy was firmly entrenched. In spite of the vociferous and politically engaged activity of the suffrage activists, victories were few. Indeed, while there are no reports of women seeking the vote being lynched or shot, in fact, the struggle on the street was difficult, even dangerous. Women involved were regularly arrested, and in jail suffered numerous indignities, including physical attacks. On marches and at rallies and vigils they were harassed and verbally assaulted, if not worse. And the suffragists learned that women could be as intransigent opponents as the most troglodytic men: there were significant numbers of women's organizations dedicated to keeping women from securing the franchise. On a daily basis, women seeking the vote faced calumnious assaults from editorial writers, journalists, and authors of political screeds and broadsides.

And yet matters were more complicated than this. In fact, some women were voting, at least in limited circumstances. As early as 1855, widows and unmarried women who owned property could vote on school issues in Kentucky, while taxpaying women in Michigan secured the vote on school matters in the same year. By 1912, women (and not just taxpaying women) could vote in school elections in thirty states and territories. Between 1887 and 1917 women in fourteen states gained the franchise for municipal elections involving tax or bond issues. And by 1919, on the eve of the Nineteenth Amendment, women could vote for president (or at least in the primary or at nominating conventions) in seventeen states.[63]

But in a sense the dam began to break in 1869, when the territory of Wyoming provided full enfranchisement for women. This was followed quickly by the territories of Utah (1870), Washington (1883), and Montana (1887). By 1919, sixteen states and the territory of Alaska fully enfranchised women.[64]

While it could be argued that the national climate regarding women's suffrage had changed sufficiently by the end of World War I, as well as the existence of full women's suffrage in at least some parts of the United States, and that it was not a great leap to the passage (1919) and ratification (1920) of the Nineteenth Amendment, in fact there was nothing inevitable about it. The Nineteenth Amendment had first been introduced in 1878, as well as in every year afterward until it finally secured the necessary two-thirds congressional vote. Even the adoption in 1912 of a women's suffrage plank in Theodore Roosevelt's Bull Moose Party platform was not enough to spur passage for seven more years.

Indeed, final ratification of the amendment was very much in doubt. Most Southern states were decidedly hostile to it. As luck would have it, Tennessee became the thirty-sixth state to vote on ratification. The outcome of the state senate vote could not be predicted in advance, and indeed turned almost on serendipity. The youngest member of the senate, twenty-four-year-old Henry Burn, who had declared against the amendment, suddenly voted in favor; his was the deciding vote.

Later it was learned that Burn had received a telegram from his mother, which he held in his pocket, urging him to "be a good boy" and vote for women's suffrage. For his trouble, Burn had to jump out a third floor window of the Capitol and go into hiding in the attic to keep from being dismembered by outraged amendment opponents.[65]

What was behind all this? Why did it take so long for women in the United States to secure the right to vote? The easy answer is male chauvinism, of course; men didn't want women leaving hearth and home to participate in the act of voting, traditionally an exclusively male activity. A better answer is cultural inertia; for nearly two thousand years there was no Western impulse—at least not in any formal, organized, or institutional manner—to permit women to vote or, indeed, to participate in public affairs in any but the most tangential way. A woman's place, whether she was married or not, was at home, not in the public square. While it would be incorrect to say that the idea of women's suffrage did not exist before the publication of Wollstonecraft's treatise, in fact as a political and social movement it had little traction prior to the nineteenth century. Undoubtedly the role that women on both sides of the Atlantic played in the antislavery movement, whose roots lay in the first decades of the nineteenth century, served as a major catalyst for events that culminated in the Seneca Falls convocation in the summer of 1848.

Indeed, the wonder is not that it took so long for American women to secure the franchise but that it happened at all. Efforts to include women were slow and sometimes painful, as noted women activists for suffrage were not infrequently severely mistreated. The United States was very slow to grant the right to vote to women. New Zealand was the first nation to do so, and that did not happen until 1893. Some twenty-six nations worldwide gave women the franchise before the United States finally did in 1920.[66]

All sorts of objections were raised during the nineteenth century to the idea that women should be able to vote. To the modern reader they may seem bizarre and ridiculous, but there seems little doubt that they held great currency a century ago and more. While it is not possible to list all of the objections here, a few can briefly be mentioned: women are not capable of voting; women are different from men, less rational and more emotional; all women tend toward the hysterical and thus need not be taken seriously; women are too weak to vote ("Once a woman arrived [at the polls] she would have to mingle among the crowds of men who gather [there] . . . and to press her way through them to the ballot box. Assuming she reached the polling place, she might get caught in a brawl and given women's natural fragility, she would be the one to get hurt"[67]); it's a woman's job to take care of the household and family, and to raise children, not to vote; dire consequences would occur if women secured the vote, including jeopardizing national security ("Allowing women to vote would lead to foreign aggression and war"[68]); allowing women to vote would increase fraud, because they could hide extra ballots in their "voluminous sleeves" and thus cast multiple votes.

Women, of course, fought back at every turn, and made it very clear that these accusations and attitudes were baseless. Howard Zinn quotes Rose Schneiderman of the Garment Workers, who at a feminist rally at Cooper Union denied that if women could vote they would lose their essential femininity:

> Women in the laundries . . . stand for thirteen or fourteen hours in the terrible steam and heat with their hands in hot starch. Surely these women won't lose any more of their beauty and charm by putting a ballot in a ballot box once a year than they are likely to lose standing in foundries or laundries all year round.[69]

In spite of sensible statements like this one, notions and rationalizations denying women's suitability as voters persisted. And there was, in fact, a very powerful political force preventing the rapid spread of women's suffrage in the United States: many women opposed it. It was not solely men who successfully kept women from voting. As Sara Hunter Graham points out, even as the women's suffrage movement had a kind of renaissance at the beginning of the twentieth century, so did opposition increase as well.[70] Many of the opposing organizations were well funded and organized, and counted among their members urban women of substance and social prominence. But opposition extended into smaller towns and villages as well, and as we noted, it was especially pronounced in the conservative Southern states. It wasn't until pro-suffrage activists and organizations made the leap from social movement to skillful, savvy political lobby that the tide of public opinion began to turn in their favor.[71]

To reiterate, there was nothing inevitable about women's securing voting rights in the United States, unless one wants to adopt a history-as-progress perspective. In the case of women's suffrage, such an interpretation would be unjustified. Women's suffrage in this country was achieved only after decades of blood, sweat, and tears, repeated setbacks, and enormous dedication on the part of skilled, committed leaders such as Susan B. Anthony, Lucretia Mott, Elizabeth Cady Stanton, and a number of others. Indeed, the ultimately successful struggle for women's suffrage achieves meaning only when seen in the context of the long tradition of American disenfranchisement; it didn't have to happen, but the fact that it did only after Herculean labors shows just how intransigent and grounded were the forces allied against it.

Chinese Immigrants

Disenfranchisement as public policy can also be seen in the case of the vast waves of immigrant groups that came to the United States beginning in the decades before the Civil War, and which grew to tsunami proportions from the 1870s until World War I. Indeed, virtually all groups—national, ethnic, and religious—whose origin was not northern Europe or the British Isles experienced substantial, in some cases severe, levels of discrimination, including denial of the franchise. Irish Catholics and eastern, central, southern, and southeastern European immigrants (many of whom were Catholic or Orthodox), as well as Jews and Russians, were the victims of especially harsh levels of discrimination.[72]

But perhaps no group of immigrants in American history, with the exception of Africans brought to these shores as slaves, were treated as badly as Asians, particularly the Chinese. Indeed, it would hard to argue that the status of the Chinese in the United States between the years following the Civil War and the onset of World War II was anything more than a nano-step above that of economic and political slaves.

Chinese immigrants came to California as early as 1815, but substantial numbers did not begin to arrive until the gold rush days of the 1850s. The earliest immigrants were apparently well received, because they were for the most part successful merchants, businessmen, artisans, and professionals who contributed to the nascent California economy.[73]

Once gold was discovered, however, large numbers of unskilled Chinese laborers (often called "coolies") arrived, in part to work in the goldfields but mainly to buttress the service sector required to support the gold rush as cooks, peddlers, storekeepers, day laborers, and track layers. They were willing to work very long hours for extraordinarily low wages. Most were single men who worked for a time and then returned to China with their savings; others stayed, but sent money back to their homeland and in some cases paid to bring family members and compatriots to California. They lived frugally in enclaves, often because they were not allowed to live elsewhere. By 1851 it was estimated that there were 25,000 Chinese in California, mostly in and around San Francisco.[74]

Those who worked in the mines were sometimes victims of hate crimes; about one-third of the miners in California were from the American South, and they brought their racial attitudes with them. But more generally, as the number of Chinese immigrants rose—by 1870 there were about 100,000 in California[75]—attitudes toward them turned sharply negative. Resentment grew among whites, as the Chinese were willing to take jobs that whites considered dirty and demeaning, and for very low wages. Nowhere was this more clearly apparent than during construction of the transcontinental railroad during the 1860s. About 10,000 Chinese workers built the western leg of the Central Pacific Railroad, nearly 90 percent of the total work force. About 1,000 Chinese died on the job during the construction, as the work was dangerous and backbreaking. Not only was the role of Chinese workers in building the railroad unrecognized and unappreciated, whites commonly expressed hostility toward Chinese for taking "their" jobs and for working for low pay. It is symptomatic that when the railroad was completed in 1869, no photographs taken at Promontory Point, Utah, where the final spikes were driven into the ground, included Chinese workers.[76]

Attitudes toward the Chinese became increasingly harsh as the 1870s dawned, particularly when an economic depression slowed the California economy. During this same time in other parts of the United States, attitudes toward former black slaves also began to harden and Northern white support for them to dissipate. The growth of American imperialist ideas and "white superiority" gave rise to deeper feelings of antipathy and hostility toward peoples of color worldwide. In California, the Chinese found themselves targets of vitriol and hatred, and victims of violence and rioting.[77] They were even, perhaps especially, resented because they refused to accept Christianity.

Pressure to limit Chinese immigration began in earnest in California during the 1870s, and culminated in Congress's passage of the Chinese Exclusion Act in 1882. This infamous legislation was the only one of its kind ever passed by the U.S. Congress, insofar as it targeted a particular group for state-sanctioned discrimination against immigration. It halted all immigration of Chinese laborers into the United States (exceptions were made for students, diplomats, and a few others) and, most importantly, prohibited Chinese already living in the United States from becoming citizens. Thus, in one bold stroke, the Chinese were denied the benefits of citizenship, including the franchise. Citizenship was not stripped from those Chinese who were already citizens, but the historical evidence suggests that even they were rebuffed in their efforts to vote.

The Chinese Exclusion Act was renewed in 1892 and made permanent in 1902. As a result of these laws, Chinese were victimized, scapegoated, and discriminated against in very much the same way Southern blacks were as a result of Jim Crow laws.[78] Local ordinances were passed forbidding Chinese from living in some counties. Riots drove many from their homes. In cities, they were forced to live in segregated enclaves, derisively called "Chinatowns" by whites. Women Chinese immigrants were especially victims of harassment, the result of an effort to drive them away and thus decrease the size of the Chinese population. Many Chinese simply left. In 1890 there were about 108,000 Chinese in America; by 1920 the number had fallen to 62,000.

In addition, Chinese living in the United States were required by the Exclusion Acts to carry a "certificate of identity." It was the only time in our history that a group was singled out to possess and produce on demand such a document. Further, Chinese (and other Asians) seeking to come to the United States were required to pass through California's infamous "Angel Island." More than one million Asians were held in this facility between 1910 and 1940. For Chinese, the experience was especially difficult and hostile. Many immigrants were detained for months, even years, ostensibly to check documentation but more probably as a form of harassment and discrimination. Angel Island was not at all comparable to Ellis Island in New York harbor; it was a government mechanism designed to keep Chinese out rather than welcome them to this country.[79]

The Chinese Exclusion Act was finally repealed in 1943, presumably because China was an ally of the United States during World War II. It would be wrong, however, to assume that the demise of these laws ended discriminatory practices against Chinese Americans. Just as African Americans continue to bear the burden of racial prejudice, Chinese Americans find themselves victims of indifference and hostility. The Asian American Legal Defense and Education Fund (AALDEF) has recently documented cases (AALDEF Report to Congress, March 19, 2009) in which U.S. citizens of Chinese and other Asian descent were not allowed to vote, in part because of noncompliance with Voting Rights Act language requirements, but in some cases because local voting officials refused to recognize these voters' credentials (especially in the case of first-time voters). These officials also engaged in other harassment practices, including illegal demands for identification. AALDEF also reported 214 hate crimes against Asian Americans in the United States, as well as the use of overtly racist tactics designed to keep them away from the polls on Election Day 2004 in New Jersey.[80]

Conclusion

My investigation of three groups in this country—African Americans, women, and Chinese Americans underscores the point of this chapter: disenfranchisement of targeted populations has long been part of the public policy of this nation. Other groups could also be held up as examples of American policies of disenfranchisement. Native Americans and Alaskan indigenous populations come to mind. Indeed, it may be fair to say that the policy of extending the franchise to immigrant groups existed only in carefully controlled, limited circumstances (as we saw in Chapter 1). In the main, most groups that did not consist of white Anglo-Saxon Protestant men were widely prevented from voting.

Eventually women secured the franchise because of the Nineteenth Amendment; whatever problems women have in voting today are generally not a function of their gender but of something else. But for African Americans and Chinese Americans, the struggle to vote continues. Hard data and anecdotal evidence from the 2000, 2002, 2004, and 2006 elections reveal that these two groups continue to be the victims of discriminatory practices whose purpose is to prevent them from voting. And so it is for other groups; evidence from California in 2006, for example, reveals that other Asian American citizens, especially Vietnamese, were prevented from voting. Other examples of similar ilk surfaced in the 2008 elections.

This chapter forces us to look at a question posed earlier, and to which we will return again: how far do Americans really want to extend the franchise, especially to nonwhite fellow citizens? This same question will form the basis of our investigation in the next chapter, when we will look at the disenfranchisement of some other population groups, those who are even further outside "mainstream" America than African Americans and Chinese Americans.

Notes

1. Deborah Stone, *Policy Paradox* (New York: W.W. Norton, 1998), p. 37.

2. David L. Weimer and Aidan R. Vining, *Policy Analysis,* 2d ed. (Englewood Cliffs, NJ: 1992), Chapter 1.

3. Data for this section draw heavily from the tables in Alexander Keyssar, *The Right to Vote* (New York: Basic Books, 2000), pp. 339–402.

4. Ibid., p. 340.

5. Ibid., pp. 340–341.

6. Ibid., p. 341.

7. Ibid., pp. 340–341.

8. Ibid., p. 54.

9. Ibid., pp. 54–55.

10. New Hampshire was the first state to eliminate property requirements, in 1792. American Civil Liberties Union, Voting Rights Act Timeline. Viewed at www.votingrights. org/timeline/?year=1700, accessed July 13, 2010.

11. Keyssar, *The Right to Vote,* p. 348.

12. Ibid., pp. 349–353.

13. See the expert testimony of Eric Foner, *Gratz v. Bollinger* (02–516), 539 U.S. 244 (2003). Viewed at www.vpcomm.umich.edu/admissions/legal/expert/foner.html, accessed October 10, 2007.

14. Ibid.

15. Ibid.

16. Keyssar, *The Right to Vote,* p. 354.

17. Ibid., p. 354.

18. As late as the mid-twentieth century, journalist Edward R. Murrow could quote a Southern farmer as saying, "We used to own our slaves, now we rent them." Edward R. Murrow, *Harvest of Shame,* CBS Reports, November 25, 1960 (videotape).

19. See, for example, the Louisiana Black Code of 1865, which sharply curtailed the economic activity in which blacks could engage. Viewed at http://lsm.crt.state.la.us/cabildo/cab11.htm, accessed July 13, 2010.

20. See V.O. Key, Jr., *Southern Politics in State and Nation* (New York: Vintage Books, 1949); C. Van Woodward, *Origins of the New South* (Baton Rouge: LSU Press, 1951); Woodward, *The Strange Career of Jim Crow* (New York: Oxford, 1966); J. Morgan Kousser, *The Shaping of Southern Politics* (New Haven: Yale University Press, 1974); Foner, expert testimony.

21. Numan V. Bartley and Hugh D. Graham, *Southern Politics and the Second Reconstruction* (Baltimore, MD: Johns Hopkins University Press, 1975).

22. Woodward, *The Strange Career of Jim Crow.*

23. See United States Department of Justice, Civil Rights Division, "Introduction to Federal Voting Rights Laws," July 25, 2008. Viewed at www.usdoj.gov/crt/voting/intro/intro_a.htm, accessed July 7, 2009.

24. *U.S. v. Cruikshank,* 92 U.S. 542 (1875).

25. *U.S. v. Reese,* 92 U.S. 214 (1875).

26. See the discussion at www.gpoaccess.gov/constitution/html/amdt15.html, and U.S. Supreme Court Center, www.justia.us, 2005. Viewed online at http://supreme.justia.com/constitution/amendment-15/07-congressional-enforcement.html. Both viewed July 7, 2009.

27. Race, Voting Rights, and Segregation, "Techniques of Direct Disenfranchisement, 1880–1965." Viewed at www.umich.edu/~lawrace/disenfranchise1.htm, accessed July 7, 2009.

28. U.S. Census of Agriculture, 1920 and 1930, Chapter 1, "Farms and Farm Property." Viewed at http://www2.census.gov/prod2/decennial/documents/03337983v4ch02.pdf, accessed July 13, 2010.

29. *Breedlove v. Suttles,* 302 U.S. 277 (1937).

30. Keyssar, *The Right to Vote,* pp. 368–369.

31. Kousser, *The Shaping of Southern Politics,* pp. 374–379.

32. "Techniques of Direct Disenfranchisement."

33. Any number of analysts have pointed out that the instructions accompanying the

use of electronic voting, whether by optical scanning equipment, touchscreen, Internet, or something else, constitute a de facto literacy test.

34. Key, *Southern Politics;* Koussar, *Shaping of Southern Politics;* Steven F. Lawson, *Black Ballots* (New York: Columbia University Press, 1976).

35. Key, *Southern Politics;* Donald Strong, *Urban Republicanism in the South* (University: Bureau of Public Administration, University of Alabama, 1960); Richard K. Scher, *Politics in the New South,* 2d ed (Armonk, NY: M.E. Sharpe, 1997).

36. *Grovey v. Townsend,* 295 U.S. 45 (1935).

37. "Techniques of Direct Disenfranchisement."

38. *Smith v. Allwright,* 321 U.S. 649 (1944).

39. See David Chalmers, *Hooded Americanism* (Durham, NC: Duke University Press, 1987). See also the publications of the Southern Poverty Law Center, viewed at www.splcenter.org/index.jsp, accessed July 7, 2009.

40. Lawson, *Black Ballots,* p. 135, quotes a Mississippi judge in 1954 as saying, "Over 95 percent of the negroes of the South are employed by white men or corporations controlled by white men. A great many negro employees will be discharged and a deplorable situation will arise for the negro."

41. John Egerton, *Speak Now Against the Day* (Chapel Hill: University of North Carolina Press, 1994), p. 360.

42. Ibid.

43. Readers who have not already done so are well advised to see the classic film *To Kill a Mockingbird,* one of the few Hollywood efforts to deal seriously and realistically with a lynching.

44. Lawson, *Black Ballots,* pp. 132, 136–137, 148.

45. Numan V. Bartley, *The Rise of Massive Resistance* (Baton Rouge: LSU Press, 1969).

46. Pat Watters and Reese Cleghorn, *Climbing Jacob's Ladder* (New York: Harcourt, Brace and World, a Harbinger book, 1967), pp. 363–375.

47. David J. Garrow, *Protest at Selma* (New Haven: Yale University Press, 1978).

48. Bartley, *Rise of Massive Resistance;* Florence Mars, *Witness in Philadelphia* (Baton Rouge: LSU Press, 1977).

49. Frances Fox Piven, Lorraine C. Minnite, and Margaret Groarke, *Keeping Down the Black Vote: Race and the Demobilization of American Voters* (New York: The New Press, 2009).

50. This is a theme that runs deep in the writings of Jonathan Kozol. See, for example, *The Shame of the Nation* (New York: Crown, 2005).

51. Mary Wollstonecraft later married the famous poet Percy Shelley and took his name. She is probably better known as the author of one of the first gothic novels in English, *Frankenstein,* first published anonymously in 1818, but then again in 1831 in a third edition under her own name.

52. Worcester Women's History Project, "World Anti-Slavery Convention and Lucretia Mott," by Karen Board Moran. Viewed at www.wwhp.org/Resources/Slavery/mott.html, accessed July 9, 2009.

53. The Susan B. Anthony Center for Women's Leadership, University of Rochester, "U.S. Suffrage Movement Timeline, 1792–present." Viewed at www.rochester.edu/SBA/suffragetimeline.html, accessed July 9, 2009.

54. Exploring Constitutional Conflicts, "Women's Fight for the Vote: The Nineteenth Amendment." Viewed at www.law.umkc.edu/faculty/projects/ftrials/conlaw/nineteentham.htm, accessed July 9, 2009.

55. Keyssar, *The Right to Vote,* p. 54.

56. Ibid.

57. Susan B. Anthony Center, "Timeline."

58. Ibid. See also, Documents 28–30, in Mari Jo Buhle and Paul Buhle, *The Concise History of Woman Suffrage* (Urbana: University of Illinois Press, 1978).

59. See Sara Hunter Graham, *Woman Suffrage and the New Democracy* (New Haven: Yale University Press, 1996), p. 6.

60. See Rosalyn Terborg-Penn, *African American Women in the Struggle for the Vote, 1850–1920* (Bloomington: Indiana University Press, 1998).

61. See Ann D. Gordon, ed., *African American Women and the Vote, 1837–1965* (Amherst: University of Massachusetts Press, 1997), especially Rosalyn Terborg-Penn, "African American Women and the Vote: An Overview," Elsa Barkley Brown, "To Catch the Vision of Freedom: Reconstructing Southern Black Women's Political History, 1865–1890," and Janice Sumler-Edmond, "The Quest for Justice: African American Women Litigants, 1867–1890." See also Jewell L. Prestage, "In Quest of African American Political Woman," *Annals of the American Academy of Political and Social Sciences,* vol. 15, American Feminism: New Issues for a Mature Movement, May, 1991, esp. pp. 93–95.

62. *Minor v. Happersett,* 88 U.S. 162 (1874).

63. Keyssar, *The Right to Vote,* pp. 399–401.

64. Ibid., p. 402.

65. Exploring Constitutional Conflicts, Blue Shoe Nashville, "The Nineteenth Amendment and the War of the Roses," viewed at www.blueshoenashville.com/suffragehistory. html, accessed July 9, 2009.

66. Women's Suffrage, "Women in Politics," viewed at www.ipu.org/wmn-e/suffrage. htm, accessed July 9, 2009.

67. Quoted in "The Arguments of the Anti-Suffragists," viewed at www.history.rochester. edu/class/suffrage/anti.html, accessed July 9, 2009.

68. Quoted in ibid.

69. In Howard Zinn, *The Twentieth Century,* rev. and updated ed. (New York: Harper Perennial, 1998), p. 60.

70. Graham, *Woman Suffrage and the New Democracy,* Chapter 3.

71. Ibid., Chapter 1.

72. Janelle Wong, *Democracy's Promise* (Ann Arbor: University of Michigan Press, 2006).

73. Think Quest, "Immigration, the Journey to America: The Chinese," n.d. Viewed online at http://library.thinkquest.org/20619/Chinese.html, accessed July 9, 2009.

74. Ibid.

75. "Chinese Immigration to the United States," n.d. Viewed online at http://nhs.needham. k12.ma.us/cur/kane98/kane_p3_immig/China/china.html, accessed July 12, 2009.

76. Think Quest, "Immigration: The Journey to America: The Chinese."

77. See the collection of documents on Chinese immigration especially geared toward educators in the Library of Congress, "Teaching with Primary Sources," viewed online at http://lcweb2.10c.gov/learn/features/timeline/riseind/chinimms/chinimms.html: see especially "The Chinese in California, 1850–1925," a collection of documents, viewed at http://memory.loc.gov/ammem/award99/cubhtml/cichome.html. Both accessed on July 12, 2009.

78. See Maryland State Archives, "The Chinese Exclusion Act," 2005. Viewed online at http://teachingamericanhistorymd.net/000001/000000/000136/html/t136.html, accessed July 12, 2009.

79. "Immigration Station," A National Historic Landmark, 1998–2009, viewed online at www.angelisland.org/immigr02.html, accessed July 12, 2009.

80. Asian American Legal Defense and Education Fund, Testimony on Renewal of the Voting Rights Act, June 13, 2006; see also its final report, "Asian Americans and the Voting Rights Act." Viewed online at www.aaldef.org/docs/AALDEF_Sen_VRAreport_ rls_2006.6.13.pdf, accessed July 12, 2009.

3

Disenfranchising the Marginalized

In this chapter we will look at the disenfranchisement of a number of nonmainstream groups of Americans: felons, noncitizens, the mentally and physically disabled, language minorities, those under eighteen years of age, and the homeless. Based on the way these groups are treated in the United States, it appears that Americans don't want their members to vote. Indeed, these groups are generally viewed as outside the "mainstream" of American life, and are often ostracized, ignored, and discriminated against. They are, from a political standpoint, marginalized to the point of exclusion. The marginalization of each of these groups is arbitrary, capricious, and unreasonable, based solely on cultural shortsightedness and prejudice. Except in a few instances, their exclusion is completely unjustified.

It is essential that we discuss why Americans choose to disenfranchise members of these groups. Perhaps most importantly, there are powerful arguments in favor of including these groups in the list of those eligible to vote. The fact that Americans don't want these groups to vote is not a valid reason for denying them the franchise. Next, there is inconsistency across the states in the way the franchise is extended to or denied these groups; the prohibition is not universal in the United States. Thus, issues of fairness and equity rear their important heads. Finally, other democracies extend the franchise to at least some of these population groups. The fact that their roofs have not caved in, nor have their democratic governments been undermined because these groups vote, suggests that denying these marginalized populations the right to vote is unjustified.

Convicted Felons

In 2004, more than 5,250,000 persons who had been convicted of a felony were denied the right to vote in the United States. Of this number, some 63,000 were in jail on Election Day; 478,000 were on parole; 1.3 million were in prison; 1.3 million were on probation; and 2 million had completed their sentence.[1]

Convicted felons are the single largest group of disenfranchised adults in the nation. Public policy aimed at preventing felons from voting goes back to medieval times, when "civil death" was attached to those guilty of committing heinous crimes. These individuals, even if released from prison, were permanently denied any form of civil rights.

In the United States, disenfranchisement of felons became common in the South (and in some Northern states as well) following the Civil War. Disenfranchisement laws were designed primarily as "insurance" against recently enfranchised ex-slaves who might try to vote. But the list of crimes causing disenfranchisement was peculiar, to say the least. Mississippi included a provision in its 1890 state constitution for disenfranchising those convicted of burglary, theft, arson, and obtaining money under false pretenses, but not for robbery or murder. As Mark Mauer notes, a Mississippi Supreme Court decision a few years later observed that "blacks engaged in crime were 'given rather to furtive offenses than to the robust crimes of the whites.'"[2] Alabama, Louisiana, South Carolina, and Virginia rapidly followed suit. And these provisions lasted well into the twentieth century. Alabama's laws disenfranchising those committing offenses of "moral turpitude" were not struck down until 1985. Mississippi did not disenfranchise rapists and murderers until 1968, although for years it barred many petty offenders from voting.[3]

Currently, states differ substantially on the degree to which felons are allowed to vote, including those who are no longer in prison. The U.S. Constitution is silent on the question of felons' voting rights, thus allowing individual states to create whatever policies they please. Forty-eight states and the District of Columbia do not allow felons in prison to vote; Maine and Vermont do, along with the Commonwealth of Puerto Rico.[4] Thirty-two states disenfranchise felons on parole; twenty-eight felons on probation. In fourteen states felons are de facto disenfranchised for life because restoration of voting rights is an exceptionally onerous process, often requiring a gubernatorial pardon, clemency, complex and costly administrative appeals, or special acts of the state legislature (possibly with an extraordinary majority).[5] In six of these states, restoration of voting rights is essentially impossible, while in the eight others it is extraordinarily difficult.[6]

Florida, the nation's fourth largest state, leads the country in the number of disenfranchised felons: nearly 1.2 million in 2007. By contrast, California has only a quarter that number, 238,000; Texas, 523,000; and New York, 122.000. Illinois, the nation's fifth most populous state, has 46,000 disenfranchised felons.[7]

But the absolute number of disenfranchised felons is not the real story. A much more serious matter is the fact of racial discrimination in the conviction and sentencing of felons. Approximately 3 in 10 black males can expect to be disenfranchised during some portion of their lifetime, given present rates of incarceration. According to Demos, a nonpartisan public policy research and advocacy group, the average disenfranchisement rate is nearly five times higher for blacks than for nonblacks because of felony convictions. In the states that permanently disenfranchise felons, about 1 in 4 black males is affected. Felon laws also heavily impact Hispanic males and discriminate against them: about 16 percent of Hispanic males will be imprisoned because of felony convictions during their lifetime, compared to slightly more than 4 percent of white males.[8]

Where did these numbers come from, and why are they so overwhelmingly discriminatory against African Americans and Hispanics? According to most specialists, the answer lies in the war on drugs during the 1970s through the 1990s. Between 1972 and 1996, incarceration rates in the United States quadrupled. Public expenditures against crime, especially drug-related crime, rose from $4.6 billion in 1965 to more than $100 billion in 1993. Much of the attention of the criminal justice system was focused on blacks and Hispanics, because they were made the scapegoats responsible for America's rapidly growing drug culture.

What is now abundantly clear is that most of the drug-related felons were and are nonviolent. Most of the crimes that they committed did not result in loss of life, injury, or damage to property. But federal and state sentencing guidelines, including mandatory sentencing, created during America's get-tough, law-and-order response to drug crimes, forced the hands of judges. They had little or no choice but to incarcerate those convicted. As a result, the prison population mushroomed, and it was overwhelmingly comprised of Hispanics and blacks. According to a recent Pew study, this trend has continued into the twenty-first century.[9]

And yet it is very curious why those convicted of felonies should lose the right to vote. Committing a crime—especially one that is essentially nonviolent—would seem to have little to do with qualifications for voting. It is not as if felons lose all rights: they can, after all, still own property and securities, and file lawsuits. They are required to pay income taxes on any taxable income they may have while serving time. It is impossible to argue convincingly that felons lack a "stake" in America, a point repeatedly made by those wanting to disenfranchise them; clearly they do, and not infrequently the stake includes a financial one. Nor can the argument stand that because of their crimes they have relinquished or forfeited any possible stake they may have had in the life of the nation and their community; how would that possibly be the case?

Moreover, many other modern nations allow prisoners, including convicted felons, the right to vote. Canada, Denmark, France, Israel, Japan, Kenya, Norway, Peru, South Africa, Sweden, and Zimbabwe are among them. Recently, the European Court of Human Rights ruled that Britain's disenfranchisement of 48,000 prisoners violated the European Convention on Human Rights.[10] In this country, the Sentencing Project noted some years ago that depriving citizens of a political right should only be undertaken for compelling state reasons and only to the extent necessary to further those interests.[11] But, as the Project states, proponents of felons' disenfranchisement have yet to succeed in pointing out what state interest is advanced by denying felons the right to vote.

In general, proponents of felon disenfranchisement make three arguments to justify the practice: convicted felons have violated the "social contract" and thus lose the rights of citizenship; the nation needs to protect itself against voter fraud; and convicted felons would vote in such a way as to weaken the criminal justice system. All of these arguments are bogus.

The "social contract" thesis is a useful philosophical argument, but has little practical consequence. What social contract have felons violated? Is it the Constitution? The Constitution is arguably the result of a social contract but is not the contract itself. In any case, as noted earlier, the federal Constitution is completely silent on the question of felonies and voting rights, so it is not clear what part of the contract—or Constitution—felons have violated. In the case of state constitutions, while convicted felons have clearly violated laws based on constitutional language, it is not necessarily clear that they have violated the social contract. Are statutes, constitutional provisions, and the social contract the same, or co-equal? Hardly.

Moreover, are all felons equally guilty of violating the social contract? One could perhaps make a case—although I do not—that a convicted serial rapist or ax murderer has seriously violated the social contract. What about the felon whose crime was nonviolent? What is the justification for taking away his or her rights as well? In these instances, does the punishment truly fit the crime?

The social contract argument also ignores the racial dimension of felony convictions. It is clearly another "cover" for discriminating against blacks and Hispanics: Do the social contract theorists actually believe that blacks and other minorities are more inclined to break the contract than whites? What's the evidence for this? To suggest that they do, based on race or ethnic felony conviction rates, is tautological reasoning at its worst.

The other arguments for disenfranchisement are even more specious. Although Republicans, in particular, have hyped the presence of widespread voter fraud in recent years, in fact very little fraud has ever been uncovered. There is no evidence that convicted felons who have served their time and had their voting rights restored are any more inclined to engage in voter fraud than the rest of the voting population.

And to argue that felons would support candidates or causes designed to weaken the criminal justice system is just silly. This would require the presence of "pro-crime" or "pro-criminal" candidates, platforms, and agendas on the electoral stage. It is safe to say that none of these would have the slightest chance of succeeding, whether felons vote or not.

Why, then, do we continue public policies designed to prevent felons—and too often, ex-felons—from voting?[12] Reasons abound, but the following are central.

First, felons are afflicted with the "mark of Cain." For many, a felon can never fully repay the damage his or her crime caused, especially if it is a particularly heinous one. As a result, felons bear a stigma that cannot be erased. Second, many would hold that felons, even those who have supposedly "paid their debt to society," are morally defective, guilty of moral turpitude as well as their specific crime. As a result of this black stain on their character, they should not be allowed to vote. The basis for this attitude is, of course, that voting is a privilege and not a right, to be awarded the virtuous and denied the malefactor. But was we have seen, voting is not a privilege, and cannot be denied a person because of some alleged character flaw. Indeed, character tests are explicitly forbidden in the determination of voter qualifications.

Next, racial prejudice is a major force denying felons and ex-felons the franchise. When compounded with felony conviction rates, the underlying racism and prejudice of too many white Americans toward blacks is multiplied, providing yet another excuse not to let blacks vote. In this regard, Hispanic American felons are scarcely advantaged over blacks; they too bear the burden of prejudice and racism against them.

One can only speculate what the status of felon disenfranchisement would be if most convicted felons were white middle-class males. There would doubtless be some, perhaps many, Americans who are not ready to give the franchise to felons no matter who they are. But minus the racial dimension, it is likely that the hard-line attitude that other Americans hold toward felon disenfranchisement would be mitigated to a significant degree.

Finally, many Americans, especially Republicans, have a very practical political reason for not granting felons the franchise: they are likely to vote Democratic. African Americans, in particular, have been shown to vote Democratic at rates exceeding 90 percent, at least in some elections. Non-Cuban Hispanic voters also vote heavily Democratic, although not at the extraordinary rates of African Americans.[13] It is true that minority voters tend to have lower turnout rates than whites, thus mitigating to some extent their ability to increase Democratic vote totals. But sociologists Jeff Manza and Christopher Uggen have documented that even with their lower turnout rates, minority felons could have changed the outcome in some seven U.S. Senate races between 1978 and 2000 if they had been allowed to vote.[14] If even a fraction of the approximately 2,500 ex-felons denied the right to vote in Florida in the presidential election of 2000 could have voted, the outcome undoubtedly would have been different.

Noncitizens

Why would anyone think it appropriate for noncitizens to vote? They are not members of the political community, they just happen to be "living here," and some have no intention of ever becoming citizens. They have, the argument goes, no stake in this country and thus should not have the franchise. As we saw from the vitriolic public discussions over immigration during George W. Bush's second term, expressions of complete outrage, peppered with fulminations of bigotry, were heard when the issue of permitting noncitizens to become full-fledged Americans with voting rights emerged.

But there is every reason to support giving legal noncitizens the vote. Noncitizens are in fact members of the American social, political, and economic communities. In general, they enjoy the same rights, especially First and Fourteenth Amendment rights, that citizens do. They can own property. They can buy and sell securities, including government bonds. They pay taxes. They can hold jobs and own businesses. They send their children to public schools, no questions asked. They are not prohibited from serving on juries. They can and do serve in the armed forces; as of 2004, when the Iraq War was in high gear, some 37,000 non-citizens were so doing.[15]

Thus the argument that noncitizens have "no stake" in the United States makes no sense. But one cannot help wondering if the waves of immigrants to the United States in the last thirty years had been Anglo-Saxon and northern European rather than Asian, southeast Europeans, Arabs, Muslims, and especially Hispanics, there would be such hostility directed against them, and fuss over their right to vote.

Opponents of noncitizen voting also claim that the franchise is a privilege (that word again!) that can accrue only to those who take the trouble to become citizens. Fox News characterized opponents to noncitizen voting as believing that voting is a "a sacred privilege and responsibility of the American citizen," and went on to quote the director of the Center for Immigration Studies (a right-wing think tank) as saying "Giving voting rights . . . to non-Americans 'just fundamentally cheapens citizenship.'"[16]

What is odd about all of this is its total denial of the history of noncitizen voting rights in the United States. In fact, between 1776 and the mid-1920s, noncitizens could vote in some forty states and U.S. territories, in local, state, and even federal elections.[17] According to Ron Hayduk, a New York City academician who has spent his career researching the history of noncitizen voting and is also an advocate of noncitizen voting rights, in the history of the United States, noncitizens were allowed to vote for a longer period of time than they were not. Indeed, their voting rights were curtailed in the 1920s amid the wave of xenophobia that swept the country during the period following the end of World War I, including the so-called "Red Scare."[18]

The disenfranchisement of noncitizens is not trivial because of the numbers involved. In California alone one in four residents is an immigrant.[19] Nationally, over 20 million immigrants are denied the right to vote. In Los Angeles, about one-third of the voting age population (VAP) is composed of noncitizens; in New York City the figure is 22 percent. In seven states and the District of Columbia, the noncitizen VAP is about 10 percent of the population.

The numbers alone reveal why opposition to noncitizen immigrant voting rights persists: given the size of the populations involved, they could strongly influence the outcome of elections. Indeed, it is no exaggeration to say that they could literally take over some city and county governments, and have a much greater influence at the state level than they currently do. For many Americans this is not acceptable.

Opponents of noncitizen voting rights ignore the fact that there are some twenty nations, including the European Union, that allow at least some noncitizens to vote.[20] And they overlook the jurisdictions in the United States that in recent years have extended the franchise to noncitizens, at least for local elections.[21] Chicago, for example, has allowed noncitizens to vote in school board elections since 1988 on the grounds that since their children attend public schools, these parents should have a say on the composition of the board and its policies. The Bay Area Immigrant Rights Coalition has for years been pushing for similar voting rights for noncitizens in San Francisco.[22] Several communities in Maryland, as well as Amherst and Cambridge in Massachusetts, and the City Council in Washington,

D.C., have approved measures to allow noncitizens to vote in local elections.[23] The New York City Council has considered a similar measure, but Mayor Michael Bloomberg has opposed it.[24] Between the 1960s and early 2000s, noncitizens could vote in decentralized school board elections in New York City; the practice ended when New York abolished local school districts and boards.

Opponents of noncitizen voting are quick to point out that in those places where noncitizens can vote, turnout is miniscule, even nonexistent. From that they infer this is evidence that affording noncitizens the franchise is a mistake, because until they become citizens they do not take voting seriously.[25] In fact, these opponents ignore an important reality: noncitizens, even immigrants with green cards, are often anxious and fearful of confronting government authority (which would include local voting officials), worrying that their status might be jeopardized. There are even bona fide American citizens—black males come to mind—who avoid contact with authority figures, especially from law enforcement, since the experience is so often unpleasant, or worse. In addition, as one looks for reasons why noncitizens vote in low numbers, one has to consider such factors as how elections/candidates/issues are publicized, language barriers, the unwillingness of many employers to allow wage-earners time off to vote, and lack of language assistance at polling places. It is no wonder, then, that turnout in some areas where noncitizens can vote has been so limited. In fact, researchers have pointed to other data: in areas where noncitizens can vote, there is increased interest in pursuing citizenship.[26]

Other issues arise. All of the discussion of allowing noncitizens to vote applies only to legal aliens. Illegal aliens are always excluded. While understandable given the political climate in this country, this view is also shortsighted and unfair. It ignores two crucial facts: first, there is no federal policy (thanks to a recalcitrant Congress) through which illegal immigrants can become legal. Until there is, illegal immigrants—who pay taxes, work, and contribute to the economy at local, state, and national levels—are permanently disenfranchised. Second, there is a large black market in fake or forged green cards. Thus, it is not always as easy as it seems to tell legal from illegal aliens, and it may well be the case that illegal aliens with counterfeit cards already have the franchise, which raises a serious question of double standards. A better approach is to create a national policy by which illegal immigrants can become legal; once this is in place, the problems of legal or illegal immigrants, and the black market in forged or counterfeit documents, evaporate.

As it also happens, many legal aliens are disenfranchised because of severe time constraints they face in getting their green cards or, indeed, citizenship. Data reveal that there is now at least an eighteen-month wait beyond the minimum required for citizenship for the 1.4 million immigrants currently in the pipeline to complete the process.[27] No one is sure when this backlog will dissipate. What is clear is that most of these immigrants are Hispanic and likely to vote Democratic. Partisan pressures in Washington are at least partially responsible for the long delay these immigrants face in securing their voting rights.

Finally, opponents of noncitizen voting fail to recognize that most immigrants want to become American citizens. In fact, the number of naturalized citizens in the United States has increased dramatically in recent years. In the early 1990s, there were only 6.5 million naturalized citizens; by 2002 there were 11.3 million.[28] About 625,000 were naturalized in 2006 alone.[29] Asians, Europeans, and Canadians are the most likely to naturalize within ten years of arrival, and Mexicans the least; however, the rate across national groups varies considerably.[30]

What these data show is that contrary to the vitriol often hurled at immigrants, most of them want and intend to become citizens. Undoubtedly there are also many who do not. But most understand that even before they become citizens, they have a stake in this nation. They should be allowed to vote.

The Mentally and Physically Impaired

Large numbers of Americans suffer from mental disabilities or physical challenges every day. Too often members of these groups are deprived of the right to vote, either by law or practice.

According to the National Institute of Mental Health,[31] in any given year about one in four persons eighteen and older—in other words, the voting age population—suffers from some form of diagnosable mental disorder. Most of these are minor and temporary, and with proper treatment are successfully resolved. But about 6 percent of this group—1 in 17 persons—suffers from a more serious mental disorder, sometimes more than one. It is this population whose voting rights are most at risk. Similarly, between 6.2 and 7.5 million Americans are afflicted with some form of mental retardation; the VAP in this group also are regularly denied the right to vote.[32]

Some forty-four states restrict the franchise for individuals suffering from mental illness or impairment, either by constitutional provision, statute, or case law.[33] The language used to disenfranchise these individuals is often archaic, demeaning, and disrespectful: the terms "idiots," the "insane," "morons," or "lunatics" are still found. Some thirty-two states that have presumably more modern language also disenfranchise individuals "found to be suffering from mental incompetence or incapacity."[34] Eleven states disenfranchise persons placed under guardianship or conservatorship, and there are states that continue to disenfranchise those who are institutionalized because of their mental condition.

It is well known that at least until well into the twentieth century, those suffering from mental illness or retardation were regarded as abnormal, and treated as pariahs or worse. Historical literatures abound that describe, graphically, the ways in which people who had mental disorders were treated, whether in institutions or by families. Who has not heard of insane asylums, and the way in which even "respectable" people went for amusement to watch and mock the inmates? Those whose families kept them at home, often sequestered away from view and interaction with others, were generally mistreated, and not infrequently left to die. Even today it is not clear that all of the prejudicial attitudes against people with mental disorders have disappeared.

Because of these attitudes, states put constitutional provisions or laws on the books to ensure that those with mental disorders could not vote. Underlying these prohibitions were a number of assumptions about voting, all based on the idea that obtaining the franchise was a privilege, not an inherent right: these individuals were not normal, they were "defective," irrational, and out of control; they could not think "properly" and thus could not make "informed" choices while voting.

These assumptions cannot withstand scrutiny. Modern mental health care professionals and jurists both agree that the determination of who is sufficiently mentally ill or retarded to be denied voting rights leaves everything to be desired. In fact, the criteria used in making such determinations are now recognized as constitutionally and legally vague and clinically nonspecific.[35] It is clear that many individuals suffering mental disorders are capable of making decisions about voting. Nor is there any evidence that their way of doing so differs significantly from the voting population as a whole.

Matters become even more complicated for those persons who are institutionalized or placed under guardianship. Most states prevent such individuals from voting.[36] But the evidence reveals that many, perhaps even most, individuals who have been institutionalized or placed under guardianship for mental illness are nonetheless quite capable of voting. Their particular condition may in fact have nothing whatsoever to do with the thought processes needed to make voting decisions.[37] Yet, as scholars have shown, often their status as institutionalized persons or those under guardianship has been viewed by courts as prima facie evidence that they should be denied the franchise.

There is a subset of the institutionalized that has emerged in recent years, posing a unique set of problems for voting rights: nursing home residents. The number of such persons now approaches 2 million nationally. Most of the individuals in nursing homes do not suffer from mental disorders, but about 14 percent have been diagnosed with Alzheimer's disease.[38] Alzheimer's disease is but one form of dementia; the percentage of nursing home residents who suffer from all forms of dementia is substantially higher than the 14 percent cited above.[39]

Many—perhaps most—nursing home residents have not had their voting rights removed by courts. But many cannot independently exercise their franchise because of their infirmities. Thus, family members or nursing home staff generally cast ballots for them if they still want to vote. As the Dana Foundation observes, this leads to potential abuse and corruption of the electoral process. Most nursing homes have no mechanism or process in place to ensure that residents' votes are cast in the manner that the patient wishes, nor is there any accountability to the patient, or his or her family, to show that the votes were properly cast, or, indeed, cast at all. And in any case the secret ballot is completely compromised. In a state such as Florida, which contains nearly 700 nursing homes, any manipulation of residents' votes could significantly affect the outcome of elections.

To try to deal with the disenfranchisement of persons with mental disorders, the American Bar Association (ABA) created a standard by which courts could determine if a person with mental problems should be allowed to vote: "Any person who is able to provide the information, whether orally, in writing, through an interpreter or interpretive device or otherwise, which is reasonably required of all persons seeking to register to vote, shall be considered a qualified voter."[40] The Bar Association anticipated that this information would include only "minimal data such as name, age, address, and proof of citizenship."[41] Obviously some individuals with severe impairments or illness would not be able to reach even this modest standard; but the consensus of modern mental health professionals is that many, perhaps most, could do so and thus should be allowed to vote.

Undoubtedly this standard of the American Bar Association is a step forward. But three hurdles need to be overcome if it is to be effective. First, it has to be implemented. State laws, and in some cases constitutions, need to be revised and replaced with the ABA language to ensure that the standard is put in place. Second, it has to be applied fairly and uniformly, with standards sufficiently specific so that arbitrary decisions by courts, no matter in which states, are minimized or eliminated. Finally, it is possible to use even the minimal ABA standards as either literacy or character tests. Both are illegal. It would be both shameful and inexcusable if such tests were resurrected under the guise of the ABA standards as a means of keeping individuals suffering from mental disorders from voting.

Individuals with physical disabilities face comparable challenges to voting. Following virtually every election one learns of voters with physical disabilities who were not able to vote: for example, there are reports of voters with cerebral palsy who were not allowed to cast a ballot because local officials thought they were drunk or having a "fit," even though neither constitutes legal grounds to take away someone's franchise.[42] In other instances, voters theoretically allowed to vote could not do so: the building housing the polling station was not accessible, no "curbside" voting opportunity existed, no assistance was rendered the disabled person (including helping them into the building), the voting machines were not user-friendly for certain kinds of handicaps, or something similar.[43]

It is difficult to determine exactly how many Americans have some sort of physical impairment. Disability Statistics reported that in 2002, about 13.5 million noninstitutionalized Americans aged eighteen to sixty-four (a substantial but not total portion of the voting age population) indicated some kind of physical limitations on their ability to work.[44] This represents about 8 percent of the work force. However, the actual percentage of Americans with some kind of disability appears to be much greater. Some estimates suggest that one out of every five Americans has some kind of disability, but this includes mental as well as physical impairments. At the dawn of the twenty-first century, more than 2 million Americans were confined to wheelchairs; about 6 million used a cane, crutch, or walker; 18 million over the age of fifteen had difficulty carrying a ten-pound weight; and 25 million had difficulty negotiating stairs of ten steps.[45]

For some, simply getting to the polling station is a major issue, especially for those who are completely paralyzed or may have to travel with special equipment.

To say, as some have, that these voters should cast ballots absentee is no argument at all; voters have a right to vote in the way they want, and many of the disabled prefer to do so like nondisabled persons. Besides, they may be physically unable to request an absentee ballot or comply with the requirements for voting absentee. For others who can physically get to a polling station, there may be problems entering the facility: lack of ramps, lack of elevators, difficult stairs, and narrow doorways can be serious impediments. The blind and visually impaired, of course, must rely on others to cast ballots on their behalf unless Braille ones are available, which is not always the case. Trusting another person to cast one's ballot not only requires a leap of faith; it also compromises the secret ballot. Amputees and people whose arms and hands are disabled must also rely on assistance, although it must be said that getting rid of punch-card voting systems has helped those whose manual dexterity is impaired.

Four separate pieces of federal legislation require that voters with physical disabilities be accommodated when they choose to cast a ballot. The most important is the 1990 Americans with Disabilities Act (ADA). It requires that physically challenged persons have access to basic public services; "however it does not strictly require that all polling place sites be accessible."[46] Second, the Voting Rights Act (1965) requires that "any voter requiring assistance to vote 'by reason of blindness, disability, or inability to read and write may be given assistance by a person of the voter's choice. . . .' "[47] Finally, the 1993 National Voter Registration Act (more commonly called the "Motor Voter Law") required that agencies, including nonprofits, assist physically challenged voters to register.[48] The "Help America Vote Act" (HAVA, passed 2002) also required that polling stations be accessible to the blind and others with physical disabilities, and provide information about voting to those with disabilities.

The problem with all of this is that the laws and rules have not been sufficiently enforced. Studies indicate that voters with disabilities are 10 percent less likely than the nondisabled to register to vote and, of those who are registered, 20 percent less likely to vote.[49] A study of counties in upstate New York revealed that only 10 percent were compliant with state and federal requirements for accommodating persons with disabilities. In its monumental study of voting rights for the disabled, the U.S. Government Accountability Office (GAO) found that only 16 percent of polling places in its survey had no impediments to disabled persons; 56 percent had potential impediments even in those places that offered curbside voting, and 28 percent had impediments where there was no curbside voting.[50]

Physically impaired voters in both Florida and California have sued state and federal officials to force compliance with ADA and other requirements. But it is not clear that even successful disposition of these lawsuits will remove all of the hurdles handicapped voters face. As noted, the ADA does not require that every polling station be accessible to the disabled, which then requires that disabled persons make arrangements with local voting registrars to vote in a place other than their precinct if it is not accessible, and that help be provided for them once they arrive. Too many local officials simply do not want to be bothered. As the GAO points out, providing full accommodation at every polling station would be enormously expensive, and neither the federal government, states, nor counties have the means to provide the needed resources.

And yet while these may all be legitimate concerns, none is acceptable as a reason why the physically challenged have difficulty voting. Clearly, a double standard for voting (as well as many other aspects of society) exists with respect to the mentally impaired and physically challenged. Both groups face hostility, indifference, and insensitivity from fellow Americans. Unless and until these attitudes change, it is unlikely that people with mental and physical disabilities will find anything but the most minimal efforts to accommodate their desire to vote. This can most charitably be described as a national disgrace.

Those Under Eighteen

On July 1, 1971, the Twenty-sixth Amendment to the Constitution was ratified, thereby lowering the voting age from twenty-one to eighteen. In fact, Congress had passed a law changing the voting age to eighteen in 1970, but the U.S. Supreme Court struck down parts of it that required eighteen-year-olds be allowed to vote in state elections.[51] In response, the Congress proposed the Twenty-sixth Amendment; it was ratified more quickly than any other amendment in U.S. history.[52]

It was also one of the least controversial amendments ever proposed and ratified. At the time, eighteen-year-olds were being sent to Vietnam in vast numbers; thousands were killed or seriously—often permanently—injured. None could vote. A popular slogan created at the time helped propel ratification: "Old enough to die, old enough to vote." It was difficult to oppose the slogan's logic.

The amendment granted the franchise to about 11 million new voters, those between eighteen and twenty-one. The 1972 elections were the first in which they were eligible; about 55 percent were estimated to have cast ballots.

Although the eighteen-year-old vote is now well established, proposals that the voting age be lowered to sixteen have been put forth and generally strongly opposed in most parts of the United States in spite of the fact that the idea has enjoyed support among such key opinion leaders as the *New York Times* and CNN.[53] Reasons offered by opponents sound familiar, because they are the same ones that were used to keep blacks, women, and other marginalized groups from having the franchise: sixteen-year-olds are not mature enough to make independent judgments; they are erratic and irresponsible in their behavior; they don't follow politics and thus cannot make informed decisions; they cannot own property and therefore have no stake in electoral outcomes; even if they had the franchise they would not use it because "everybody knows" young people don't vote; they would use their vote foolishly by supporting celebrities or backing ridiculous initiatives (such as abolishing schools) put forward by politicians pandering to young voters.[54]

None of this makes any sense, and fails to rise to the level of justification. Most of the objections can quickly be brushed aside as silly, irrelevant, or just wrong. For example, there is no constitutional or legal requirement in any state that voters demonstrate "maturity" in order to vote. As used by opponents, this is nothing more than a prohibited character test.

But there are more serious matters. It is simply not true that sixteen-year-olds have no stake in our social, political, and economic communities. They pay taxes (sales taxes, most assuredly), and since many sixteen-year-olds hold jobs, they pay income taxes as well. Children and youth are singularly unrepresented in our political system; because they cannot vote they have to rely on surrogates. Lowering the voting age might well force politicians to pay more attention to adolescent interests. Today's youth are the owners and inheritors of our national debt; should they not have a say in how the debt is created and paid off? Finally, they are expected to obey laws and—this is a key point—if they run afoul of the law (especially if the matter is a potential felony) they are not infrequently treated like adults and tried as adults in court. In most states sixteen-year-olds are eligible to obtain a driver's license.

Indeed, this latter point deserves further consideration, because it leads to the heart of the question of whether or not sixteen-year-olds are capable of making judgments about voting. Americans accept the idea that sixteen-year-olds can drive a car, pick-up truck, SUV, or a van weighing thousands of pounds in heavy traffic at 70 miles an hour.[55] But many of those same individuals would question the judgment of that same teenager to vote. Thus, the question arises: which situation poses the greater potential public danger, a teenager casting a ballot or one driving a heavy vehicle (potentially a lethal weapon) at high speed in traffic? The answer is self-evident.

As it also happens, opponents of under-eighteen voting also ignore the fact that in some places teenagers under eighteen can actually vote. Some nine states allow them to vote in primaries if they will be eighteen by the date of the next general election.[56] Proposals are on the table in Massachusetts, New York City, Baltimore, Texas, and Maine to allow sixteen- and seventeen-year-olds to vote.[57] None has yet been passed, but the issue is still on the radar screen. In California—where else?—a state official has proposed a proportional voting system: fourteen- and fifteen-year-olds would get one-quarter of a vote, and sixteen- and seventeen-year-olds would get one-half.[58] The proposal has not been laughed off the table. The president of prestigious Bard College, Leon Botstein, has strongly supported lowering the voting age to sixteen, arguing, "we have overrated the childlike aspects of adolescence."[59]

A number of other nations also permit sixteen-year-olds to vote, including Austria, Brazil, Cuba, Nicaragua, and the Isle of Man. Germany permits sixteen-year-olds to vote in some purely local elections, as does one of the Swiss cantons. Slovenia permits sixteen-year-olds to vote if they hold a job. And the issue is very much on the table in New Zealand, Australia, England, and Canada. Only one nation—Iran—appears to have gone the other way in recent years, when it raised the voting age from fifteen to eighteen following some significant defeats of the government in local elections.

Most of the reasons given by opponents of granting the franchise to sixteen-year-olds are just window dressing and rationalization. They fear the expansion of the voter pool because it greatly increases uncertainty over the outcome of elections. A sudden increase of several million teenagers in the voting age population could change the political landscape and adversely affect entrenched political interests. Better to keep teenagers in their place, label them immature and lacking in judgment, and buy them off by letting them drive cars. Better that than giving them the right to vote.

Language Minorities

At present about one in five residents of the United States has an immigrant parent.[60] About the same proportion (19.7 percent in 2006) speak a language other than English at home.[61] Most of the non-English households speak Spanish (about 28 million); Chinese is a distant second (2 million), with other Indo-European, Asian, and a variety of other languages (including Arabic) also common.[62] More important is the growth in the number of people over five years of age and households whose primary language is not English. In 1990 there were about 31.8 million non-English-speaking residents of the United States. By the 2000 census, there were 47 million over five years of age, an increase of 19 percent.[63] By 2006, there were an additional 8 million non-English speakers, most of them using Spanish as their primary language. According to the census, some 11 million of these residents spoke English either "not well" or "not at all" (about 23 percent). Of this group, about 4.4 million households were "linguistically isolated," that is, no one in the household over fourteen years of age spoke English "very well."[64]

There is nothing especially new about these data, except for the enormous increase in non-English-speaking U.S. residents since the 1970 census. The last thirty-plus years have seen an explosion of immigration into the United States. In 1970 there were approximately 10 million foreign-born residents in this country; the estimate for 2006 was 37.5 million, an increase of 73 percent.[65] Not all of the immigration was legal.[66] Indeed, the data cited do not differentiate between legal and illegal immigrants.

But since the United States has always been a nation of immigrants, the presence of non-English speakers (or readers) has presented voting officials with a major problem: how to accommodate them, given that ballots for most of our history were printed only in English? Were translators to be provided? Could ballots be printed in languages other than English? Could non-English speakers bring aides into the polling station to help them negotiate the ballot? Should speakers fluent in other languages be available at polls to offer assistance?

Until 1975 there was no federal law to provide answers to these questions, and rarely did state law address them either, although some states and counties (especially in California) did make at least modest efforts to accommodate non-English speakers. As a result, too often language minorities were not allowed to vote. This was true even for voters who were otherwise legitimately registered. They were denied because of uncooperative local officials, or because they were deficient in English and could not negotiate the ballot, or both.

It was for this reason that the 1965 Voting Rights Act (VRA) was amended in 1975, and again in 1982 and 2007, to protect language minorities.[67] The original legislation did not make provisions for them, focused as it was on securing the franchise for African Americans. However, evidence soon surfaced that other minority groups in the United States, especially Spanish-speaking residents in the Southwest and elsewhere (including Puerto Ricans in New York City[68]) were being denied access to ballots solely on the basis of language. So were natives of Alaska, Native Americans throughout the United States, and Asian-language-speaking populations primarily along the West Coast but also in other enclaves, such as Houston.

As a result of the 1975 and later amendments, some 496 jurisdictions—states and counties[69]—were covered by one of two sections of the Voting Rights Act: 4(f)(4) and 203.[70] The triggering mechanisms that bring jurisdictions under these sections differ slightly, but essentially at least 5 percent of the population in a jurisdiction must constitute a single language group; it must comprise more than 10,000 persons; represent more than 5 percent of persons of voting age population; or constitute more than 5 percent of Native Americans of a single language group living on one reservation. The illiteracy rate of the language minority must also exceed the national average, that is, they speak English less than "very well."[71]

Covered jurisdictions must provide all election materials—not just ballots—in the language used by the relevant minority, must offer language assistance at polling stations, and must allow language minorities to have an assistant of their choosing with them at the polls. Languages covered by the required criteria are limited to Spanish, Asian languages (especially Chinese, Japanese, and Korean, although recently Tagalog has been added to the list), and Native American and Alaskan languages. Some in these latter groups pose special problems because there is no written form of the language, or has not been until recently.

While the existence of these language accommodations is widely known, what is not well known is how effective the provisions are in covering language minorities. The answer is that the record is very mixed.[72] Indeed, one would have to conclude from the available evidence that in too many places the language minority provisions of the Voting Rights Act are not implemented very well at all. A Berkeley study revealed that of 67 jurisdictions surveyed, only 1 in 7 could provide voting materials in a language other than English. The authors of this study further pointed out that states ranged widely in their degree of compliance, with five—Colorado, Kansas, Massachusetts, Nevada, and Rhode Island—having especially low rates.[73] As hearings and investigations concerning renewal of the Voting Rights Act proceeded in 2006, it became very clear that discrimination against Native Alaskans, Hispanics, Native Americans, and Asians continued. Many were denied access to ballots in required languages, or were not provided language assistance at polling stations. In a number of Asian-language communities and in some Hispanic election districts, ballots were mistranslated, and in other cases mistakes were made during the effort to render candidates' names in Asian-language alphabets so that they were incomprehensible. Many language minorities were also subject to verbal abuse and humiliation by local voting officials. Nor were these isolated instances. Thousands of complaints were filed, and scores of instances of discrimination against language minorities have been documented, especially by the Asian American Legal and Education Defense Fund.

Indeed, these last points bring us to the heart of the matter. Why do we have to have special legislation to protect language minorities so that they can vote? Why don't we make coverage of the Voting Rights Act universal? Why cannot legitimately registered voters be accommodated at polling stations regardless of whether they speak English, Tagalog, Urdu, Swahili, or a nonwritten Alaskan or Native American language? Leaving out the latter as special cases, computer technology is now sufficiently sophisticated so that any ballot in any jurisdiction could, in a matter of moments, be translated on-site into literally hundreds of languages and then printed to accommodate voters, at very little cost depending on how on-site computers and printers are networked. So why don't we do this? Why don't we accommodate any voter who would prefer a ballot to be available in a language other than English, not just those covered by the VRA?

For some—perhaps many—Americans, the idea of a linguistically tailor-made ballot is unacceptable, even abhorrent. Reasons vary, other than "that's not the American way," or "I just don't like that idea." Some would argue on the basis of cost—why bother to print any ballots if we are just going to have to reproduce them in various languages on-site? Why not just print them all at the individual polling station, wouldn't that be cheaper? For others, "exceptions" cause anxiety. Standardization of procedure is the only way to ensure equality and fairness, or so the argument goes. Others just don't like the idea that some voters will not or cannot read and speak English.

But there are more sophisticated opponents of ballots for language minorities as well. While the arguments vary, they essentially devolve into the notion that a "nation" cannot exist peacefully unless it has a common, "official" language. Thus, we hear frequent calls for constitutional amendments and accompanying legislation to make English the official language of the United States, which presumably would prevent ballots and other election materials from being printed in languages other than English.

But as we have seen in the case of other marginalized groups, such objections are bogus. American cities have always been polyglot, veritable towers of Babel. There is no legal or cultural basis for forcing people to speak English. There are even exceptions to the requirement that, to become a citizen, an individual "must be able to read, write, speak, and understand words in ordinary usage in the English language,"[74] and in any case this standard is sufficiently broad and nonspecific as to be unenforceable. Non-English speakers are not very different, in social and political terms, from those who speak English. They hold jobs. They own property. They pay taxes. They can travel freely within the United States and, depending on their residency status and documents if they are immigrants, outside of it as well, and return. And, just like English speakers, they must obey the law and are afforded equal protection rights under the law. Why treat them differently at the ballot box?

Moreover, it is not necessarily clear that linguistic homogeneity is a prerequisite for peaceful democracy. Examples are legion. Canada is closest in proximity to the United States, and while it is true that the linguistically and politically separatist Québécois movement is robust and noisy, no serious observer believes that it threatens to tear the country apart. Switzerland has thrived for centuries with German, French, and Italian populations living side by side. Israel is linguistically very diverse because of its varied immigrant (and native) populations. Belgium manages with two languages living together. Ireland has seen a resurgence of a Gaelic-speaking population, but it is hardly falling apart as a result; likewise, in Wales the increasing popularity of Welsh as a lingua franca has not resulted in its secession from England.

But perhaps most crucially, attacks on non-English speakers and efforts to keep them from exercising the franchise are based on inaccurate data. It is assumed that most individuals, and most households, that do not speak English as their primary language, or at all, are immigrants. This is far from true. Nationally, in 2000, of the 47 million persons in the United States who spoke a language other than English, 46 percent were native born. These individuals are, of course, citizens of the United States by virtue of having been born on U.S. soil or in one of its territories. Of the population who could not speak English "very well"—that is they were "linguistically isolated"—nearly 6 million were native born.[75]

This population is not evenly distributed throughout the country. In California, for example, there were 1.2 million native-born citizens who could not speak English "very well." In Texas the number was 952,000; New York, 570,000; Florida, 316,000, and so on down the list.[76] There is every reason to believe, based on census estimates in mid-decade, that these numbers have increased substantially since 2000.[77] What this means is that more and more "linguistically isolated" citizens find that their voting rights are at risk due to the failure of state and county officials to comply with the requirements of the Voting Rights Act, or merely due to the fact that they do not live in "covered" jurisdictions, even though they are native-born U.S. citizens.

In any case, the arguments against allowing non-English speakers to vote are irrelevant. The reason is twofold. First, under the U.S. constitutional system a fundamental right cannot be denied a person because he or she does not speak English. Nowhere in the Constitution is there a provision that says rights only apply to those who speak English. Second, individuals cannot be forced to learn English in order to secure their rights. Again, there is nothing in the Constitution that compels individuals to become English speakers to ensure that basic rights apply to them. There may be perfectly good reasons to encourage non-English speakers to learn the language; for example, one thinks of enhancing educational and employment opportunities. And there may be very effective ways to encourage them to do so—one thinks of offering tax incentives, for example, or other kinds of tangible benefits such as paying people to learn. But it is not legally or ethically acceptable to use the Constitution as a club to force people to learn English in order for them to exercise their voting rights.

Finally, opponents of allowing non-English speakers to vote using ballots in their language have suggested that because of their unfamiliarity with English, these potential voters are not aware of the political candidates and issues in this country—national, state, or local—and thus cannot make informed decisions. But information about American politics is widely, and sometimes spectacularly. Available to non-English speakers in their native languages. South Florida presents a useful case in point. There are at least eight Spanish-language radio stations in Miami, including the flamboyant Univision station "Radio Mambi" (710 AM). Some of these are primarily music and entertainment media, but Mambi and one or two others consist mainly of political news and commentary, mostly focused on Cuba and Latin America but with substantial, if idiosyncratic, coverage of American politics. There are also four Spanish-language television stations in South Florida, including Telemundo, Univision, and two independents, each of which has a significant news component.[78] Spanish-language radio and television stations also abound in California, Arizona, and Texas; they can also be found across the nation, especially in metropolitan areas that have large Hispanic populations. Also scattered across the United States are some sixteen Chinese-language radio stations. Increasingly important are online and Internet radio broadcasts in such languages as Japanese, Vietnamese, and Arabic that cover issues of U.S. affairs and politics.

The point is, non-English speakers living in the United States have any number of outlets—not even mentioned were newspapers, magazines, and newsletters[79]—from which to learn about American politics, candidates, and issues. For those who somehow feel voters have to be "knowledgeable" in order to cast votes responsibly, there is absolutely no reason why most non-English speakers cannot qualify, even though there is no requirement that they so demonstrate.

The Homeless

The last consistently disenfranchised group of marginalized Americans we shall discuss is the homeless. No one really knows how many homeless people there are in the United States. Serious problems exist in defining what "homeless" means, most especially because in the majority of cases, homelessness is a temporary condition. And there are great methodological difficulties in locating and identifying the homeless for the purpose of counting them.

The National Coalition for the Homeless has attempted to synthesize the most authoritative data derived from the U.S. Conference of Mayors, the National Law Center on Homelessness and Poverty, the Urban Institute, and comparable sources.[80] In surveyed cities, the homeless were found to be 42 percent African American, 39 percent white, and 13 percent Hispanic, on average. Most—51 percent—are single males. Seventeen percent are single females. Some 30 percent are families with children. About 16 percent are mentally ill, and 26 percent are substance abusers. Thirteen percent are employed. About 200,000 are veterans.[81] The average period of homelessness in surveyed cities is about eight months.

Numerically, it is estimated that over the course of a year 3.5 million people, 1.35 million of them children, will experience homelessness. On a given night in October, according to the National Law Center on Homelessness and Poverty and the Urban Institute, about 444,000 people from some 346,000 households were likely to be homeless; in February the number rises to 842,000 from 637,000 households.[82] These figures are corroborated elsewhere, if not in precise numbers, then in order of magnitude.[83]

There are a number of reasons why the homeless are disenfranchised. Some, of course, are too young to vote: aside from children who are part of homeless families, some 2 percent of all homeless people are unaccompanied minors. Those who are mentally ill or who are substance abusers may not know how to register and vote, or may choose not to do either. But the overwhelming reason why the homeless cannot vote is that they usually are unable to document that they are legal residents of a state or county. Establishing legal residence generally requires that individuals have permanent addresses.[84] By definition, the homeless do not.

The problem occurs both for registering and for obtaining a ballot at the polls. Only one state—North Dakota (which has no voter registration)—does not demand proof that an individual is a resident. Most states require documentation of residence or proof of legal residence. New Hampshire, for example, insists that registrants "Have a permanent established domicile in the State of New Hampshire." West Virginia demands proof that the individual "Live in West Virginia." Wyoming states that registrants must "Be an actual and physically *bona fide* resident of Wyoming."[85]

Examination of registration forms from forty-eight states plus the District of Columbia and the National Mail Voter Registration form[86] reveals that potential registrants must indicate an address where they live. Most homeless people cannot provide such an address unless they offer their last permanent address and hope it works. In many states, voters must also verify their address when they show up at the polls, even if it is with a document such as a utility or phone bill. In such instances, the homeless voter wishing to cast a ballot will not be allowed to do so unless, again, he or she offers the last permanent address and it is accepted.[87] This puts the homeless person in a dicey ethical and legal position, because in claiming a residential address, he or she is not telling the truth.

As noted, homelessness is generally a temporary condition. When the home-less person finds a permanent domicile, he or she will be able to vote. But this is hardly the point. More troubling is the fact that in the United States, homelessness means disenfranchisement, the loss of a basic civil right. But there is more. Because voter registration requires proof of a permanent address, and casting a ballot often requires verification of it, we can assert that these requirements constitute a means test, something that was supposedly discarded in the nineteenth century. We shall leave the point for now, but return to it elsewhere.

Conclusion

Why do we disenfranchise so many groups of people in the United States? The word "groups" is important in the last sentence. It is not as though a few individuals are singled out for disenfranchisement. Rather, entire segments of the population are denied the right to vote.

While explanations are legion, let me just advance two. As I noted in the first chapter, there is an interest among those who control the election machinery in this country—at all levels and in both parties—in controlling the scope of electoral conflict. Doing so allows predictability. The problem with the marginalized groups we discussed is that their political behavior is completely unknown. How would sixteen- and seventeen-year-olds vote, for example? The only group about whom it is possible to make an educated guess are felons, since the preponderance are black and most blacks vote Democratic. The Republicans cannot accept this likelihood, and even Democrats don't want to be known as the party of felons. So it is in the interest of both parties to ensure that they be relegated to the sidelines, and not allowed into the game.

Then there is the second reason. Marginalized groups are viewed as different, separate, pariahs, even freakish (especially in the case of mentally and physically impaired people). Voting is too often seen as a privilege for "regular" people, not those whose characteristics or behaviors put them outside of what we regard as "really American" or "fully qualified." So they are pushed aside, and while they may be bona fide citizens (including noncitizens who eventually are naturalized) they hardly enjoy the fruits of citizenship.

But matters go beyond regarding most of the groups discussed in this chapter as nonmainstream, as outliers. There is something more pernicious at work. By denying some of these marginalized individuals the right to vote, and by making it very difficult for others, we have actually established a double standard for voting. Those who are somehow "different" must pass tests that most Americans do not face, test that are indeed illegal: this could be a form of character/maturity/judgment test (as for felons, immigrants, the mentally impaired, or those under sixteen), a physical test (those with impairments), or a means test (the homeless). It might not be obvious to most Americans that this is what we are doing, but it is the reality. Unless and until these tests, whether explicit or implicit, are removed, we will continue our policy of disenfranchising—in some cases illegally, but in every case unethically, even immorally—people who are "different."

The conclusion, then, is obvious. There are major portions of our population who are deliberately prevented from casting ballots. Whether this happens by constitutional fiat, law, or practice is irrelevant. The truth is, all of these examples are evidence that disenfranchisement is a matter of public policy in this country.

Notes

1. Demos, "Restoring Voting Rights to Citizens with Felony Convictions," Spring/Summer 2006. Available at www.demos.org/home.cfm, accessed January 7, 2009.

2. Mark Mauer, "Disenfranchisement of Felons: The Modern-Day Voting Rights Challenge," *Civil Rights Journal* (Winter 2002): p. 2. Available at http://findarticles.com/p/articles/mi_m0HSP/is_1_6/ai_106647782, accessed January 9, 2009.

3. Ibid.

4. Demos, "Restoring Voting Rights," p. 3.

5. Mauer, "Disenfranchisement of Felons," p. 1.

6. Eva Kuras, "Unworthy Citizens," *Z Magazine,* May 2005, p. 2. Available at www.thirdworldtraveler.com/Election_Reform/Ex-Felons_Denied_Vote.html, accessed January 7, 2009.

7. American Civil Liberties Union, "Disenfranchised Felons by State." Available at www.aclu-wa.org/detail.cfm?id=238, accessed January 9, 2009.

8. Demos, "Restoring Voting Rights," pp. 2–3. See also Friends of Justice, "Pew Report Blasts Mass Incarcerations," February 29, 2008. Available at http://friendsofjustice.wordpress.com/2008/02/29/pew-report-blasts-mass-incarceration, accessed January 9, 2009; and Pew Charitable Trusts, "Groups Push to Expand Ex-Felon Voting," September 23, 2008. Available at www.pewtrusts.org/our_work_report_detail.aspx?id=44418, accessed September 23, 2008.

9. See the Pew Center on the States, *One in 100: Behind Bars in America* (Washington, DC: Pew Center, 2008); see also Pew Charitable Trusts. Available at www.pewtrusts.org/our_work_report_detail.aspx?id=44418, accessed January 9, 2009.

10. Demos, "Restoring Voting Rights," p. 2.

11. The Sentencing Project, www.sentencingproject.org/Default.aspx; see also http://supreme.justia.com/us/405/330/case.html, accessed January 9, 2009.

12. Elizabeth Hull, *The Disenfranchisement of Ex-Felons* (Philadelphia: Temple University Press, 2006).

13. Exit polls from the 2008 presidential election indicate that African Americans voted at rates above 90 percent for Democrats, and Hispanics at 67 percent. Even younger Cuban American voters broke with their Republican tradition to support Barack Obama, if not all down-ticket Democratic candidates. See www.cnn.com/ELECTION/2008/results/polls.main, accessed November 13, 2008.

14. Jeff Manza and Christopher Uggen, *Locked Out: Felon Disenfranchisement and American Democracy* (New York: Oxford University Press, 2006).

15. Bay Area Rights Coalition, www.immigrantrights.org/news052804.asp, accessed January 10, 2009.

16. Fox News, www.foxnews.com/story/0,2933,120080,00.html; see also Mark Krikorian, Center for Immigration Studies, www.cis.org/articles/2004/markoped041804.html. Both accessed January 10, 2009.

17. Jan Frei, "Noncitizens Have the Obligations of Citizens, So Why Not the Right to Vote?" April 27, 2006. Available at www.alternet.org/blogs/echochamber/35585, accessed January 9, 2009. Ron Hayduk, untitled essay, www.immigrantvoting.org/Articles/Haydukessay.pdf, accessed January 10, 2009.

18. Ron Hayduk. *Democracy for All* (New York: Routledge, 2006).

19. "Mobilize the Immigrant Vote," 2008, www.mivcalifornia.org, accessed September 8, 2008.

20. Ron Hayduk and Michele Wucker, "Immigrant Voting Rights Receive More Attention," *Migration Information Source,* November 2004. Available at www.migrationinformation.org/Feature/display.cfm?id=265, accessed January 10, 2009.

21. Michele Wucker and Ron Hayduk, "The Immigrant Voting Project," *World Policy Institute,* n.d. Available at www.worldpolicy.org/projects/IMV/index.html, accessed January 10, 2009.

22. May Chow, "Push for Non-Citizen Vote in School Elections," *Asian Week,* May 28, 2004; available at www.immigrantrights.org/news052804.asp, accessed September 8, 2008. The measure was defeated at the polls in a popular referendum. Felicia Mello, "Immigrant Voting Measure Defeated in San Francisco," *UC Berkeley Graduate School of Journalism,* November 2, 2004. Available at http://journalism.berkeley.edu/projects/election2004/archives/2004/11/proposition_wou.html, accessed September 8, 2008.

23. Hayduk and Wucker, "Immigrant Voting Rights Receive More Attention."

24. Sewell Chan, "Immigrant Voting Bill," *New York Times,* April 6, 2006. Available at http://query.nytimes.com/gst/fullpage.html?res=9F05EFD71030F935A35757C0A9609C8B63, accessed January 10, 2009; see also Frankie Edozien, "Let Immigrants Vote: Activists," *New York Post,* February 20, 2007. Available at www.nypost.com/seven/02202007/news/regionalnews/let_aliens_vote__activists_regionalnews_frankie_edozien.htm, accessed January 10, 2009.

25. Reynolds Holding, "Voting Block," *Time Magazine,* April 12, 2007. Available at www.time.com/time/magazine/article/0,9171,1609804,00.html, accessed October 3, 2008; Immigrant Voting Project, "Recent Articles About Noncitizen Voting Rights," 2007. Available at www.immigrantvoting.org/material/articles.html, accessed October 3, 2008.

26. Chow, "Push for Non-Citizen Vote."

27. Ibid.; Chen, "Curbing the Immigrant Vote," *The Nation,* blogs, State of Change, January 30, 2008. Available at www.thenation.com/blogs/campaignmatters?pid=277767, accessed October 17, 2008.

28. Sarah Margon, "US in Focus: Naturalization in the United States," *Migration Information Source,* May 2004. Available at www.migrationinformation.org/USFocus/display.cfm?ID=225, accessed October 17, 2008.

29. John Simanski, "Naturalizations in the United States: 2006," *Annual Flow Report,* Department of Homeland Security Office of Immigration Statistics, May 2007. Available at www.dhs.gov/xlibrary/assets/statistics/publications/Natz_01_Sec508Compliant.pdf, accessed January 10, 2009.

30. Bryan C. Baker, "Trends in Naturalization Rates," Fact Sheet, Office of Immigration Statistics, Department of Homeland Security, December 2007. Available at www.dhs.gov/xlibrary/assets/statistics/publications/ntz_rates508.pdf, accessed January 10, 2009.

31. National Institute of Mental Health, "Statistics." Available at www.nimh.nih.gov/health/topics/statistics/index.shtml, accessed October 10, 2008.

32. Mental retardation is a nonspecific condition that is generally diagnosed in childhood. Not all children who suffer from retardation survive to adulthood. The figures just mentioned do not differentiate between the total afflicted population, children, and the voting age population.

33. Statistics in this paragraph are from Paul S. Applebaum, " 'I Vote, I Count': Mental Disability and the Right to Vote," *Psychiatric Services* 51, no. 7 (July 2000). Available at www.psychservices.psychiatryonline.org/cgi/reprint/51/7/849, accessed May 16, 2008.

34. Ibid.

35. See, for example, "Mental Disability and the Right to Vote," Notes, *Yale Law Journal* 88, no. 8 (July 1979). Available at www.jstor.org/pss/795691, accessed May 16, 2008; Jane Galt, "Asymmetrical Information." Available at www.janegalt.net/blog/

archives/004899.html, accessed January 10, 2009; A. Ann Woolfolk, "Voting by Incompetent Persons," Delaware Office of Attorney General, June 19, 2000. Available at
http://attorneygeneral.delaware.gov/office/opinions/2000/00ib11.htm. Accessed May 16,
2008; Nancy Maurer, "Voting Rights," *New York State Commission on Quality of Care,
Quality of Care Newsletter,* no. 11 (May–June 1982). Available at www.cqc.state.ny.us/
counsels_corner/cc11.htm, accessed May 16, 2008; Kay Schriner, Lisa A. Ochs, and
Todd G. Shields, "The Last Suffrage Movement," *Publius* 27, no. 3 (1997). Available at
http://publius.oxfordjournals.org/cgi/content/abstract/27/3/75, accessed May 16, 2008;
Kay Schriner and Lisa A. Ochs, "Creating the Disabled Citizen," *Ohio State Law Journal*
62 (2001). Available at http://moritzlaw.osu.edu/lawjournal/issues/volume62/number1/
schriner.pdf, accessed May 16, 2008.

36. "State Voter Registration Requirements," About.com, U.S. Government Info, n.d.
Available at http://usgovinfo.about.com/blvrbystate.htm, accessed October 10, 2008; "State
Laws Affecting the Voting Rights of People with Mental Disabilities," n.d. Available at
www.ndrn.org/issues/voting/resources/state_voting_rights_MD_laws%5B062304%5D.
pdf, accessed October 10, 2008.

37. Schriner and Ochs, "Creating the Disabled Citizen."

38. National Center for Health Statistics, "Alzheimer's Disease," August 8, 2008. Available at www.cdc.gov/nchs/fastats/alzheimr.htm, accessed October 10, 2008.

39. David A. Drachman, "Fading Minds and Hanging Chads: Alzheimer's Disease and
the Right to Vote," DANA Foundation, January 1, 2004. Available at www.dana.org/news/
cerebrum/detail.aspx?id=1258, accessed October 10, 2008.

40. Quoted in Applebaum, "'I Vote, I Count.'"

41. Ibid.

42. Kay Schriner and Douglas Kruse, "People with Disabilities and Voting," *Center for
an Accessible Society,* n.d. Available at www.accessiblesociety.org/topics/voting, accessed
October 10, 2008.

43. Ibid.

44. "Disability Statistics," Online Resource for U.S. Disability Statistics, *Cornell
University,* n.d. Available at www.ilr.cornell.edu/edi/disabilitystatistics/glossary.cfm?g_
id=243&view=true, accessed October 10, 2008.

45. "Housing First, A Special Report," *NPR News.* Available at www.npr.org/news/
specials/housingfirst/whoneeds/physdisabled.html, accessed October 11, 2008.

46. General Accounting Office, *Voters with Disabilities* (Washington, D.C., October 2001),
p. 18. Available at www.gao.gov/new.items/d02107.pdf, accessed October 11, 2008.

47. Ibid., p. 19.

48. National Voter Registration Act. Available at www.usdoj.gov/crt/voting/nvra/ac-
tiv_nvra.php, accessed September 11, 2008; Schriner and Kruse, n.d.

49. Schriner and Kruse, "People with Disabilities and Voting."

50. GAO, *Voters with Disabilities,* p. 8.

51. *Oregon v. Mitchell,* 400 U.S. 112 (1970).

52. National Youth Rights Association, "Top Ten Reasons to Lower the Voting Age," n.d.
Available at www.youthrights.org/vote10.php, accessed January 12, 2009.

53. Anya Kamenetz, "You're 16, You're Beautiful, and You're a Voter," *New York
Times,* February 6, 2008. Available at www.nytimes.com/2008/02/06/opinion/06kamenetz.
html?_r=1&hp&oref=slogin, accessed January 12, 2009; Pam Belluck, "Sixteen Candles,
But Few Blazing Trail to the Ballot Box," *New York Times,* August 26, 2007. Available at
www.nytimes.com/2007/08/26/weekinreview/26belluck.html, accessed January 12, 2009.
See also Young Philly Politics, youngphillypolitics.com, "Let's Lower the Voting Age for
Municipal Elections," April 5, 2007. Available at http://youngphillypolitics.com/let_s_low-
er_voting_age_municipal_elections, accessed January 12, 2009; BBC News, "Demands to
Lower Voting Age to 16," May 4, 2005. Available at http://news.bbc.co.uk/2/hi/uk_news/

politics/vote_2005/frontpage/4511267.stm, accessed January 12, 2009; and National Youth Rights Association, "Top Ten Reasons to Lower the Voting Age."

54. For a brief overview of opponents' views, see Alastair Enderby, "Voting Age, Lowering," International Debate Education Association, February 22, 2007. Available at www.idebate.org/debatabase/topic_details.php?topicID=588, accessed January 12, 2009. See also No Right Turn, "Lowering the Voting Age," June 21, 2007. Available at http://norightturn.blogspot.com/2007/06/lowering-voting-age.html, accessed January 12, 2009; ACT, "Government to Consider Lowering the Voting Age," September 26, 2007. Available at http://the-riotact.com/?p=5888, accessed January 12, 2009; Philip Hensher, "Politics Does Not Require an Influx of Idealism, *The Independent* (London), December 11, 2003. Available at http://findarticles.com/p/articles/mi_qn4158/is_20031211/ai_n12729374, accessed January 12, 2009.

55. In 2004, the curb weight of an average American automobile was 3,240 pounds; in 1975 it was 3,730 pounds. See David A. Buckingham, "Aluminum Stocks in Use in Automobiles in the United States," *United States Geological Service*, n.d. Available at http://pubs.usgs.gov/fs/2005/3145/fs2005_3145.pdf, accessed January 12, 2009.

56. Belluck, "Sixteen Candles."

57. Ibid.; Stephanie M. Skier, "City Council Moves to Lower Voting Age," *Harvard Crimson,* March 25, 2002. Available at www.thecrimson.com/article.aspx?ref=180754, accessed January 12, 2009; Catadromous, "Lowering the Voting Age in Minnesota," *Daily Kos,* February 8, 2008. Available at www.dailykos.com/story/2008/2/8/17830/88904/679/452905, accessed January 12, 2009.

58. Julie Patel and Kate Folmar, "Senator Seeks Lower Voting Age," Mobilize.org, March 9, 2004. Available at www.mobilize.org/index.php?tray=release&tid=top407&cid=84, accessed January 12, 2009.

59. Belluck, "Sixteen Candles."

60. Frank Rich, "The Grand Old White Party Confronts Obama." *New York Times,* February 17, 2008. Available at www.nytimes.com/2008/02/17/opinion/17rich.html?hp, accessed October 3, 2008.

61. U.S. Census Bureau Newsroom, "New Census Bureau Data Reveal More Older Workers, Homeowners, 'Non-English Speakers,'" press release, U.S. Census Bureau, September 12, 2007. Available at http://todaysseniorsnetwork.com/more_older_workers.htm, accessed July 24, 2010.

62. U.S. Census Bureau, "American Fact Finder," United States S1601–Language Spoken at Home. Available at www.census.gov/Press-Release/www/releases/language3.pdf, accessed October 3, 2008. See also Paul Siegel, Elizabeth Martin, and Rosalind Bruno, "Language Use and Linguistic Isolation," U.S. Census Bureau, February 12, 2001. Available at www.census.gov/population/socdemo/language/li-final.pdf, accessed October 3, 2008.

63. Hyon B. Shin and Rosalind Bruno, "Language Use and English-Speaking Ability 2000," U.S. Bureau of the Census, Census 2000 Brief, October 2003. Available at www.census.gov/prod/2003pubs/c2kbr-29.pdf, accessed October 3, 2008.

64. Nova Southeastern University, "Vulnerable and Hard-To-Reach Population Fact Sheet: Non-English Speakers," October 2006. Available at www.nova.edu/allhazards/forms/non_english.pdf, accessed October 3, 2008.

65. Federation for American Immigration Reform, "Immigration's Impact on the U.S," January 2008. Available at www.fairus.org/site/PageServer?pagename=research_research9605, accessed October 3, 2008.

66. Associated Press, "Non-English Speaking Households on Rise," *St. Petersburg Times,* October 9, 2003. Available at www.sptimes.com/2003/10/09/Worldandnation/Non_English_speaking_.shtml, accessed October 3, 2008.

67. See, for example, National Commission on the Voting Rights Act, "Protecting Minority Voters," June 27, 2006. Available at www.votingrightsact.org; Project Vote, "A Summary of

the Voting Rights Act, 1965," May 24, 2006. Available at http://projectvote.org/fileadmin/
ProjectVote/pdfs/A_Summary_of_the_Voting_Rights_Act.pdf; Wan J. Kim, Statement
Before the Committee on the Judiciary, United States Senate, Concerning Enforcement of
the Voting Rights Act, May 10, 2006. Available at www.usdoj.gov/crt/speeches/wjk_sjc_5–
10–06.pdf ; ACLU, "Voting Rights Act—Timeline," n.d. Available at www.votingrights.org/
timeline/?year=1971; Wade Henderson, "Voting Rights Reauthorization," *National Voter,*
June 2006. Available at http://findarticles.com/p/articles/mi_m0MLB/is_3_55/ai_n16689803;
Ann Marie Tallman, "Statement Regarding Reauthorization of the Temporary Provisions of
the Voting Rights Act," United States House of Representatives, Judiciary Subcommittee
on the Constitution, October 18, 2005. Available at www.votingrightsact.org/congresstest/
testimony_pdfs/annmarie_tallman.pdf. All references accessed October 3, 2008.

68. Doug Muzzio, "Voting Rights Act," *Gotham Gazette,* June 2003. Available at www.
gothamgazette.com/article/voting/20030610/17/420, accessed October 3, 2008.

69. Section 4(f)(4) applies to three states (Alaska, Arizona, and Texas) and nineteen
counties in six others (California, Florida, Michigan, New York, North Carolina, and North
Dakota). James Thomas Tucker, Testimony Before the U.S. House of Representatives
Committee on the Judiciary, Subcommittee on the Constitution, May 4, 2006. Available at
www.votingrights.org/resources/downloads/tucker050406.pdf, accessed October 3, 2008.
Section 203 jurisdictions include fifteen states: Arizona, California, Colorado, Connecticut,
Florida, Illinois, Kansas, Massachusetts, New Jersey, New Mexico, Nevada, New York,
Rhode Island, Texas, Washington. See Michael Jones-Correa and Israel Waismel-Manor,
"Verifying Implementation of Language Provisions in the Voting Rights Act," in *Voting
Rights Act Reauthorization in 2006,* ed. Ana Henderson (Berkeley: Earl Warren Institute on
Race, Ethnicity and Diversity, University of California, Berkeley Public Policy Press, 2007),
Chapter 7. Available at www.law.berkeley.edu/centers/ewi-old/research/votingrights/vra/
ch%207%20jones-correa%20waismel-manor%203–9-07.pdf, accessed October 3, 2008.

70. Kim, Statement Before the Committee on the Judiciary, May 10, 2006.

71. Tucker, Testimony, May 4, 2006.

72. Sandra Guerra, "Voting Rights and the Constitution: The Disenfranchisement of Non-
English Speaking Citizens," *Yale Law Journal* 97, no. 7 (June 1988). Available at http://links.jstor.
org/sici?sici=0044–0094(198806)97%3A7%3C1419%3AVRATCT%3E2.0.CO%3B2–6,
accessed October 3, 2008.

73. Jones-Correa and Waismel-Manor, "Verifying Implementation of Language Provisions in the Voting Rights Act."

74. U.S. Bureau of Citizenship and Immigration Services, "General Naturalization
Requirements," n.d. Available at www.uscis.gov/portal/site/uscis/menuitem.5af9bb95919
f35e66f614176543f6d1a/?vgnextoid=12e596981298d010VgnVCM10000048f3d6a1RCR
D, accessed October 3, 2008.

75. U.S. Census Bureau, Census 2000, Summary File 3, Table PCT12, Internet release
date February 25, 2003. Available at www.census.gov/population/cen2000/phc-t20/tab06.
pdf, accessed October 3, 2008.

76. U.S. Census Bureau, Census 2000, Summary File 3, Table PCT12. In some local areas,
non-English speakers can be the rule, not the exception. For example, in Hialeah, Florida's
fifth-largest city, located in Miami-Dade County, 2000 estimates revealed that 93 percent
of the population over five years of age spoke no English at home. See Nova Southeastern
University, "Vulnerable and Hard to Reach Population Fact Sheet," n.d.

77. U.S. Census Bureau, "New Census Bureau Data Reveal More Older Workers, Homeowners, Non-English Speakers," September 12, 2007.

78. I am indebted to Ms. Alina Mejer, honors student in "Beyond the Beltway: Politics
in States, Counties, and Communities," Spring 2008, for supplying this information.

79. See, for example, "The Citizen," *Gotham Gazette,* March 2008. Available at www.
gothamgazette.com/citizen/mar08, accessed October 3, 2008.

80. National Coalition for the Homeless (NCH), "How Many People Experience Homelessness?" NCH Fact Sheet no. 2, June 2008. Available at www.nationalhomeless.org/publications/facts/How_Many.pdf, accessed November 21, 2008.

81. Paul Riekhoff, "O'Reilly Downplays Number of Homeless Veterans," Huffington Post, January 16, 2008. Available at www.huffingtonpost.com/paul-rieckhoff/oreilly-downplays-number_b_81900.html, accessed November 21, 2008. Political commentator Bill O'Reilly of Fox News created a national controversy when he denied that any veteran was homeless. However, even he was forced to retract his statement upon presentation of substantial evidence to the contrary.

82. "How Many People Experience Homelessness?"

83. Martin Kasindorf, "Nation Taking a New Look at Homelessnes, Solutions," *USA Today*, October 12, 2005. Available at www.usatoday.com/news/nation/2005-10-11-homeless-cover_x.htm, accessed November 21, 2008.

84. In many states, those registering to vote can instead provide an address where they receive mail, but post office boxes are not acceptable. No data could be found on whether or not homeless people receive mail. In some states, people who live in rural areas can draw a map if their domicile does not have an actual street address. But it is not clear if this applies to the homeless, even those who live in "camps" with other homeless people, in spite of the fact that some of the camps seem to be at least semipermanent.

85. About.com, "State Voter Registration Requirements," n.d. Available at http://usgov-info.about.com/blvrbystate.htm, accessed November 21, 2008.

86. Federal Elections Commission, "The National Mail Voter Registration Form," n.d. Available at www.fec.gov/votregis/vr.shtml, accessed April 11, 2008.

87. Providing a false address for legal/identification purposes is of course a violation of state law, but we will leave such niceties aside for the moment.

Part II

The Mechanics of Voting

Part II of this book focuses on the mechanics of voting. In Chapter 4, we look at how people qualify to vote, what they have to do in order to vote, and how their efforts can be stymied when they try to do so. Chapter 5 examines the technology of casting ballots, and the pitfalls of that seemingly simple act.

4

Keep You from Voting? Yes, We Can!

At the conclusion of many naturalization ceremonies in this country, the new citizens are often offered registration materials so they can sign up to vote on the spot. Sometimes this opportunity is provided by local voting officials, sometimes by representatives of one or the other of the political parties. The idea is that there is no better time to introduce the new Americans to the rights and responsibilities of citizenship. Voting is surely one of the most important of these. Rare are the instances in which the new citizens decline to take advantage of the offer. What they don't realize, in the glow of the moment, is that even though they may have filled out the form, signed it, and handed it to the attendant voting functionary, they still might not be able to vote when the next election rolls around.

The truth is, the process of becoming a voter in the United States is difficult, arduous, and fraught with pitfalls. It is doubtful that any other nation makes it harder for citizens to vote than the United States. In this chapter we will look at what one has to do in order to become a voter. We will first examine the process of qualifying and registering. Then we will move to what happens step-by-step when the potential voter shows up at the polling place—assuming he or she can find it—and requests a ballot. We will also consider the voter who wants to vote early or absentee. At each step of the process—no matter how small it might seem—the wheels can come off and the voter will be turned away, unable to cast a ballot.

Qualifying

Before a prospective voter can register, he or she must first qualify. That is, the voter must meet certain prerequisites before his registration form will even be considered. Individual states establish the criteria for qualification; the Tenth Amendment reserves to the states the right to determine qualifications for voting, modified only by the Thirteenth, Fourteenth, and Fifteenth Amendments, the Voting Rights Act, federal court decisions, and federal rules and regulations, primarily emanating from the Civil Rights Division of the Department of Justice.

There is remarkable uniformity across the states in qualifications for voting. All require that prospective voters be citizens of the United States and have reached eighteen years of age by the time of their first election; several states allow pre-registration at sixteen or seventeen, but not (except in a very few instances) voting.

All but a few states also require state residence, and generally residence in the county or jurisdiction where the citizen intends to vote. Likewise, all but a handful disenfranchise felons, but there is some variation here. Most require that ex-felons have had their civil rights restored before they can register; in other states those rights are automatically restored upon completion of their sentence. Most states also disenfranchise those who are in prison, whether or not they committed a felony. Some states—Mississippi is an example—list crimes for which disqualification and hence disenfranchisement is a consequence; Arizona includes treason on its list.

More than thirty-five states deny the franchise to those who have been found by a court to be mentally incompetent, institutionalized for mental reasons, or are under guardianship. Twelve states require that prospective voters affirm that they are not registered in another county or state, or have a different legal residence from the one they wish to claim for voting purposes. Alabama requires that prospective voters take an elaborate oath of allegiance before they can qualify; Florida and some other states require that the signature on its registration form (to be discussed below) include acceptance of a loyalty oath. And some states have what can charitably be called idiosyncratic criteria for disqualification; Massachusetts, for example, requires that applicants "not have been convicted of corrupt practices in respect to elections." Wisconsin disqualifies anyone who made or profited from "a bet or wage[r] depending on the result of an election."[1]

What are the consequences of these prerequisites to registration? The most important is not how many different population groups are included, but how many are left out: noncitizens, those under eighteen, felons (or in some cases just those in jail), and the mentally impaired. We saw in the last chapter that more groups than these are disenfranchised as a matter of practice if not always by actual law, but it is notable that these four are singled out and prevented by state constitutional provision, statutes, or rules and regulations from qualifying as voters. Once codified, these stipulations become very difficult to change.

And we can say that in the United States, conceiving and codifying qualifications for registering is an example of the politics of exclusion. Americans often like to talk about the inclusiveness of our democracy, and the importance of both the franchise and political participation generally. But in fact this is true only in a limited sense. Those satisfying the qualifications for registration are almost exclusively limited to "mainstream" population groups in this country.

Registration

Students of election laws and rules have repeatedly demonstrated that the greatest single impediment to increasing voter turnout in the United States is voter registration. As Jason Halperin notes in his exhaustive study of registration laws in the states, "the single most important reason for the drastic decline in voter turnout during the twentieth century stems from the burdensome and outdated voter registration laws most states implemented at the turn of the century."[2]

During much of the nineteenth century, voting was mainly an unregulated activity, especially in nonurban areas. Women could not vote at all, and by the late 1880s freed slaves in the South, who could vote in the years immediately following the Civil War, lost their franchise. But white males for the most part could vote; essentially all they had to do was show up on Election Day to cast a ballot. Sometimes more than once. Rarely were they asked to do more than state their name and sign that they had come to vote (or make an X if they were illiterate). And not infrequently they were rewarded with whiskey and other refreshments, even a little cash, for their trouble. There was nothing in place comparable to what we would now refer to as "registering to vote."

In cities of the East and Midwest, political parties took control of voting. As their organizations developed into powerful machines, their grip on the mechanics of voting reached strangulation proportions. When immigrants began flooding American shores after the Civil War, urban political machines organized and mobilized different national and religious groups (depending on which party sought them) into blocs of voters. These groups, for whom the machines provided modest levels of social services, were expected to vote as the machine directed them. Registration scarcely existed, and the secret ballot hardly at all. Immigrants came to the polls and voted as they were told—citizenship was not always a precondition of voting then, and in any case the machines controlling elections ignored any such requirements. In many cases, the "poll workers," who were actually street-level functionaries of the political machines, filled out the ballots for the immigrants. It was a cozy arrangement, totally corrupt and devoid of any public accountability.

Change began as the Progressive movement picked up steam. The term "Progressive" is actually a misnomer in this context. The Progressives were very conservative when it came to voting rights. And, while they stood for many things, the Progressives were decidedly hostile to the waves of immigrants coming to the United States, that is, except for those from northern Europe and the British Isles. But they feared and held in contempt those from central, southern, and southeastern Europe, Poland and Russia, and China. Nor did the Progressives in the South have much use for ex-slaves and their descendents.

While the Progressives did indeed target corrupt urban political machines for extinction, they were just as much concerned about the avalanche of immigrants invading the country. If they could not stop them from disembarking, they could at least block them from voting. Indeed, in their view they could kill off the machines by keeping the immigrants away from the polls, since the former essentially stood on the backs of the latter. Thus, the Progressives began a campaign to disenfranchise immigrants and other undesirables.

Voter registration was a powerful tool that they developed to regulate who could vote and who could not. Establishing and institutionalizing (through constitutional provisions and state laws) elaborate constructs of preconditions and qualifications for voting became common. Also common were complex procedures for registering those who at least met the prerequisites; registration meant that the machines could control the extent of political participation, particularly voting.

In the South, Progressivism took an even more pernicious turn.[3] Late in the nineteenth century there were fewer European immigrants in the South than in the North and Midwest, but there were large numbers of blacks. Accordingly, Progressives actively participated in the institutionalization of Jim Crow laws to prevent former slaves from voting. Poll taxes, literacy tests, and character testaments were the most common mechanisms used to prevent blacks from registering; in most cases they were institutionalized by law. But they were not the only ones; terror and other forms of intimidation could also be used to ensure that blacks didn't even try to register, or to vote, if by some mischance they were able to do so.

Thus, by the dawn of the twentieth century, voter registration procedures had been put in place throughout the nation. Their effect was to sharply limit access to the ballot box. Fast-forwarding to the beginning of the twenty-first century reveals that even though registering to vote is not as onerous as it was when first introduced, it is still a device that is designed to limit, and has the result of curtailing, voting in America. It is an almost exquisite instrument of disenfranchisement, another example of how public policy in this country is designed to keep people from casting ballots.

Some will object that this discussion is overblown. How difficult is it, really, to register to vote? You get the form, you fill it out, you mail it in, and it's done. A week or two later a voter registration card arrives by return mail and you are ready to vote. Some states even let you register online now. What's the big deal?

The answer is that the devil is in the details. The process of registering to vote is long, cumbersome, and fraught with pitfalls. A blunder at any step of the way can result in rejection of the application form, disqualification, or delay in successfully completing the process.

Before looking at the registration process, it needs to be said that voter registration is easier now than a generation ago. This is because of the National Voter Registration Act of 1993, more commonly known as the "motor voter law." Under provisions of the law, people can register to vote when they obtain or renew their driver's licenses at their Department of Motor Vehicles rather than having to go to the office of their county voting registrar or supervisor. They can also get the forms at other government offices that provide social services, such as welfare departments or those assisting the disabled. And, while not required by the motor voter law, other types of public agencies such as libraries often have voter registration materials on hand for patrons. Some stores—grocery chains, for example—have also made registration forms available to customers at their courtesy desks.[4] In all states except Massachusetts it is possible to download either the state or national voter registration form on a computer, print it out, complete it, and mail it in. A few states—Washington is an example—even allow online registration, which does indeed shorten the process.

In spite of these considerable improvements, it is not at all clear that voter registration figures in the United States have risen substantially since passage of the motor voter law. In 1990, about 67 percent of the voting age population was registered; in 1998, 62 percent. This fell slightly by 2002—a nonpresidential election year—to 61 percent, and rose again in 2004 to 65 percent.[5]

Initially, scholars studying the impact of the motor voter law found that its influence on increasing voter registration was slight and generally limited to those under thirty and those who moved within two years of Election Day. But more recent research suggests otherwise, especially if we consider the way in which registration rates vary by race and ethnicity. The U.S. Census reported that in 2006—a nonpresidential election year when both registration rates and turnout tend to dip—69.5 percent of whites were registered (71.2 percent non-Hispanic white), 60.9 percent of blacks, 49.1 percent of Asians, and 53.7 percent of Hispanics.[6] What has become increasingly well recognized is the disparity in registration rates between the poor (defined as those on public assistance) and the nonpoor. Demos estimates the gap at over 19 percent.[7] However, Demos points out that in those states that vigorously implement the provisions of the 1993 motor voter law by encouraging those on or seeking public assistance to register, registration rates among the poor have risen appreciably; the study points to Missouri, Virginia, and North Carolina as having particularly successful initiatives.

Thus, we can recognize that the motor voter law has at least made access to voter registration materials easier for many people. But even with these materials in hand, the voter's problems do not shrivel up and go away. For the purposes of this discussion, only Florida's form will be reviewed, although I examined the forms of all forty-eight states that provide them online, plus the National Voter Registration Form and District of Columbia form.[8] As noted earlier in this chapter, qualifications prerequisite to voting are fairly consistent across the nation, and the registration forms that require the prospective voter to attest to them are quite similar. Florida's form does contain one or two idiosyncratic elements that are not found in all or even some other states; nonetheless it is more typical than not of the rest of the nation.

Florida requires that its form be completed with a ballpoint pen using black ink.[9] Pencil, blue ink, or some other writing medium is not acceptable, although it is not clear if the application is invalid if something besides a black ballpoint pen is used. The form itself consists of sixteen lines of questions (some lines contain more than one question). Eight of the lines are required, that is, they must be completed fully; the other eight consist of optional items.

Seven of the required lines can be anticipated: certification that the applicant is a U.S. citizen; not a felon or if so, his or her voting rights have been restored; and not adjudged mentally incompetent with respect to voting, or if so, his or her rights have been restored; date of birth indicated in a very specific format (MM/DD/YYYY); name (including suffix); and legal residence (street number, apartment if applicable, city, county, zip code). Applicants must also provide their Florida driver's license or Florida ID number; if they have neither, they must indicate by writing the word "none" in the box provided, as well as the last four digits of their Social Security number. Finally, applicants must sign and date the form; the signature represents acceptance of an oath that is printed to the left of the signature box: "I do solemnly swear (or affirm) that I will protect and defend the Constitution of the United States and the Constitution of the State of Florida, that I am qualified to register as an elector under the Constitution and laws of the State of Florida, and that all information provided in this application is true."

The form does not indicate whether or not failure to provide the required information is grounds for rejection of the application. What happens if the applicant does not offer his or her birth date in the manner prescribed? What happens if he or she does not write out the word "none"? The oath itself is highly problematic: why should a voter have to swear or affirm a duty to protect and defend the U.S. and Florida constitutions? The U.S. Constitution makes no such demand on prospective voters. For many individuals, having to take a loyalty oath is not just distasteful but a violation of one's civil liberties. Suppose the prospective voter crosses out the oath; is the application then invalidated, even if it still is signed?

Indeed, the only clear statement indicating how the applicant could invalidate the application comes at the bottom, where the statement "Invalid without signature or mark of applicant" is printed. It is not clear if the date is included in this stipulation.

What all of this means, of course, is that voting officials—local and state—have immense discretion as to accepting or rejecting the voter's application.[10] The fact that the prospective voter has very little way of telling ahead of time if the application will be accepted or not makes the whole registration process very much a willy-nilly, hit or miss, roll-of-the-dice proposition.

There is an additional matter. Applicants must provide a legal residence, including street address (Florida, unlike some states, makes no provision on its registration form to draw a map indicating the location of residence in case there is no street address, which is not uncommon in rural areas). What does it mean to demonstrate a legal residence? One has to offer evidence that he or she actually can be found at a particular place. Implied is some concept of being settled, if not permanently, then at least for some unspecified period; most states have gotten rid of long residency requirements, although not completely. In any case, the idea of a legal residence is to show that the applicant is not a bum, a vagrant, a transient, or indeed, merely homeless; that is, he or she is a person worthy of the franchise. According to the instructions accompanying the Florida registration form, this evidence can be a bank statement, government check, paycheck, utility bill, or "other government document."

While most of us take things like this for granted, some people cannot provide the required kind of information. We saw earlier that homeless people generally cannot. Institutionalized or hospitalized people are probably uncertain as to their address, or which one to put down; some may be unable to write, and it is not clear that surrogates can fill in the information. There are also people who do not have bank accounts, are not connected to utilities, and who receive no paycheck. Those who are extremely poor; those living in isolated, especially rural, areas; the very elderly in urban areas, particularly if they are mentally impaired or are completely alone—all of these population groups might have trouble providing the needed documentation in order to vote. Undoubtedly there are other such population groups.

But what is perhaps most shocking about all of this is that the requirement of demonstrating a legal residence constitutes a means test. The evidence needed to prove legal residency implies the possession of material resources by the applicant, or at least the ability to pay for electricity or water or a telephone. Those with no demonstrable resources cannot vote. Means tests continue in the United States.

Some readers might object that demonstrating a legal residence makes sense. After all, the argument might run, if a person does not have to show that he or she is actually grounded in a place with at least some degree of permanence, what is to stop him or her from going from polling place to polling place on Election Day and voting several times, or crossing county and even state lines to do the same thing? Requiring evidence of a residence is essential to prevent voter fraud, some would say. We will return to the issue of voter fraud later.

I am not suggesting that there is something necessarily wrong with having to show a legal residence for someone who has one. I certainly do not condone cheating and voter fraud of the kind just mentioned. But I do suggest in this chapter that forcing potential voters to provide evidence of a legal residence is unfair, because some people who otherwise should be qualified to vote cannot produce this proof. In other words, exceptions and substitutes must be made, and requirements waived when extenuating circumstances exist. Ways must be found to prevent discrimination against those who cannot satisfy the residence or means requirement and thus are unable to vote. But there is nothing on the political horizon to suggest that some kind of accommodation for these people will be put in place anytime in the near future.

For the sake of argument, though, let us assume that the prospective voter has completed the registration form. His or her next step is to ensure that it is sent, dropped off, or delivered to the proper local voting officials, usually found in a county office. Addresses are generally listed on the registration materials and are frequently listed on the Web sites of local voting officials' agencies. Alternatively, in those states that so permit, the application can be filed online.

One would assume that this is a matter of routine and that, shortly, a voter registration card would be mailed to the applicant. But further complications can arise that will prevent him or her from being able to vote, particularly if the election is to occur soon. We leave aside the sometimes erratic manner in which the U.S. Postal Service delivers snail mail; the possibility that when the registration form reaches the relevant county officials, it is misplaced; or that in the event of an online submission, the transmission gets lost in cyberspace rather than going to the appropriate agency. And we pass over the numerous reports, often anecdotal, from those trying to register, especially for the first time, who did not receive their registration cards back from local voting officials in time for the next election. All of these things can and do happen.

More serious matters erupt when local voting officials begin to examine the received applications. Earlier we noted that they have vast discretion in deciding which applications are valid and which are not. But not only are there no clearly defined standards of acceptability across states, often within states, across counties, and even sometimes within individual elections offices there is no consistency; one clerk may accept an application, another may interpret the form differently and reject it.

Some of these issues affect African American voters disproportionally. Professor Michael McDonald has shown that in Florida, at least, African American voters have had particular registration problems because apartment numbers and street addresses cannot be reconciled with those on file on approved address lists. The same is true because of errors with zip codes. Too often, according to McDonald, black voters are not registered due to these discrepancies.[11] It is entirely likely that the "Florida syndrome" affecting black voters is manifested in other states as well.

A further problem results from a key provision of the Help America Vote Act (HAVA) of 2002.[12] States are required now to build and maintain master lists of registered voters. The laudable goal of this requirement is to prevent the situation, well documented in Florida in 2000, in which thousands of voters could not exercise their franchise because the records kept by local registrars and the state list of alleged felons were fatally flawed. But HAVA requires that the state voter lists have also to be compared to other statewide databases, for example (and most commonly) those for driver's licenses maintained by Departments of Motor Vehicles; lists of welfare clients are also used. If these do not match precisely, the prospective voter will not be registered or, if he or she is, will not be allowed to vote upon appearing at the polls.

For example, a voter may list his name for the driver's license as "John A. Smith." But for voter registration, he may write "John Albert Smith." The state will generally regard these as two different people, and even if the same address and birth date are shown, his voter registration will be disallowed or canceled. Or he may list his name on the voter application form as "John A. Smith," but signs it at the bottom as "John Albert Smith." It's still the same person, but either the local voting official or the state list might well kick it out. This phenomenon is called the "no match, no vote" rule, and it is a mechanism for disenfranchising voters whose names on various lists (including ID cards) don't match master lists. It has become an all too common way of keeping people from voting, and indeed in the 2008 presidential election the U.S. Supreme Court forced Ohio not to apply the "no match, no vote" rule when it was clear that the person was one and the same.

Indeed, as other studies have shown, state master lists are only as good as they are up-to-date and accurate. Numerous flaws have been found.[13] Duplication of names and birth dates across states continues to be common; a study by the *Orlando Sentinel* found 68,000 occurrences across the states of Florida, Georgia, and the Carolinas; the *Charlotte Observer* found more than 60,000 in just the Carolinas alone. Voter purges are sometimes carried out willy-nilly, and neither state lists nor individual voters are notified. Voters who seek to register through third parties (an issue we will return to shortly) are not always certain if their registration was successful. Applicants whose names happen to match those of celebrities or other famous people ("George Clooney," "Britney Spears," "George W. Bush") often find their registrations disregarded as fraudulent or frivolous, or held up pending presentation of further evidence that they are not the same person as their namesake.

In short, too often voters are left in ambiguous positions with respect to the status of their registration. When they arrive at their polling place, they might be turned away for reasons that have nothing to do with them, or for reasons that have nothing to do with the way they filled out their application.

As important as these issues are, they take secondary position to another one—the continuing existence of state residency requirements for registration. We noted earlier that before an individual can register, he or she must meet a residence requirement of some days or weeks as a precondition or qualification in the vast majority of states. In most, but not all, of these states, the qualification residence requirement is also a voter residence requirement. In other words, a person must not only have lived in the state for a certain length of time in order to qualify to register, he or she must also register to vote within a specified period (usually the same) before the election in order to be able to vote. At the end of the business day on the indicated number of days prior to the election, the books close. If the person is not registered when the clock strikes on that day, he or she will not be able to vote. In a large majority of states, this period is over twenty days; in a significant number it is twenty-nine or thirty days.

Why the "waiting period"? The answer varies from trying to ensure that transients don't vote to preventing voter fraud to making sure that the local voting registrar has enough time to process registration forms prior to the election to hoping that the voter learns enough during the incubation period to make an "informed" decision at the polls. All of these claims are bogus, particularly the latter, as it stretches somewhere between character and literacy tests. Sometimes one also hears that the waiting period is essential to maintaining political stability and continuity. Why these are more important than encouraging people to vote, and enhancing the likelihood that they will do so, is not at all clear.

The real purpose behind registration residency requirements is to control access to the polls. In areas where the population is especially mobile—college and university towns are good examples—local power structures want to be able to regulate who can vote in order to maintain their positions and protect fellow officeholders, as well as entrenched interests. The same is true in states where the population is mobile and immigration widespread—Colorado, Florida, Arizona, New Mexico, Texas, and California come to mind. To say that voting officials take a conservative view of who should vote is an understatement. It is not in their interest to have the polls flooded by unpredictable newly registered voters, so they are kept away.

But the fact that some states—Maine and Maryland, for example—have no waiting period and have not been ripped asunder gives lie to the argument that one is needed to ensure political stability and continuity. True, Maryland has witnessed more voter fraud and political corruption scandals than most other states, but this has more to do with the political culture of the state, its traditions of "politics as usual," and its patterns of doing state business than with the absence of a waiting or incubation period.

It would seem that there is no legitimate reason for states to maintain residence requirements between registration and the actual casting of ballots. The effect of maintaining them is to prevent late deciders, those who have recently moved into the area, purged voters, and those who simply missed the deadline from voting. It is another example of employing public policy to disenfranchise potential voters.

In the end, we can legitimately ask if we need to continue the process of voter registration at all, or at least as most states have been carrying it out. The process is arduous, often arbitrary, and does not lead to a guarantee that the successful registrant will be able to cast a ballot. One state—North Dakota—does not require voter registration. Granted, it is a relatively homogeneous, underpopulated state. But that is not the point; the point is that there is no evidence that because North Dakota does not require people to register to vote, elections there are rife with corruption and fraud. Quite the contrary, in fact. It is my position that serious consideration be given to eliminating the practice of voter registration as it is carried out in most of the United States. Or, if that is too much to ask, I advocate moving to same-day registration, to be discussed in the next section. But to continue registration of voters as most states practice it is to perpetuate an unfair, and completely unnecessary, mechanism of voter disenfranchisement.

Same-Day Registration (EDR)

Some eight states—Idaho, Maine, Minnesota, New Hampshire, Wisconsin, Wyoming, North Carolina, and Montana—have allowed "same-day" registration (often called "Election Day registration," or EDR) for voters for several years; Maine, Minnesota, and Wisconsin have had it since the 1970s.[14] Since January 1, 2008, Iowa has joined this small group.[15] It is likely that more states in the future will allow same-day registration. It appears to be an idea whose time has come.[16] Currently, some twenty-one states are considering adopting same-day registration, as is the national government for federal elections.[17]

The idea is not new. It has floated in and out of the national political agenda for decades. Jimmy Carter pushed it during his administration, at least briefly, before it ran into a brick wall of opposition. While the mechanics of same-day voter registration differ somewhat across the states that have adopted it, the general idea is the same. Individuals show up at their polling place on Election Day and present an ID card. This is generally a valid driver's license showing current address.[18] For those without a driver's license, some other evidence of a permanent address is acceptable. For example, in Iowa, nondrivers can present a residential lease, property tax statement, utility bill, bank statement, paycheck, government check, U.S. passport, U.S. military ID, employer-issued ID, or some similar kind of document. Both Iowa and Minnesota make special provision for college students, who can present their university or college ID card, fee card, or something similar.

What has been the effect of EDR in those states that have adopted it? Several studies and reports suggest that it has had a positive impact on voter turnout.[19] In fact, the Institute for Southern Studies found that turnout in EDR states is as much as 10 percent higher than in those without it; Demos reports that in 2004, EDR states had a 12 percent higher turnout than others; in 2008 Demos claimed EDR increased voting by 8 percentage points, and Iowa had a comparable increase that year.[20] Demos also gives evidence that EDR addresses a number of other key voting issues: it encourages "late deciders" to vote, as it doesn't matter if their interest was piqued only after the registration books closed; it allows those who may have been purged from the voter rolls to cast votes on Election Day; it encourages new, especially young, voters to participate; it allows highly mobile, and low-income, voters to participate; it obviates arbitrary voter registration deadlines; it is cost effective, as studies indicate that EDR elections are no more expensive than non-EDR ones; and it does not promote voter fraud.[21] In addition, the former secretary of state of Montana claims that in his experience, EDR prevents confusion at polling places as to who is eligible to vote and who is not, and actually expedites the voting process because it prevents long lines of voters from forming as the eligibility of individual voters is determined.[22]

Perhaps most importantly, EDR eliminates the need for provisional ballots on Election Day. HAVA allows the use of these ballots at polling places when a voter's registration cannot be verified on-site. But the problem with provisional ballots is that they cause delays in voting at the polls, since voters have to line up while eligibility is determined, and more significantly, they delay the vote count. Provisional ballots are not always counted the same day as the election, often only days later (and sometimes not at all). In the case of close votes, this delay means that determination of the winner is suspended and the results ambiguous. It also opens the door to charges of vote fraud, as opponents vie to determine whose votes really "count." But none of this happens with EDR. There are no provisional ballots, since all votes are cast immediately upon registration. And all votes are counted the same day (the only ones that might not be are absentee ballots, and those that show defects and are contested). Thus, election results are determined much more quickly than with provisional ballots, with greater accuracy, and with much less rancor.

There is, of course, opposition to same-day voter registration, although it is difficult to characterize since it ranges across a number of issues.[23] Partisanship represents one divide on EDR: Democrats tend to like it because they feel it favors lower-income people likely to vote for them; Republicans oppose it for the same reason. Local voting officials often oppose it, arguing it would make their lives more difficult and election costs would increase; this latter point is usually asserted rather than demonstrated, because most of the evidence is that same-day registration does not increase costs. Some opponents argue that EDR takes away states' rights to run elections in the way they choose. Others claim it will increase voter fraud since it would be hard to prevent a voter from acquiring multiple identity and residence documents and voting numerous times, including across county and even state lines. Others simply say it will "cheapen" the electoral process, whatever that means.

These claims are worthless. Local voting officials are notorious foot-draggers when it comes to changing election procedures, because they have to learn to run elections differently from their accustomed procedures. When pressed to show how voter fraud has increased in those states with same-day registration, opponents cannot deliver the goods because, as we will see shortly, there is so little same-day election fraud in this country anyway. Sophisticated computer networking that connects databases across counties and states can certainly monitor same-day registrants and catch whatever potential fraud might exist. Others claim that the technology to allow for same-day registration has not been proven; on the contrary—it has, repeatedly, as it is very different, much simpler, and much more reliable than the technology of, say, e-voting with touchscreens.

Indeed, one would have to conclude that inertia and a certain Ludditism, as well as partisan fears, are at the base of opposition to same-day registration. As for cheapening the electoral process, this would seem to be a hard position to sustain, given that EDR makes voting accessible to more people, and expedites the process of casting and counting ballots. Rather than cheapening the process, it should be asserted that it adds value to the electoral process, because more people can participate more quickly, and outcomes can be determined faster and more efficiently. But it is clear that some people don't see this added value as a positive step.

Third-Party Registration

In recent years, states have moved to restrict efforts by organizations other than local voting offices and political parties to conduct voter registration drives. In truth, these "third-party" registration efforts have been around for a long time. The League of Women Voters, for example, has conducted voter registration (and education) efforts for decades, generally very successfully. Other, essentially private organizations have also sought to carry out voter registration activities.

However, national attention was drawn to some of these efforts before and after the 2006 midterm elections. In particular, CBS News reported that a national campaign by ACORN (Association of Community Organizations for Reform Now) had committed grievous errors in its voter registration drives in Philadelphia, Ohio, Denver, and elsewhere. ACORN used incorrect forms, did not always provide signatures, listed faulty addresses, and made other errors. Thousands of potential voters were denied registration because of their errors of omission and commission. There are also confirmed reports of thousands of voter registration applications—from ACORN and other third-party groups—which local voting officials simply ignored, or tossed aside.[24]

As a result, states moved rapidly to regulate third-party registration efforts. Unfortunately, many of the regulations adopted in some states smacked of ugly partisanship, usually by Republicans who claimed they were fighting voter fraud.[25] In fact, they were trying to make sure minorities and lower-income groups who might vote Democratic would be kept off the rolls; these were the special focus of ACORN registration efforts, which accounts for the Republican assault on it. States that moved to regulate third-party voter registration drives included Arizona, Florida, Georgia, Louisiana, Michigan, Minnesota, and Ohio.[26]

Not all of the regulations imposed were severe, but those in Florida and Ohio were draconian. Severe penalties and fines, potentially amounting to several thousand dollars per registered voter depending on the nature of the offense, could be imposed on organizations not following correct procedures. These were so restrictive as to virtually eliminate any possibility they could engage in voter registration efforts.[27] The League of Women Voters in Florida simply abandoned its traditional drives.

Lawsuits were filed in both Florida and Ohio to prevent enforcement of these regulations, and in both states federal judges enjoined officials from enforcing them pending further litigation.[28] As of this writing, it is not clear what the disposition of these cases will be, or whether or not the Florida and Ohio rules will be overturned or allowed to stand.

During the 2008 presidential campaign, the Republican Party in a number of states again attacked ACORN, which continued its voter registration drives, for engaging in fraudulent registration practices. While investigations revealed that ACORN had indeed made some mistakes, they were far fewer than the number alleged. There was virtually no evidence that the errors rose to the level of voter fraud.[29]

Nonetheless, it has to be said that efforts to stop third-party groups from registering voters has had a chilling effect. As noted, the League of Women Voters ceased registration efforts in some states. Nongovernmental agencies, such as stores, that had offered registration forms to customers in a number of states, pulled them. This hardly seems like a recipe for extending the franchise to new voters.

Polling Places

Let us assume that a hypothetical voter has valid registration and identification materials in hand (more on the latter later), and he sets out to vote. The first task is to find the proper polling place, that is, the location to which he has been assigned by local voting officials in order to cast a ballot.[30]

This is not always as easy as it seems. In most states the address of the polling place is usually printed on the voter registration card, along with the name (if any) of the school, church, or other building in which voting is to take place. Of course, if the voter has gone to the polling place previously, he or she will generally remember where it is and simply head to it. The problem arises when he or she arrives and discovers it is no longer a place to vote.

Usually local voting officials will notify voters when the location of polling places has been changed, or if the voter has been assigned to a different precinct, ward, or voting district from the previous one because the boundary lines were redrawn. The notification generally comes by mail. But there is considerable evidence (mainly anecdotal, yet frequent enough to give it weight) that local officials don't always do so. More commonly, they don't do so in a timely fashion, and the voter does not note the location change. Of course, it also happens that the voter pays no attention to the notice mailed to him or her, in which case it is not the fault of local officials that he or she went to the wrong place to vote.

But it also happens that in at least some states—Texas is a good example—local registrars are infamous for changing the location of polling places almost willy-nilly, and often so close to Election Day that prospective voters are bamboozled when they try to find them. Travis County (Austin—home of a large university campus) notes on its Web site, in fact, that "polling places are subject to change up until election day."[31] One can only speculate as to the reasons why local voting officials would engage in such practices, but a reasonable guess would be that it has something to do with regulating—especially limiting—voter turnout.

Well, it might be objected, so what? It is, after all, the voter's responsibility to find out where he or she is supposed to vote ahead of time. No argument there, except for the preponderance of evidence that local officials do not always do a good job of notifying voters of polling place changes, thereby unnecessarily disenfranchising some voters. But, the objections continue, with the proliferation of cell phones all the voter need do is call the local registrar and find out the new location. Again, no argument, except that on Election Day local voting officials' offices are generally swamped with phone calls, and it might take an hour or more for a voter standing on a street corner or cruising around in his or her car to get through. Many voters on their way to work, on their lunch hour, or heading home, will lose patience and forget about voting. This also constitutes disenfranchisement, functionally if not legally.

Fortunately, help is at hand. Almost all states, and many counties, provide on-line assistance to voters to locate their polling place. Voters need simply type their address onto the form found on voting officials' Web sites, and the location of the polling place to which they have been assigned will be shown. Data are shown in real time, so that even in those instances in which local officials redrew precinct lines or changed polling locations at the last minute, voters can find where they are to vote. There is no doubt that this is a big improvement, but of course it only works for those with computers or Blackberries and iPhones having Internet access; the continuing digital divide in this country means that it is much less likely to help poor people than those who are better off.

Does polling place location influence voter turnout? Are people more likely to vote if they don't have to travel long distances to do so? The evidence is not fully clear. In general, it seems to depend on where the voter lives. In cities, where voters are used to traffic congestion and may well be accustomed to using public transportation, distance to polling places does not seem to influence the decision of whether or not to vote; of course, in densely populated urban areas, precincts or wards or election districts are geographically small and voters don't have to go far to find their polling place. In rural areas, voters may be used to driving ten or more miles over sparsely populated roads for all sorts of reasons, and doing so to vote is nothing out of the ordinary unless conditions are so bad (floods, snowdrifts, a bridge outage) that the roads are impassable. Suburban voters seem to be the most sensitive about traveling to vote, especially if traffic is heavy and congestion bad. While "upper limits" are hard to gauge, at least some analysts suggest that voters who have to struggle more than five miles or so through fierce traffic in order to vote might well decide not to bother.

Most polling places are located in schools, public buildings, and churches.[32] Outside of central cities, the operative consideration for choosing a location seems to be availability of parking space. Schools and churches, especially the latter during weekdays, offer the most. Following incidents throughout the country in which strangers entered school grounds and caused injury and worse to students, school officials have become skittish about allowing voters, whose behavior they cannot regulate, on campus. Thus in recent years there has been a substantial movement to put polling places in churches, as any voter who is a child predator will not find likely targets unless the church has a school attached, but reasonable levels of supervision can keep voters and children apart.

The main problem with using churches as polling places is that it raises church-state separation issues. Using church facilities to conduct elections creates an entanglement between church and state upon which both the federal and most state constitutions frown. It can further be argued that because of the costs of running the election, compensation to the church for use of its facilities involves at least indirect and possibly direct aid to the church, something that many state constitutions forbid.[33]

Some states have become conscious of the constitutional issues that arise through use of churches as polling places. Alaska, for example, notes that some people are uncomfortable going into a church to vote because of personal beliefs and convictions, even as it recognizes that in some sparsely populated areas a church might be the only building suitable for a polling place. In these instances, Alaska allows the voter to go to another polling place if there is more than one in the precinct and cast a "questioned" (provisional) ballot, or to vote absentee if not.[34] Other states appear not to be so flexible. As a matter of policy, it might behoove states to find suitable polling places other than churches in the future, and to allow objectors to cast ballots in other venues besides churches. Early and absentee voting to some extent reduce the pressure on the individual voter, but do not address the underlying constitutional conundrum that using church facilities for voting raises.

What happens when a voter shows up at the wrong polling place? Perhaps he or she has moved and not bothered to reregister; perhaps the location was changed and he or she is unaware that it was. In previous years, in general the voter was out of luck. Officials at polling places would not usually allow the person to vote. As a result of HAVA, though, many local voting officials have taken a more flexible approach and allowed the voter to cast a provisional ballot, to be counted once it was confirmed that the voter was in fact legitimately registered but simply showed up at the wrong place. However, standardization of this procedure has not been established, and practices vary widely across the nation. There are many reports of legitimately registered voters going to the wrong polling place and not being given provisional ballots, or discovering later that even if they were, these were not counted. In order to extend the franchise to as many legitimately registered voters as possible, it would seem that use of provisional ballots under the circumstances mentioned should become universal. Of course, same-day registration eliminates the problem completely, and saves time, money, and administrative snafus.

A related issue is whether or not the jurisdiction provides a sufficient number of polling stations to accommodate all potential voters. Local voting officials try to use various formulas to determine how many are needed. And they are quick to point out, legitimately so, that adding more polling stations adds to the cost of the election. On the other hand, it is not always clear that there are enough conveniently located polling stations to accommodate all potential voters fairly. Indeed, while hard data are lacking, there are more than a few reports that it is easier to access polling stations in some parts of a jurisdiction than others. This raises issues of fairness, with accompanying questions of racial and social class bias.

Once our registered voter has located his polling place, he needs to make sure he shows up while it is open. This too can be problematic, depending on where he lives, his employment, his life style, and his desire to vote.

Most states—thirty-three in fact—open their polls at 7:00 or 7:30 A.M. Fourteen open at 6:00 or 6:30. Two—Idaho and Nebraska—don't open until 8:00 A.M. But in a number of states, local voting officials can set their own opening hours. In Maine, for example, polls can open as early as 6:00 A.M. or as late as 10:00; New Hampshire's opening hours vary between 6:00 and 11:00 A.M.; some polling places in Vermont open as early as 5:00 A.M. or as late as 10:00.[35]

Closing hours also vary widely. Twenty-three states close at 7:00 or 7:30 P.M., and twenty at 8:00 or 8:30 P.M. But three states—Hawaii, Indiana, and Kentucky—close at 6:00. Three other states—Iowa, New York, and Rhode Island—close at 9:00 P.M., although hours across the latter can vary.[36]

In the vast majority of states polls are open for twelve or thirteen hours. But Hawaii's are open for only eleven hours (7:00 A.M. to 6:00 P.M.), the shortest of all fifty states plus the District of Columbia (excepting those areas in Maine, New

Hampshire, and Vermont that might open late). New Jersey's polls are open for fourteen hours (6:00 A.M. to 8:00 P.M.), and New York's fifteen (6:00 A.M. to 9:00 P.M.). Oregon actually has the most hours available for voting, since the state uses mailed ballots over a period of a few weeks, and voters can mark and send in ballots at any time during that period.

Do the hours when the polls are open make any difference in voter participation? The answer is potentially yes, although there is little hard data on the subject. States that offer more hours to voters potentially afford more people the chance to vote. Perhaps more significantly, limiting hours may cause hardships, even discrimination, for some voters. For example, those who start work at 5:00 or 5:30 A.M. may have difficulty getting to polls, even if they leave work by early afternoon, as fatigue, the chores of daily life, children, schooling, and second jobs may prevent their getting to polls while they are still open. Many hourly wage employees cannot afford to take time to go vote. Those working graveyard shifts might have difficulty getting to polls while they are open, as they are sleeping or working other jobs during that period. Many workers, including those on salary, simply cannot take time off from their jobs to travel to the polls and then return to work. Some employers are not sympathetic to employees who may want to do so, especially wage earners. In an increasingly global economy, workers who track and trade in distant markets may have to keep their eyes glued to computer screens the entire time their polling station is open and cannot afford to break away to get there.

It can be argued that those who want to vote will make the effort to do so regardless of their employment status, family responsibilities, other jobs, schooling, and so forth. That is true. On the other hand, the question is whether voters with certain types of jobs face additional, and often troubling, barriers to voting from those who work "normal" 8:00 to 5:00 jobs. This extra burden placed on them, which is both problematic and troubling, in the end may cause them to not vote.

Alternatives to Polling Places

Expansion of opening hours at polling places would solve many of the issues just mentioned; for example, if all polling places were open from, say, 5:00 A.M. to midnight, it is likely that more people could find their way to vote. Candidates and the media, of course, would not like this idea at all, since it would delay by hours the counting of ballots and the determination of winners. Local election officials would not like the idea either since longer hours would add greatly to the cost of manning polling places (assuming enough poll workers could even be found to cover the extra hours). Nor have local voting officials been receptive to expanding the number of polling stations, generally citing a paucity of suitable sites, increased costs at a time of shrinking public budgets, and difficulties in finding skilled personnel to run the added facilities as major reasons for their opposition.

But it is possible to expand opportunities for people to vote without relying on increasing the number of polling places or their opening hours at all; alternatives exist.

The most promising of these alternatives is what is known as "early voting," although in some states it is more formally called "in-person absentee voting."[37] Fundamentally, early voting consists of opening the polls early so that voters have a considerable period, in some cases a month or more, to cast ballots. Local voting officials establish one or more locations in their jurisdiction to which voters can come during open hours and vote, regardless of their address or assigned precinct in the jurisdiction. Often these polling places are open weekends as well as during the workweek.

Some thirty-one states have what is called "no excuse" early voting. This means voters casting early ballots need not offer any reason for choosing to vote before Election Day. Another four states plus the District of Columbia offer early voting for those with an excuse, although it is not always clear what constitutes an acceptable excuse (absence from the jurisdiction on Election Day is the most common one). Nor does the record reveal if any early voter has ever been turned down for lack of an acceptable excuse in these five jurisdictions. Sixteen states do not allow early voting as of this writing.[38]

States vary considerably in the length of time given to early voting. Most are in the two-to-three-week range, again often including weekends. But Wyoming opens its early voting polls forty days before the election; Virginia opens them forty-five days before the November general election and thirty days before others. Vermont allows a thirty-day period, Texas seventeen days, Utah fourteen, Nebraska thirty-five, Florida fifteen, Georgia one week, and so forth. Some states require that voters go to the county administration building to cast early ballots, but most allow satellite sites to be established; voters can cast ballots at the location of their choice.

Does early voting increase turnout? The evidence is that it has a positive effect.[39] The problem in making the determination is heavily methodological: in an election in which overall turnout increases because it is competitive, controversial, even exciting, or one in which overall turnout is depressed, it is difficult to separate out the independent effect of early voting from other forces influencing what was happening anyway. Expensive postelection surveys are necessary to make this determination with any degree of certainty.

On the other hand, anecdotal evidence suggests that early voting is a boon to certain types of voters. Older voters who do not want to endure potentially long lines on Election Day at their regular polling place or the hurly-burly that often accompanies them speak favorably of early voting. Those whose jobs do not allow them to get to the polls on Election Day also like it. Sometimes local circumstances can make a difference. For example, during the 2004 presidential election the Reverend Jesse Jackson made a number of visits to urban areas with substantial African American populations, speaking at rallies; at the conclusion of those rallies he sometimes led voters to early voting locations, with subsequent media reports that many people voted who might not have done so otherwise. Voters who want or need to vote early but do not wish to go through the hassle of getting an absentee ballot also like early voting, since there is almost no red tape involved. Reports about the fall 2008 elections are still coming in, but there are numerous accounts of greatly increased voter turnout because of early voting in those states that allow it.

On balance, early voting has a great deal to recommend it, and it is likely that more states in the future will adopt it. If it is combined with same-day registration it will unquestionably make voting easier and more accessible to many people. Indeed, that is the point. If the goal is to provide greater opportunities for people to vote, then early voting is a winner. Whether or not it independently increases voter participation is less important than that it opens doors for potential voters that previously were closed.

Another alternative to voting at polling places is "vote by mail" (VBM), practiced in Oregon. It is a relatively simple, cost-effective election procedure, which by all accounts works very well.[40]

VBM was adopted by Oregonians in 1998, and first used in 2000. All elections in the state are now run this way, as no polling places exist anymore. Every registered voter in the state receives a ballot in the mail roughly two weeks prior to the election. No mail forwarding is permitted; those not deliverable are returned to local voting officials. In the envelope addressed to the voter are a ballot and a "secrecy" envelope into which the voter places her completed ballot. The secrecy envelope must be signed on the outside so that signatures can be checked by local voting officials; this is the primary means of ensuring security and protection against possible fraud. Ballots must be returned by 8:00 P.M. on Election Day, at which time they are opened and counted.[41] Postmarks don't count; the ballots must actually be in the hands of voting officials by the designated time. Ballots need not be mailed in; they can be delivered personally to local voting officials or dropped off at a number of approved locations.[42]

What is the effect of VBM? Does it work? Indirect evidence suggests that it does. It is difficult to assess, for the reasons mentioned before, whether or not it independently increases voter turnout; the methodological problem in Oregon is compounded by the fact that there is no "control group" of polling places with which to compare VBM turnout. However, what is clear is that in recent elections voter turnout in Oregon has been extraordinarily high, reaching nearly 87 percent in one contest.[43] Both Priscilla Southwell and Paul Gronke report that Oregonians like the vote by mail system very much, and find it much more convenient than going to the polls; this was true across all demographic and partisan groups. Southwell shows that particularly women, homemakers, the disabled, and those aged twenty-six to thirty-eight like it.[44] There is no evidence that it favors a higher turnout of either Democrats or Republicans. Gronke reports that ballot integrity is much better served with VBM than with traditional absentee ballots. And there is general agreement that the VBM system does not increase the cost of elections.

In short, voting by mail as an alternative to voting at polling places is a concept that other states need to consider adopting. It is particularly suited to the physically challenged, whose problems with voting were detailed in the previous chapter; to shut-ins; and to those who are hospitalized, institutionalized, or in nursing homes. It eliminates the need for absentee ballots for all but those who live overseas. Indeed, it is ideally suited to a population that spends long hours in the workplace, has complicated lives outside of work that take a significant portion of its time and attention, and may hold more than one job or attend school after work—in fact, a large proportion of the American people. Like early voting, VBM is an idea whose time has come.

There is another way for Americans to vote without physically having to go to a polling place: absentee ballots. These require requests, often in writing, by voters to local voting officials that they be sent a ballot, which they then mark and return, usually by mail; in some limited instances e-mail and faxed returns are possible (in which case the secrecy of the ballot is compromised). There is often a time limitation on absentee ballot requests, for example, in many states none can be entertained less than a week prior to the election because of the problem of turn-around time. Absentee ballots are usually counted on Election Day, although in some states counting can continue even afterward if the ballot is postmarked on or before Election Day; in the presidential election of 2000, overseas absentee ballots in Florida were counted for some ten days after the election and accounted for the 537-vote difference between George W. Bush and Al Gore.

All states permit absentee ballots. Twenty-eight do not require an excuse, while the remainder do. Four states—California, Colorado, Montana, and Washington—offer permanent, no-excuse absentee ballots, that is, voting officials automatically mail a ballot for each election to voters who have made a request; no additional requests are needed.[45]

On the face of it, absentee ballots would seem to have much to commend them, as they are a kind of variant on voting by mail discussed previously. For the elderly, infirm, handicapped, and others they might be ideal, especially if they are of the permanent, no-excuse kind. For citizens living abroad who wish to vote, they are essential. But in fact, absentee ballots offer none of the advantages either of early voting or the VBM system used in Oregon. They are cumbersome and awkward to use, and open wide the door to unfairness and potential corruption and fraud.

The reason for this has to do with reforms enacted by most states in the 1990s and 2000s, following major scandals. Indeed, the long history of absentee ballots is one of fraud and corruption. It was commonplace during the twentieth century for political machines, candidates, and campaigns to use absentee ballots to steal elections: "voting cemeteries," creating fictitious lists of voters, casting multiple ballots, and other illegal practices, were almost standard election procedures in some, especially urban, areas. Indeed, it is fair to say that to the degree there has been electoral fraud in the United States, the use of absentee ballots to subvert the electoral process accounts for a preponderance of it.

By the late 1990s things had gotten out of hand. The 1998 mayoral contest in Miami had to be voided by federal courts and a revote scheduled because of fraudulent use of absentee ballots. The razor-thin 2004 gubernatorial election in

Washington could not be resolved until June 2005 because of irregularities associated with absentee ballots, a significant number of which allegedly were "lost." Scholars have also noted absentee ballot fraud in Colorado, Michigan, New York, Mississippi, and a host of other locations.

To try to limit the extent of abuse, states began to crack down on the availability of absentee ballots. In the bad old days, it was not unusual for campaigns to designate individuals whose job was to go the local voting officials' offices, pick up absentee ballots, distribute them to voters (whether or not they had been requested), wait while they were filled out, and return them to the central office. Even the dimmest of imaginations reveals how fraudulent such practices could become.

While each state has its own procedures for dealing with absentee ballots and none is necessarily typical, Florida's reforms are at least illustrative of efforts to clean up the abuse of absentee ballots. They also show the length to which the state went to impose a very cumbersome process for absentee voting, presumably to minimize its use.[46] Perhaps most significant are strict rules about when absentee ballots can be requested and returned (overseas ballots have more flexibility), and more importantly, tight limitations on the ability of second parties to request and secure absentee ballots for an individual. Now, the designee can pick up only two absentee ballots (in the past they could pick up bushelfuls); the designee must be a member of the requestor's immediate family, meaning "the voter's spouse or the parent, child, grandparent or sibling of either the voter or of the voter's spouse."[47] And the designee must provide his or her name, address, driver's license, relationship to requestor, and a signature. Thus, people with no immediate family cannot request an absentee ballot using a second party. This creates a clear double standard between those who have and those who do not have immediate relatives.

Once the ballot is filled out the requestor can mail it back, drop it off, or have someone else do so. However, the ballot must be signed so that local voting officials can compare signatures; failure to sign voids the ballot, while other ballots have been disqualified on the grounds that the signatures did not match (for example, officials may have "Mary J. Smith" on file but the ballot is signed "Mary Smith"). It is no longer necessary for the voter to have his signature witnessed in Florida, which was a requirement in the past.

Absentee ballots likely will continue to be with us for the foreseeable future. For voters living abroad or servicemen and -women stationed in other lands, absentee ballots seem essential. Eventually absentee ballots for these voters will be replaced by Internet or e-mail voting, but as we will see in the next chapter, that is years and possibly decades away.

But for "everyday" voters, early voting and Oregon's VBM system are easier, cheaper, less cumbersome, and less onerous on both voters and officials. Errors by voters in both early voting and VBM are much easier to deal with than in absentee ballots. And ballots cast through early voting and VBM are much more likely to be counted than absentee ballots; there are many reports of absentee ballots, even if legitimate, never being counted, especially if the election is not close. It would seem, then, that absentee ballots could eventually become the dinosaurs of election practices, to be replaced by more efficient and effective means of casting ballots.

Voter Purges

I noted earlier that our hypothetical voter may arrive at his correct polling place, with his registration card, during open hours, and still find that his voting status is in limbo. One of the most common reasons for this is that his name has been purged from the voter lists and he is no longer considered registered.

Local voting officials have been in the voter purging business for a long time. There are many possible reasons for purging a voter's name. Voters who fail to cast ballots over a period of time (usually two or more consecutive general elections) almost always find their names removed from the rolls. Local officials may have learned that they moved out of the jurisdiction or perhaps registered in another one. Some may have died. The voter may have been convicted of a crime (presumably a felony, but there is evidence that some officials have removed names for a misdemeanor conviction), or the voter's name may have showed up on list of alleged felons. And so on.

There are two important points to address regarding purging. First, as the American Civil Liberties Union (ACLU) and Demos have shown in their study of voter purging, states vary widely in purging practices.[48] There is no national standard for removing names from voter lists. As a result, voters are treated very differently across the nation, and what constitutes grounds for purging in one state is not valid in another. Multiple standards always raise issues of fairness, and in some instances they may rise to constitutional levels of equal protection of the laws.

Second, states and local voting officials are not always conscientious about notifying voters that their names have been removed from voter lists. HAVA requires that voters officially be notified (generally by nonforwardable registered mail) before their names can be purged. But any number of studies have shown that this policy is honored in the breach as much as in the practice.[49] As a result, thousands of voters across the nation have been illegally purged in recent years; especially egregious instances have occurred in Ohio in 2004 and 2006, post-Katrina Louisiana, Mississippi, Florida, and elsewhere.[50]

The issue of voter purging resoundingly entered public consciousness during the fiasco that was the Florida presidential election of 2000. There, it will be recalled, Governor Jeb Bush and Secretary of State Kathryn Harris, using the notoriously inaccurate list of alleged convicted felons they had commissioned, purged some 57,700 voters from registration rolls; some half of the purged list were African Americans, and all but about 10 percent either were wrongfully on the list, had had their voting rights restored (in most cases in other states), or were innocent.[51]

It was in response to this debacle that HAVA insisted states keep an accurate master list of registered voters. But the problem is that at least in some states voting officials continue to purge voters illegally, mostly by not notifying them or doing so arbitrarily. In Louisiana, for example, some 20,000 persons were dropped, allegedly because officials claimed they had moved and registered elsewhere after Katrina, but the evidence was never forthcoming; in post-Katrina Mississippi the number was 11,000 illegally purged, allegedly for the same reasons but again never demonstrated.[52]

Unfortunately, the whole matter has taken an ugly partisan turn. In Florida, Ohio, Louisiana, Mississippi, and elsewhere, Republicans have used their positions as secretaries of state or local registrars to purge voters, who turn out to be mainly poor and/or African American—that is, potentially Democratic voters. In most cases, the Department of Justice, already highly politicized over the issue of voter ID (as we will see in the next section), has declined to act to rescind the purges. Lawsuits have been filed to rectify the situation, but as courts move slowly there have been documented instances in these and other states that many possibly falsely purged voters were not allowed to vote in elections held while cases were pending. Thus, the partisan use of voter purging has become a powerful instrument of disenfranchisement, mainly directed at minorities and the poor.

Another form of partisan purging is the practice of "caging." Although illegal, it has not gone away. It was the subject of a lawsuit in the mid-1980s, and resurfaced from time to time thereafter. It showed up again in 2004 and possibly 2008, although data on the latter are scanty. In brief, voter caging was used by Republicans to disenfranchise otherwise eligible voters. Republican operatives would send registered letters to voters—as it turned out, mainly African Americans (many of whom were away at college or in the armed services, or were homeless)—under the guise that they were documents from voting officials checking up on addresses, with instruction not to forward. Of course, the letters were returned, and GOP staffers would then argue this was grounds for removing these individuals from voter rolls. It is not clear how many voters were actually removed from the rolls through caging. What is clear is that the practice evidently went on for decades, and while it is evidently not as prevalent as it once was, the fact that it still exists speaks volumes to the extent to which at least one political party will go in order to keep likely voters—particularly those not likely to vote for its candidates—from the polls.[53]

Voter ID

Let us assume that our hypothetical voter does not vote by mail or absentee, but decides to go to his polling place. Let us further assume that he has located it, arrives while it is open, and has his voter registration card with him. We will even assume that his name appears on the list of eligible voters in the polling place. He still might not be allowed to vote. He has to prove that he is the person he claims to be.

In the old days, that is, prior to 2000, voters seldom encountered this problem. In most places, the voter simply announced his or her name to the attending clerk, who looked it up on the list of eligible voters. Once located, the voter might be asked if he or she still lived at the same address. The voter may or may not have been asked for a voter registration card or, that failing, a driver's license or other reasonable form of identification. Then the voter would likely be asked to sign beneath his name on the list, not so much for identification purposes (as it was rare that the clerk would attempt to match signatures, or even had the means to do so) as to show that the voter did receive a ballot. This formed a record of voting to ensure the name would be carried over to the next election and not purged. It also ensured that the voter did not try to vote again later the same day.

But HAVA changed all that. It required that first-time voters who registered by mail show some form of identification when they appeared at the polling place.[54] Presumably this was to be a photo ID of some kind, but in the event the voter did not have one, he or she could provide a utility bill, bank statement, paycheck or government check, or some other official-looking document that could verify the name and current address of the voter. More ominously, HAVA did not prevent states from imposing additional, more rigorous ID requirements.

It is this latter omission of HAVA that has created enormous controversy. Indeed, with the possible exception of voter purges, no other aspect of current voting procedures causes more difficulty, and raises more conflict, than state-imposed ID laws. At present some twenty-seven states require that all voters, not just first-time ones, provide some form of ID when they go to vote. Seven of these—Indiana, Florida, Georgia, Hawaii, Louisiana, Michigan, and South Dakota—demand a photo ID, but not just any photo ID. It must be government-issued, and it must provide an expiration date.[55] But some two-dozen other states are considering similar bills, and undoubtedly over the next few years they will be put into practice,[56] including in some instances (such as Arizona already requires) proof of citizenship.[57] The latter, of course, is clearly a slap against immigrants, legal and otherwise.

To make matters worse, the controversy over ID laws, especially those requiring a government-issued photo ID or proof of citizenship, has turned into a partisan free-for-all. Republican-dominated legislatures have provided the impetus for the most rigorous, even draconian, ID requirements. Their argument is that these documents are needed to protect the balloting process from voter fraud, especially voting by illegal immigrants. In general (although not universally so), Democrats have opposed strict ID requirements; civil libertarians have absolutely opposed them. They argue that such laws are highly discriminatory, and serve to depress voter turnout.[58]

Who is right? It appears that the primarily Republican position favoring stricter requirements is the weaker one. There are three reasons. First, there is so little voter fraud happening at American polling places on Election Day as to make the "voter fraud" argument laughable. Study after study has shown that it scarcely exists at all.[59] The Century Foundation, in its examination of the very close 2004 gubernatorial race in Washington, found only six cases of alleged fraud.[60] In Ohio, more than 9 million votes were cast in the elections of 2000 and 2002; only four cases of fraud were unearthed. Since 2002, the Department of Justice has prosecuted only thirty-eight cases of voter fraud. Texas attorney general Greg Abbott, a red-meat conservative Republican zealot, spent two years and $1.4 million tax dollars looking into voter fraud, and uncovered a total of twenty-six cases, of which only eight appeared truly fraudulent.[61] One of the country's leading experts on fraudulent voting, Professor Lorraine Minnite of Barnard College, claims that her research, released by Project Vote, conclusively demonstrates that voter fraud at the polls is not a serious problem in America.[62]

A second flaw in the strict-ID requirement argument is that it does not attack the major locus of voter fraud: absentee ballots. We discussed this problem previously. Those applying for absentee ballots are exempt from HAVA and most state ID requirements. Thus, a double standard exists: where the standard needs to be tougher—in the case of absentee ballots—in fact it is lower. Those voting at polling places are subject to much stricter rules in most states. This is illogical, unfair, and bizarre.

Finally, evidence has come to light that local voting officials have substantial discretion—too much, actually—in determining whether or not a particular government-issued photo ID actually meets the necessary requirements. Most of this evidence is anecdotal and nonsystematic, but there is enough of it to suggest that the discretion given to local voting officials potentially disenfranchises some voters, even if the photo ID card they present complies with federal requirements.[63]

Civil libertarians have a much stronger argument in their objection to strict ID, especially photo, requirements. They point out that in fact these rules discriminate against the elderly, minorities, and the poor.[64] Studies show that between 6 and 10 percent of the voting age population in America does not have a government-issued photo ID; this represents between 11 and 19 million potential voters. Research in Wisconsin and Georgia indicates that blacks were only half as likely as whites to have a driver's license, and in the latter state, only 22 percent of black males between the ages of 18 and 24 had one. In Georgia, the AARP estimates that 36 percent of those over 75 do not have driver's licenses. Nationally, about 3 million disabled people do not have driver's licenses. Some Native Americans object to having their photos taken on religious grounds. In many states, potential voters are required to submit a birth certificate in order to obtain the proper voter ID; for some individuals, especially the elderly, the poor, and those who have moved frequently in their lives, this can be a hardship, while for others—including naturalized citizens—getting a birth certificate from the old country can be impossible. Finally, there is evidence provided by the Eagleton Institute of Politics at Rutgers University in a study for the Elections Assistance Commission that requiring photo ID at the polls depresses turnout, especially among minority groups.[65]

The politics of voter ID have perhaps most acutely been seen in Georgia. There, the Republican legislature imposed an especially draconian set of voter ID rules, including requiring a costly photo ID. Because Georgia is a Section 5 state under the Voting Rights Act, this new law had to be submitted to the Justice Department for preclearance. Staff attorneys in the Office of Civil Rights declined to approve the law on the grounds that it was discriminatory against the poor and African

Americans; it was also alleged that the new rules constituted a new form of poll tax because of the substantial expense it would have imposed on those seeking the required photo ID card.

However, the Bush administration overruled the staff attorneys, and pre-cleared Georgia's new law. It was a blatant, egregious demonstration of partisanship trumping rights and fairness. Enormous controversy ensued, and as of this writing, litigation filed against its implementation is still pending.[66]

Complicating the issue of voter ID was the report of the Commission on Federal Election Reform, more commonly known as the Carter-Baker Commission because of its co-chairs, former President Jimmy Carter and former Secretary of State James Baker.[67] In its September 2005 report entitled, "Building Confidence in U.S. Elections," the commission devoted considerable attention to the issue of voter ID, at least for federal elections.[68]

The commission recommended that by 2010 all voters use what it called a Real ID card, which would also serve as a nationally standardized driver's license. For those too poor or otherwise unable to secure such a card (for example, the 12 percent of the driving-age population that does not have a license), the commission recommended that states make available free a surrogate ID card containing basically the same information.[69] For those without either card who wanted to vote, the commission said that they should be given provisional ballots, to be counted once their registration was confirmed.

The report was immediately attacked by a host of critics. Most of the criticisms were those we met earlier, particularly those concerned about the impact of the ID requirement on the elderly, minorities, and other marginalized groups, as well as on voter turnout. Others worried about its assault on privacy, and its "backdoor" approach to the creation of a national ID card, something civil libertarians have long opposed. Still others thought that different types of ID should be used instead, such as fingerprints, which might create fewer problems at the polls. And others worried about the substantial use of provisional ballots, which, as we have seen, probably create more voting problems than they solve.[70]

No doubt the Carter-Baker Commission was well intentioned. However, it readily became apparent that its report was nothing more than a series of political compromises between Democrats and Republicans who could not agree on such fundamental issues as the desirability and feasibility of photo ID cards for voting and paper trails for touchscreen voting machines (more on this in the next chapter). Its effect, in terms of controversies over voter ID, was to further muddy already turbid waters.

It is of interest that the Transportation Security Administration (TSA) has contingency plans at airports for passengers who show up without an approved picture ID. The vast majority, after undergoing separate, rigorous screening procedures from those with picture IDs, are allowed to board their plane. TSA does not offer a "provisional flight status." HAVA makes no such provisions other than providing provisional ballots, which hardly seems like a plan at all. And states such as

Georgia, Indiana, and Florida, which have onerous photo ID requirements, may not even provide the voter lacking the needed document with a provisional ballot. Aside from the issue of fairness inherent here, we have to ask the very reasonable question: which potentially is a greater danger to the public, an airline passenger without a picture ID or a voter who shows up at the polls without one? If TSA can find a way around the difficulty, why can't HAVA and state and local voting officials?

On April 28, 2008, the U.S. Supreme Court entered the voter ID fray with its long-awaited decision on Indiana's voter ID law, regarded as the nation's most strict.[71] In a 6–3 decision, which was entitled the "lead opinion" rather than a majority one, Justice John Paul Stevens and five colleagues upheld the Indiana law.[72] The Court's reasoning was, to say the least, idiosyncratic. It claimed that the law was needed to protect Indiana from voter fraud, but it recognized that there was no evidence that any voter fraud had taken place. Nonetheless, it claimed that "the risk of voter fraud" was "real."[73] Thus, the decision appears to be a ruling in search of a problem. But it also claimed that the requirement of the picture ID card in order to vote did not constitute an unfair burden on poor, elderly, or minority voters; rather, the requirement was reasonable.

The decision was a total victory for those favoring strict rules as to the kind of identification voters must present in order to obtain a ballot. In general, these are Republicans, for, as noted, the voter ID issue has become intensely partisan. More importantly, the decision will allow states to forge ahead to design virtually any form of voter ID requirements they choose.

The outcry against the decision—by civil libertarians, voting rights activists, advocates for the poor, elderly, and minorities, and even moderate editorial voices— has been deafening.[74] Nonetheless, it would appear that for the foreseeable future, states will impose ever-stricter ID requirements. True, the Court did leave the door open to lawsuits from individuals who can demonstrate that the requirements cause them undue burdens. But given the present composition of the Court, and the concurring opinions of Justices Scalia, Thomas, and Alioto that would disallow such suits, it is not at all certain that federal courts will even entertain them.

Under present circumstances, the onus is on the voter to prove he is who he claims to be. This onus is misplaced. A fairer approach would be for the onus to be on the state to prove that the voter is masquerading as someone else. Given the present political climate, even with the advent of the Barack Obama administration, it hardly seems likely that this shift in responsibility would be widely viewed favorably, or adopted.

Conclusion

In this chapter, I have demonstrated that the road to the ballot box is a rocky one indeed. Qualifying to vote, registering, finding the polling station, learning if one is still on the voter list or not at the polls, and having to prove one's identity are not only cumbersome, but fraught with pitfalls. A misstep at any one point can disenfranchise an otherwise eligible voter. And the fact that what might be acceptable in one state, or even in one jurisdiction, is grounds for disenfranchisement elsewhere (including in the same state) creates a system of multiple standards; fairness is the big loser as a result.

It is of interest, then, that most of these problems can be solved relatively easily: abandoning voter registration altogether or instituting same-day voter registration, combined with early voting or voting by mail, instantly eliminate almost all of the difficulties facing the prospective voter. The thoughtful observer has to scratch his head and wonder why these remedies are not more widely used. The answer, in too many cases unfortunately, is that voting officials, party (especially Republican) officials, and entrenched political interests don't want to make voting easier or extend the franchise any farther than they have to. As a result, we continue our policies and practices of disenfranchising thousands of voters who should have the opportunity to vote but cannot, even though they have the right to do so.

Notes

1. "State Voter Registration Requirements," About.com: U.S. Government Info, available at http://usgovinfo.about.com/blvrbystate.htm, accessed July 2, 2009.

2. Jason P.W. Halperin, "A Winner at the Polls: A Proposal for Mandatory Voter Registration," *Journal of Legislation and Public Policy* 3, no. 1, p. 71, available at www.law.nyu.edu/ecm_dlv1/groups/public/@nyu_law_website__journals__journal_of_legislation_and_public_policy/documents/documents/ecm_pro_060619.pdf, accessed July 2, 2009.

3. See, for example, Anne Firor Scott, "The Southern Progressives in National Politics" (unpublished Ph.D. thesis, Radcliffe College, 1957); and George E. Mowry, *The Progressive Era 1900–1920* (Washington, DC: American Historical Association, 1972).

4. Given the blunt, even draconian, laws that many states have recently passed to curtail voter registration by third (essentially private) parties, it is not clear that these practices will continue. We will return to this point later.

5. "Voter Registration/Turnout by State," November 3, 1992, available at www.state.sc.us/scsec/sta92.htm, accessed July 2, 2009; U.S. Census, *Statistical Abstract of the United States 1992,* 112 ed., "Voter Registration," No. 438, "Voter Registration—Registered Voters, 1984 to 1990," p. 271, available at www.census.gov/prod/www/abs/statab1951–1994.htm, accessed June 30, 2008; U.S. Census, Population/Voting, Table 1, "Reported Voting and Registration by Sex and Single Years of Age, November 1998," available at www.census.gov/population/socdemo/voting/cps1998/tab01.txt, accessed July 2, 2009; U.S. Census, Population/Voting, Table 1, "Reported Voting and Registration by Sex and Single Years of Age, November, 2002," available at www.census.gov/population/socdemo/voting/p20–552/tab01.pdf, accessed July 2, 2009; U.S. Census, Voting and Registration in the Election of 2004, Detailed Tables, available at www.census.gov/population/www/socdemo/voting/cps2004.html, accessed July 2, 2009.

6. Thom File, "Voting and Registration in the Election of November 2006," Table 2: "Reported Rates of Voting and Registration by Selected Characteristics: 2006," *Current Population Reports* (Washington, DC: U.S. Census Bureau, June, 2008), available at www.census.gov/prod/2008pubs/p20–557.pdf, accessed June 10, 2009.

7. Demos Fact Sheet, "National Voter Registration Act," Demos Ideas and Action Update, June 10, 2009, available at www.demos.org/pubs/nvra_factsheet.pdf, accessed June 10, 2009.

8. North Dakota has no voter registration; Massachusetts, as of this writing, did not provide the form online.

9. Florida Voter Registration Application, available at http://election.dos.state.fl.us/pdf/webappform.pdf, accessed July 3, 2009.

10. The Republican secretary of state in Ohio ruled that voter registration forms had to be printed on eighty-pound paper; anything else would be rejected. The Black Commentator, "Black Voter Registration Breaking Records," available at www.blackcommentator.com/107/107_cover_election.html, accessed March 19, 2008.

11. Michael P. McDonald, "Analysis of Possible Address Errors on the Florida Voter Registration File," n.d., available at http://elections.gmu.edu/McDonald_Florida_Voter_Registration_Memo.pdf, accessed July 3, 2009.

12. HAVA, Pub.L. 107–252 (2002).

13. National Committee for Voting Integrity, Electronic Privacy Information Center, "Statewide Centralized Voter Registration Databases," May 23, 2007, available at http://epic.org/privacy/voting/register, accessed July 3, 2009.

14. Demos Fact Sheet, "Same Day Registration," n.d., available at www.demos.org/pubs/EDR_factsheet.pdf, accessed June 18, 2009.

15. Chris Kromm, "A Boost for Democracy: Same Day Voter Registration," *Facing South* (Institute for Southern Studies), March 9, 2007, available at www.southernstudies.org/facingsouth/2007/03/boost-for-democracy-election-day.asp; Michael A. Mauro, Iowa Secretary of State, "Exercise Your Right to Vote," available at www.sos.state.ia.us/pdfs/elections/EDRbrochure.pdf. Both accessed July 3, 2009.

16. Demos Fact Sheet, "Same Day Registration." See also Elizabeth Daniel, "A Plea for Same Day Voter Registration," *Gotham Gazette,* September 2001, available at www.gothamgazette.com/article/20010901/17/733; Ben Cannon, "Same-Day Voter Registration," *Blue Oregon,* March 20, 2007, available at www.blueoregon.com/2007/03/sameday_voter_r.html; govtrack.us, "H.R. 2457: Same Day Voter Registration Act of 2007," n.d., available at www.govtrack.us/congress/bill.xpd?bill=h110–2457. All accessed July 3, 2009.

17. Washington watch.com, "H.R. 2457, The Same-Day Voter Registration Act of 2007," n.d., available at www.washingtonwatch.com/bills/show/110_HR_2457.html, accessed July 3, 2009.

18. Minneapolis, "Election Day Registration Requirements," n.d., available at www.ci.minneapolis.mn.us/elections/election-day-registration.asp, Mauro, "Exercise Your Right to Vote"; The American Mind, "Same Day Voter Registration," January 17, 2005, available at www.theamericanmind.com/mt-test/archives/016209.html. All accessed July 3, 2009.

19. Demos Fact Sheet, "Same Day Registration"; Kromm, "A Boost for Democracy."

20. Demos Fact Sheet, "Same Day Registration."

21. Demos has published a number of important studies on EDR; all are listed (and some are downloadable) on its Web site. Demos's studies all point in the same direction—EDR increases voter turnout. See, especially, Steven Carbo and Brenda Wright, "The Promise and Practice of Same Day Voter Registration," Chapter 5 in Demos and Benjamin Griffith, eds., *America Votes* (Chicago: ABA Publishing, 2008).

22. See www.demos.org/democracydispatches/article.cfm?type=2&id=0659CAB7–3FF4–6C82–5004D7641A4348C1.

23. Charles Brace, "Bill Seeks to Ban Same Day Voter Registration," *Daily Cardinal,* January 18, 2008, available at www.dailycardinal.com/article/1586; "Our View: Same-Day Voter Registration Would Cheapen Our Cherished Right," *Gloucester Daily Times* online, February 27, 2008, available at www.gloucestertimes.com/puopinion/local_story_058065242.html; Michael Robbie, "Controversy Surrounds Same Day Voter Registration," *Orbis,* September 24, 2004, available at http://media.www.vanderbiltorbis.com/media/storage/paper983/news/2004/09/24/Issues/Controversy.Surrounds.SameDay.Voter.Registration-2471850.shtml. All accessed July 3, 2009.

24. Gregory Palast, "Vanishing Votes," *The Nation,* April 29, 2004, available at www. thenation.com/doc/20040517/palast, accessed July 3, 2009.

25. "The Acorn Indictments," *Wall Street Journal,* November 3, 2006, available at http://opinionjournal.com/editorial/feature.html?id=110009189, accessed July 3, 2009.

26. National Campaign for Fair Elections, "Barriers to Third Party Registration," n.d., available at www.nationalcampaignforfairelections.org/page/-/THIRD%20PARTY%20 VOTER%20REGISTRATION.pdf, accessed July 3, 2009.

27. Ibid.

28. Edward B. Foley, "Online Voter Registration Is the Answer," Election Law@Moritz, June 13, 2006, available at http://moritzlaw.osu.edu/electionlaw/comments/2006/060613. php; Jim Callahan, "Voting Rights in Florida, *The Democratic Party,* available at www. democrats.org/page/community/post/JBCallahan/Ct82; Advancement Project, "Voter Protection Litigation," n.d., available at www.advancementproject.org/ourwork/power-and-democracy/voter-protection/litigation.php; Amanda Adams, "Ohio Court Prohibits Harmful Rules for Third Party Registration Efforts," *OMB Watch,* February 13, 2008, available at www.ombwatch.org/node/8551. All accessed July 3, 2009.

29. In late summer 2009, the U.S. House of Representatives overwhelmingly voted to cut off federal funds to ACORN (345–75). The bipartisan vote reflected a desire to get rid of the organization; there were allegations that ACORN was involved in under-age prostitution. The evidence to support the charge was, to put it mildly, scanty. In the background, of course, was continuing irritation with ACORN by Democrats and Republicans, who saw it as out of control and perpetuating voter fraud. That there was a racial dimension to the vote is obvious. See George Moneo, "House of Representatives Vote to Defund ACORN," *Babalu,* September 17, 2009, available at http://babalublog.com/2009/09/house-of-representatives-vote-to-defund-acorn, accessed September 28, 2009.

30. Because of space limitations I leave aside the issue, raised in Chapter 1, of the number and special distribution of polling places throughout the jurisdiction. There are many reports, not all of them substantiated, that middle- and upper-middle-class voters have easier access to polling places than poorer people; ditto for white voters over black. The usual response of local voting officials is that adding more polling places is expensive because of the cost of voting machines and paying poll workers, not to mention the rent on facilities used for voting. They generally add that their budgets are already constrained and that there is no flexibility for more polling places. Whatever the merits of this argument, it seems likely that early voting and especially voting by mail (perhaps also in the future, voting via the Internet) might obviate some of the problems of access to polling places.

31. Travis County Clerk, Elections Division, "Polling Places, Saturday, May 09, 2009," available at www.co.travis.tx.us/county_clerk/election/20090509/polls.asp, September 28, 2009.

32. PollingPlace.net, n.d., available at www.pollingplace.net/encyclopedia.htm, accessed July 3, 2009.

33. The Florida constitution, for example, reads, in Article I, Section 3, "No revenue of the state or any political subdivision or agency thereof shall ever be taken from the public treasury directly or indirectly in aid of any church, sect, or religious denomination or in aid of any sectarian institution."

34. Division of Elections, State of Alaska, "Voting Information," available at www. elections.alaska.gov/voting.php, accessed July 3, 2009.

35. New Voters Project, "Polling Places," n.d., available at www.newvotersproject.org/polling-place-hours, accessed July 3, 2009.

36. Ibid.

37. Early Voting Information Center at Reed College, "Absentee and Early Voting Laws," October 23, 2008, available at http://earlyvoting.net/states/abslaws.php, accessed July 3, 2009.

38. Ibid. The sixteen states are Alabama (which had early voting but repealed it in 2001), Connecticut, Delaware, Maryland, Massachusetts, Michigan, Mississippi, Missouri, New Hampshire, New Jersey, New York, Oregon, Pennsylvania, Rhode Island, South Carolina, and Washington.

39. Paul Gronke, Eva Galanes-Rosenbaum, and Peter A. Miller, "Early Voting and Turnout," Early Voting Information Center at Reed College, n.d., available at http://earlyvoting.net/resources/ohi007.pdf, accessed July 3, 2009. See also www.earlyvoting.net/blog. Readers are reminded that in 2005 the Republican-led Florida legislature decreased the number of hours and days that early voting was permitted because too many minorities (i.e., potential Democrats) were voting. Governor Charlie Crist, at the time a Republican, did an end-run around the legislature by executive order in 2008, and returned the days and times to their former level.

40. Bill Bradbury, "Vote by Mail: The Real Winner Is Democracy," *Washington Post,* January 1, 2005, p. A23, available at www.washingtonpost.com/wp-dyn/articles/A40032–2004Dec31.html, accessed July 3, 2009.

41. Delivery envelopes in which the secrecy envelopes are contained can be opened as soon as local voting officials receive them so that the process of signature verification can proceed.

42. Multnomah County, Oregon, "Voting in Oregon—Vote by Mail," August 24, 2004, available at www.co.multnomah.or.us/dbcs/elections/election_information/voting_in_oregon.shtml, accessed July 3, 2009.

43. Bradbury, "Vote by Mail: The Real Winner Is Democracy."

44. See, for example, Priscilla Southwell, "Five Years Later: A Re-Assessment of Oregon's Vote By Mail Electoral Process," n.d., viewed online at http://votebymailproject.org/Southwell.pdf, accessed July 24, 2010, and Priscilla Southwell, "Final Report, Survey of Vote-By=Mail Senate Election, April 3, 1996, viewed online at https://scholarsbank.uoregon.edu/xmlui/bitstream/handle/1794/1268/VBM%20Full%20Report.pdf?sequence=5, accessed July 24, 2010.

45. Early Voting Information Center at Reed College, "Absentee and Early Voting Laws."

46. Supervisor of Elections, Alachua County, Florida, "Absentee Voting," n.d., available at http://elections.alachua.fl.us/voter_information/absentee_voting/index.html#AbsenteeVoting, accessed July 3, 2009.

47. Ibid.

48. Laleh Ispahani and Nick Williams, "PURGED: Will Eligible Voters Be Purged from Election Rolls?" (Demos and ACLU, October 27, 2004), available (PDF version) at http://archive.demos.org/pub299.cfm, accessed Friday, July 3, 2009.

49. Palast, "Vanishing Votes"; Lawrence Norden, Voter Purges and Challenges blog, "Ohio's Election Blueprint," April 23, 2009, available at www.brennancenter.org/blog/category/voter_purges_and_challenges, accessed July 3, 2009.

50. Anthony York, "Will John Ashcroft Really Probe Florida's Voter Purge Lists?" Salon.com, May 23, 2002, available at http://dir.salon.com/story/politics/feature/2002/05/23/florida_suits; Norden, "Ohio's Election Blueprint"; Steven Rosenfeld, "Voter Purging: A Legal Way for Republicans to Swing Elections," Alternet, September 11, 2007, available at www.alternet.org/rights/62133; editorial, "An Untimely Voter Purge," *New York Times,* November 1, 2006, available at www.nytimes.com/2006/11/01/opinion/01wed3.html; KStreet Projector, "Action Alert: Blackwell Purged Ohio Voter Rolls October 1," *Daily Kos,* October 16, 2006, available at www.dailykos.com/story/2006/10/18/85915/109; Alann Sayre, "NAACP Challenges Louisiana Voter Purge," *Washington Post,* August 31, 2007, available at http://www.washingtonpost.com/wp-dyn/content/article/2007/08/31/AR2007083100501.html; Steven Maloney, "Voter Purge Drops 20,000 from Louisiana Rolls," *New Orleans City Business,* August 27, 2007, BNET Business Publications, available at http://findarticles.com/p/articles/mi_qn4200/is_20070827/ai_n19488624. All the above accessed July 3, 2009.

51. These data are found in many places, most authoritatively in United States Commission on Civil Rights, "Voting Irregularities in Florida During the 2000 Presidential Election" (Washington, DC: U.S. Commission on Civil Rights, 2001, No. 005–902–00064–9.

52. See, for example, Stephen Maloney, "Voter Purge Drops 20,000 from Lousiana Rolls," NEW ORLEANS CITY BUSINESS, August 27, 2007, viewed online at http://findarticles.com/p/articles/mi_qn4200/is_20070827/ai_n19488664, accessed July 24, 2010; Steven Rosenfeld, "Three States Accused of Illegally Purging Voter Lists," Alternet, July 25, 2008, viewed online at http://findarticles.com/p/articles/mi_qn4200/is_20070827/ai_n19488664, accessed July 24, 2010; and Myrna Perez, "Voter Purges" (New York: Brennan Center for Justice, New York University School of Law, 2008), viewed online at http://graphics8.nytimes.com/packages/pdf/national/Brennan_Center_Report_Voter_Purges.pdf, accessed July 24, 2010.

53. See Dalia Lithwick, "Raging Caging," Slate.com, May 31, 2007, available at www.slate.com/id/2167284, accessed July 21, 2009.

54. Help America Vote Act, PL 107–252, available at www.fec.gov/hava/hava.htm, accessed July 3, 2009.

55. Amy Goldstein, "Democrats Predict Voter ID Problems," *Washington Post,* November 3, 2006, available at www.washingtonpost.com/wp-dyn/content/article/2006/11/02/AR2006110201897.html; Michael Slater and Nathan Henderson-James, "The Fraud of Voter ID Laws," Tom Paine.common sense, March 6, 2007, available at www.tompaine.com/articles/2007/03/06/the_fraud_of_voter_id_laws.php. Both accessed July 3, 2009.

56. Adam Liptak, "Fear but Few Facts in Debate on Voter I.D.'s," *New York Times,* September 24, 2007, available at www.nytimes.com/2007/09/24/us/24bar.html?_r=1&oref=slogin, accessed July 3, 2009; Ian Urbina, "Voter ID Laws Are Set to Face a Crucial Test," *New York Times,* January 7, 2008, available at www.nytimes.com/2008/01/07/us/07identity.html?_r=1&hp&oref=slogin, accessed July 3, 2009.

57. Richard L. Hasen, "Fraud Reform?" Slate.com, February 22, 2006, available at www.slate.com/id/2136776. As of this writing, Missouri is considering legislation that would require proof of citizenship in order to vote; Ian Urbina, "Voter ID Battle Shifts to Proof of Citizenship," *New York Times,* May 12, 2008, available at www.nytimes.com/2008/05/12/us/politics/12vote.html?hp. Both accessed July 3, 2009.

58. Liptak, "Fear but Few Facts."

59. Tova Andrea Wang, "Voter ID and Fraud: Prove It," The Century Foundation Web site, July 28, 2005, available at www.tcf.org/list.asp?type=NC&pubid=1067; Hasen, "Fraud Reform?"

60. The Century Foundation, "Voting in 2004: A Report to the Nation on America's Election Process (Washington, DC, The Century Foundation, December 7, 2004), viewed online at http://www.commoncause.org/site/apps/nl/content3.asp?c=dkLNK1MQIwG&b=263740&content_id={B3DA664B-B545–447F-93EC-D082C6B022D8}&notoc=1, accessed July 24, 2010. See also, The Century Foundation, "Voting in 2006: Have We Solved the Problems of 2004?" (Washington, DC: The Century Foundation, October 12, 2006), viewed online at http://www.tcf.org/publications/electionreform/votingin2006.pdf, accessed July 24, 2010.

61. Joshua Micah Marshall, "The War on (Democrats) Voting," available at www.talkingpointsmemo.com, May 18, 2008; Steven Rosenfeld, "Vote by Mail, Go to Jail," available at www.texasobserver.org/article.php?aid=2738; April 18, 2008. Both accessed July 3, 2009.

62. Slater and Henderson-James, "The Fraud of Voter ID Laws"; Steven Rosenfeld, "Project Vote Report Accuses GOP of Decades of Voter Suppression," Alternet, September 27, 2007, available at www.alternet.org/rights/63574; Erin Ferns, "Voter Fraud Myth Used to Push Voting Policies That Harken Back to the Jim Crow Era," TPM, May 7, 2009, available at http://tpmcafe.talkingpointsmemo.com/talk/blogs/project_vote/2009/05/voter-fraud-myth-used-to-push.php. All accessed July 3, 2009. The definitive study of voter fraud in America was prepared by Professor Lorraine Minnite of Barnard College for Project Vote, 2005.

63. A letter to the editor of the *Miami Herald* is a helpful example about voter ID and the discretionary power of local voting officials. It is reproduced here in full:

> ID voting dilemma
> The May 11 editorial 'Court makes a U-turn on voting rights' was on target. However, the reality is somewhat more stringent than indicated.
> I try not to use my driver's license because a while back I was not allowed to vote in one election because the poll worker noted the blue stickers—issued by mail to safe drivers—on the back of the card. The worker claimed they were forgeries.
> This year I walked to the voting place in January, presented my military ID, listed on the Official Sample Ballot as an acceptable photo ID. It was rejected because there was no signature on it. I have two different military IDs, and neither has a place for a signature.
> I went through my papers and found my signature, but no picture, on a "Bike and Ride on Transit" permit. Amazingly, that was accepted, and I voted.
> I wrote about this incident to the Elections Department in February. Nearly three months later, I have not received a response. From this I am left with no choice but to assume that poll workers are authorized to make their own rules.
> Charles R. Jones, Miami

Charles R. Jones, "ID Voting Dilemma," Readers' Forum, Miami Herald, May 16, 2008, section A, p. 16.

64. Commissioner Spencer Overton, "Dissenting Statement," Carter-Baker Dissent, n.d., available at www.carterbakerdissent.com/dissent.php; Daniel P. Tokaji, "Two Wrongs Don't Make a Right," Election Law@Moritz, September 20, 2005, available at http://moritzlaw.osu.edu/electionlaw/comments/2005/050920.php; Wang, "Voter ID and Fraud," July 28, 2005. All accessed July 3, 2009.

65. Richard Wolf, "Study: Stricter Voter ID Rules Hurt '04 Turnout," *USA Today*, February 19, 2007, available at www.usatoday.com/news/nation/2007–02–19-voter-id-study_x.htm; Christopher Drew, "Lower Voter Turnout Is Seen in States That Require ID, *New York Times,* February 21, 2007, available at http://query.nytimes.com/gst/fullpage.html?res=9403E7D8123EF932A15751C0A9619C8B63; Slater and Henderson-Jones, "The Fraud of Voter ID Laws." All accessed July 3, 2009.

66. Hasen, "Fraud Reform?"; see also Urbina, "Voter ID Laws."

67. Commission on Federal Election Reform, "Building Confidence in American Elections," Center for Democracy and Elections Management, American University, September 19, 2005, available at www.american.edu/ia/cfer/ and http://www1.american.edu/ia/cfer/report/full_report.pdf. Both accessed July 6, 2009.

68. Commission on Federal Election Reform, "Building Confidence in U.S. Elections."

69. Dan Balz, "Carter-Baker Panel to Call for Voting Fixes," *Washington Post,* September 19, 2005, p. A03, available at www.washingtonpost.com/wp-dyn/content/article/2005/09/18/AR2005091801364.html, accessed July 6, 2009.

70. Overton, "Dissenting Statement"; Tokaji, "Two Wrongs."

71. *Crawford et al. v. Marion County Election Board et al.,* No. 07–21, 472 F. 3d 949, April 28, 2008. Available at www.law.cornell.edu/supct/html/07-21.ZS.html, accessed July 6, 2009.

72. Linda Greenhouse, "In a 6–3 Vote, Justices Uphold a Voter ID Law," *New York Times,* April 29, 2008, available at www.nytimes.com/2008/04/29/washington/29scotus.html?_r=1&hp=&adxnnl=1&oref=slogin&adxnnlx=1209992705–3d+9RIqX61sk+vetnU7F5w; Robert Barnes, "High Court Upholds Indiana Law on Voter ID," *Washington Post,* April

29, 2008, available at www.washingtonpost.com/wp-dyn/content/article/2008/04/28/ AR2008042800968.html?hpid=moreheadlines. Both accessed July 6, 2009.

73. Greenhouse, "In a 6–3 Vote, Justices Uphold a Voter ID Law."

74. Editorial, "The Court Fumbles on Voting Rights," *New York Times,* April 29, 2008, available at www.nytimes.com/2008/04/29/opinion/29tue1.html?hp; Richard Hasen, Election Law Blog, "Initial Thoughts on the Supreme Court's Opinion in Crawford, the Indiana Voter Identification Case," April 28, 2008, available at http://electionlawblog.org/archives/010701 .html; and Adam Cohen, "Voting Rights Are Too Important to Leave to the States," *New York Times.* Editorial Observer, available at www.nytimes.com/2008/05/02/opinion/02fri4. html. All accessed July 6, 2009.

5

So You Cast a Ballot! Will It Count?

Voters don't count. It's the people who count the votes, who count.
—Attributed to Josef Stalin

Whether or not Marshal Stalin actually made the observation attributed to him above is not important. What is important is that the comment bores in on a major problem of elections: there is a potential disconnect between how voters in the voting booth cast their ballots and how their votes are counted. Indeed, there is a prior issue: will their votes be counted at all? In the 2000 U.S. presidential election in Florida, more than 170,000 ballots were never tallied; George W. Bush was awarded the state by a margin of 537 votes. In the 2008 Michigan Democratic presidential primary, some 30,000 ballots were never counted. Numerous other examples could be given.

Indeed, there is a long tradition of ignoring ballots and votes in America. One remembers Boss Tweed in New York City, who was completely indifferent to the outcome of the popular vote; he simply had his henchmen announce the results on the streets regardless of what the ballots may or may not have revealed.[1] And Senator Cole Blease of South Carolina is famous for his pithy remark about the 1,100 votes cast for Calvin Coolidge in his state in 1924: "I do not know where he got them. I was astonished to know that they were cast, and shocked to know that they were counted."[2]

But assuming that ballots are counted, the results might not always reflect what voters meant or intended. The famous "butterfly ballot" in Palm Beach County, Florida (where Pat Buchanan received thousands of votes apparently meant for Al Gore), demonstrated that ballot design can rob voters of their intended vote for a particular candidate. Faulty instructions can cause voters to disenfranchise themselves, as happened in Duval County (Jacksonville), Florida, where voters in 2000 were told to "vote both sides of the ballot" (presidential candidates were listed on front and back because of the large number of candidates). Following those directions literally caused over-voting and thus disqualification.[3] The struggle over the variants of "hanging chads" during the Florida recounts showed that the intent of voters can blithely, and legally, be ignored.

Thus, the seemingly innocuous and simple act of casting a vote is really an exercise in hope and faith: hope that the ballot will be counted, and faith that it will be recorded and counted accurately, according to the voter's intent. The public record reveals that too often neither hope nor faith is rewarded. The consequence is that the announced results of elections are merely probability statements, not definitive reports of what happened on Election Day. This is hardly a ringing endorsement of America's democratic system of voting.

Why should this happen? Why can't votes just be "counted"? After all, all kinds of votes are cast every day, without dispute, in a variety of contexts—from elections for class monitor in an elementary school classroom to choosing a new program chair in the local Rotary Club. Why can't we elect our public officials with a high degree of confidence in the accuracy of the outcome?

The answer goes to the heart of the questions posed in the first chapter of this book. The stakes are too important to be left to a neutral, bean-counting process. Political parties; economic, social, and political elites; major media outlets; public opinion shapers; and even some academics are too concerned about the outcomes of public elections to take a hands-off approach, with the result that our elections are carefully regulated and monitored as to who can vote, and how. Frequently this means intervention by these and other agents in the processes of voting and counting ballots to try to influence, or even determine, the outcome. Indeed, even as the splendid movie *Election* shows, a seemingly inconsequential high school election for class president can become a vehicle for the clash of corrupt interests as efforts are made to manipulate the outcome.[4]

This chapter will provide a more limited view of why we can't just "count" votes. Essentially, I will argue that this is a result of the interplay of two powerful forces: politics and technology. Politics determines who gets to vote, how, and in what manner votes will be tallied. Although the Help America Vote Act (HAVA) of 2002 has strongly influenced how American elections go forward, most decisions about voting in this country are made by state legislatures. Local voting registrars also have tremendous discretion in making these determinations, and lately the courts have entered the political thicket of vote counting. Technology is important as well, because the machinery of voting receives and records the voters' votes. As we will see, no voting technology is flawless, no voting machine is perfect, and none is exempt from potential political manipulation, although some are better than others. The question is, why do we keep using technology and machines that are flawed when simpler, cheaper, and more accurate methods are at hand?

A Brief Overview of Voting Technology, Historically Speaking

The word "ballot" apparently comes from the Italian word *ballota,* meaning a little colored ball. For over a thousand years, use of these balls was the preferred means of voting.[5] In ancient Athens those privileged to vote were given small clay balls, which they would place in the box or vessel of the preferred candidate. It was exactly the use of these balls that gave rise to the term "blackball." When candidates for membership in secret or select societies presented themselves, existing members were given white and black balls; anyone vetoing a candidate would place the black ball in that individual's box or basket, and that person would be rejected.

Use of balls for voting continued until the nineteenth century, although by then other means of casting ballots were invented. Paper ballots were apparently first used in Rome in 139 BCE. Douglas W. Jones reports that the first documented use of paper ballots in America came in 1629, when a church in Salem selected a minister.[6] But paper ballots as we know them were not often used in the United States until late in the nineteenth century. Indeed, voting in America before then was a chaotic process as more and more people were allowed to vote. Potential voters simply showed up, signed their name (or X), and announced out loud their preference(s). These would be duly recorded by clerks, and tallies compared at the end of the day. There was no secret ballot, margins of error were huge, and corrupt practices were common—even "normal" and expected. Whoever controlled the voting process controlled the outcome.[7]

In cities, preprinted ballots were common. Political parties often printed their own ballots, pre-marked. These would then be distributed by the thousands to "voters," who would deposit them in ballot boxes. Sometimes newspapers—far more overtly partisan than they are today—would preprint marked ballots that voters could tear out and bring to the polls; other times they were printed as handbills, which voters could submit as their "votes."

The "Australian" Ballot

In 1858, officials in Australia developed a new kind of ballot that was widely adopted around the world. The Australian ballot was preprinted on a standardized piece of paper that listed all of the candidates for each office. Voters would not have access to the ballots until arriving at the polls; only one ballot was given per voter. In early versions of the Australian ballot, voters would scratch out the names of candidates for whom they did not wish to vote. Later, little boxes were placed next to the names, and voters would put an X in the box or in some other manner indicate their preferred candidate. The Australian ballot was first used in a statewide election in New York in 1889; then Massachusetts moved to adopt it, with other states rapidly following.[8]

Although the Progressive movement warmly embraced the Australian ballot in its fight against machine politics and political corruption, its use had little impact on the stranglehold that many urban political machines had on state and local politics. The reason is that use of the Australian ballot implied, but did not require, voting secrecy. Loyalists of the machines at local levels could and did direct voters as to how to vote. And in any case, machines firmly controlled the vote-counting process. They had basically free rein to determine which ballots would be counted and which "lost" or disqualified. And in case of disputes, names found in cemeteries and on other lists could be used to construct whatever number of votes was needed to ensure the machine's victory.

Mechanical Voting Machines

Lever-Operated Machines

The Australian ballot was essentially displaced by the invention of mechanical voting machines, first the so-called lever machines and later punch-card devices. The
first widely used lever-operated machine was called the Myers Automatic Voting
Booth. Its initial application was in Lockport, New York, in 1892, and toward the end
of the decade it had been adopted statewide. By 1920, gear-and-lever machines were
mandated for voting in New York, Minnesota, California, Connecticut, Wisconsin,
New Jersey, Indiana, Iowa, Michigan, Ohio, Utah, Colorado, Montana, Illinois,
Washington, Massachusetts, and Kansas. In the 1960 elections, more than half of
Americans voted using some kind of lever-operated voting machine, and even as
late as 1996, more than 20 percent of Americans cast their ballots on them.[9]

How did the voter operate the machine? Older readers may recall using these
machines, but most voters under forty-five have probably never seen one. The
voter entered the booth and stood in front of a large master lever. Moving the lever
closed a privacy curtain. The voter then faced a mechanical version of an Australian
ballot. Next to each name or ballot choice (say, for a referendum or amendment)
was a small lever; moving the lever (usually, but not always, down) put an X in a
square next to the name of the desired candidate or issue choice. The voter would
go down the columns (sometimes the ballots were designed in rows, cross-wise),
moving the levers until he or she finished making choices. Voters could change their
minds and return a lever to the original position, without a vote being recorded. In
most machines safeguards were built in so that a voter could not move more than
one lever per office, thus preventing over-voting; there was no warning against
under-voting, however. In some machines a master lever at the top would allow
the voter to vote a "straight-ticket" that would record votes for all candidates of a
particular party, but many machines did not offer this option.

Then, when the voter had finished making choices, he or she would shift the
large master lever back to its original position. This action would simultaneously
open the curtain, record the votes, and return all the small levers to their original
positions in readiness for the next voter.

How did the machine work? Each small lever was connected to a wheel in the
bowels of the machine. Whenever the curtain was opened as a voter exited, the wheels
joined to the chosen levers would move one-tenth of a rotation. When the wheel
had turned ten times, it would move another wheel, the "tens" wheel, one-tenth of
a rotation. When that one got to ten, it would move a "hundreds" wheel one-tenth
of a rotation. And so on. Assuming all the wheels had originally been set to zero,
at the conclusion of voting the machine could be opened and the number of votes
counted according to the position of the wheels. Some machines also provided a
paper trail in case recounts were needed, but this was not universally true.

Lever-operated voting machines offered a number of benefits. In spite of what some readers might see as Rube Goldberg qualities, they were actually fairly simple to construct and operate. They ensured a secret ballot, and, on those models providing a paper trail, recounts were fairly straightforward. Unless there were mechanical breakdowns, they were accurate: error rates averaged less than 3 percent, according to most estimates, which made them more accurate than punch-card devices.

But lever-operated machines also presented some serious problems. They were heavy and bulky, making them difficult and expensive to move and store. Good maintenance was essential, as the wheels and levers had to be kept clean and well oiled or they would not work properly; this, too, was an expensive, time-consuming matter. Indeed, it was exactly on this point that a major weakness of lever-operated machines emerged. Mechanical failures due to metal fatigue and poor maintenance were common. If the failure occurred on Election Day, it was never clear what to do: How and when was the failure discovered? Were the ballots already cast flawed or not? Statistical studies have shown that with lever machines the number "99" for voting totals occurred far more frequently than it should have, at least when compared to the frequency of "98" and "100." The generally accepted explanation for this was a design flaw, in that some mechanical glitch between the "tens" and "hundreds" wheels kept them from working in synch.

But the greatest problem with lever-operated voting machines was that they were easy to jimmy. If not all the wheels were set to zero before voting commenced, obviously one or more candidates would have a numerical advantage from the start. Wheels connected to the levers of nonfavored candidates could be jammed or rigged so they only moved on every, say, fourth or fifth vote. Without a paper trail, it might not be possible to prove that the vote total was inaccurate, possibly fraudulent. It was exactly because lever-operated voting devices could be manipulated fairly easily that they proved no threat to entrenched political interests and powerful political machines.

Punch Cards

Punch-card voting devices were actually developed at about the same time as lever-operated ones, but came into use much later. The first known punch-card device was developed in the 1880s by an employee of the Baltimore health department, Herman Hollerith, to help tabulate public health statistics. It was so effective that the U.S. Bureau of the Census required that punch cards be used for the 1890 census. In 1896, Hollerith founded the Tabulating Machine Company to market his invention; he sold the company in 1924 to the precursor of IBM.[10]

Although punch cards were used in a wide variety of business, governmental, military, and academic contexts during the first half of the twentieth century, they were not adapted for voting until the 1960s. Apparently, they were first used in an election in 1961, in Ohio.[11] In 1964, Fulton (Atlanta) and DeKalb counties in Georgia adopted them for primary elections. In November of that year they were also used in one county in Oregon and two in California. Thereafter their use spread rapidly. As late as 1996, more than 37 percent of all American voters used some kind of punch-card device in the general election.

There were several types of punch-card machines, but they all worked on similar principles. Voters would be given a card, which they then had to insert into a slot in a machine, where it would be held steady. The machine either had a stylus available to punch out a small, dimpled portion of the card (the infamous "chad"), indicating the voter's choice, or in some instances mounted on the machine was an actual punch that could be moved up or down, aligned with the chosen name, and the chad would be punched out using hand pressure.

The ballots could vary in design. So-called "Datavote cards" actually listed the names of candidates, and voters using either the stylus or attached punch would locate the chad next to the desired name and push or punch it out. "Votomatic" systems, common in big cities where there were many offices and numerous candidates, did not list names but rather numbers. Attached to the voting booth in a (presumably) visible place were printed lists of the candidates and the number assigned to each; voters then had to locate the number of the desired candidate and punch out his or her number on the card.

Votomatic systems saved space and paper, but they were difficult to use. Errors were common, as voters had to search for the correct number next to their candidate(s) of choice, find the corresponding number on the card, and punch out the correct chad. Campaign literature and advertisements in cities and counties using Votomatic systems emphasized the candidate's number as well as the name. Still, many errors occurred with Votomatic voting machines; in fact, the error rate of these devices was at least as great as that for any other kind of voting machine ever used, including touchscreen devices.

Contributing to the error rate of punch-card voting machines, including Datavote systems, were mechanical failures. Sometimes the stylus would not punch all the way through; on other machines, the moveable punch would not align properly, or the voter would not push it firmly enough. Both situations caused the infamous chad problems that were highlighted in the Florida presidential election of 2000. Of course, chad problems had been occurring since the first use of punch-card systems. But in 2000 the fate of the presidential election literally hinged on the existence of different kinds of chads, and how voting registrars (and candidates Bush and Gore or their surrogates, the Republican and Democratic parties, and the courts) chose to interpret them. There were five possible chad problems:

- Hanging chad—one corner of the chad was still attached to the ballot
- Swinging chad—two corners were still attached
- Tri chad—three corners were attached but a hole could be discerned
- Pregnant chad—four corners were attached but a hole could be detected
- Dimpled chad—four corners attached, an indentation was present but no hole

One would think that the voter's intent could still be determined regardless of which type of chad pathology existed. But of course matters were never that simple, not with a presidential election hanging in the balance. It was for this reason that, earlier in the chapter, we noted that the problem of counting votes rests on the intersection of technology and politics. No better example of this point can be found than the matter of chads in Florida in 2000. As the recount proceeded, what seemed like a clear instance of a voter's intent to one member of the county canvassing board[12] would be objected to by another, or by an observer from a different campaign or party.[13] And so the process, and the arguing, continued until the U.S. Supreme Court shut it all down on December 12, 2000, in the case of *Bush v. Gore*[14] and effectively declared Mr. Bush the winner.

Electronic Voting: "Grasping at Straws, Rushing to Judgment"

Following the "Florida fiasco" of 2000, virtually all states moved rapidly to revamp their electoral systems. Grasping at straws and rushing to judgment,[15] they quickly adopted a variety of electronic-voting technological panaceas designed to prevent another debacle. Most of these adoptions were made without serious consideration of the consequences that the new electronic technologies (commonly called "e-voting") created for electoral politics. The rush to "do something" was facilitated by the passage in 2002 of the federal Help America Vote Act, one of the goals of which was to foster the dissemination of e-voting technology across the nation.

It is a thesis of the remainder of this chapter that the push toward e-voting as a solution to America's voting ills has been misguided. In a very real sense, reformers were looking for answers in all the wrong places. As it presently stands, e-voting causes more problems than it solves. Indeed, e-voting as currently practiced seriously undermines American democracy. We as a nation should give serious thought to substituting a simpler, easier, less-expensive, fairer, more equitable, more secure and reliable voting system—hand-counted paper ballots—while further technological developments are devised that can address the very deep-seated problems the current e-voting systems present.

As we saw earlier in the chapter, questionable ballots were at the heart of the Florida nightmare. Many of these ballots were flawed, to be sure and politics intervened to prevent a consensus on how they should be interpreted and counted, or even if they should be. But in the majority of cases, it was the technology itself that prevented a clear determination of the voter's intent. The two questionable technologies were punch cards[16] and optical scanners. Aside from the problem of chads, punch-card machines caused another headache: they jammed the card-sorting and -counting machines. The effect was to reduce to a snail's pace the recount process in many of the twenty-four Florida counties that used them,[17] allowing the national and international media to have a field day of speculation and rumormongering, encouraging political posturing by the presidential campaigns and their spin doctors, and opening the door to lawyers and courts to preempt the Florida recount process. The result, of course, was a ghastly mess.

But mechanical problems were not the only technical glitches in Florida's voting. Forty-one counties used some form of paper ballot read by optical scanners; sixteen of these used central tabulation procedures in which the ballots are read by a machine in a single location, and twenty-five used a precinct-level scanning process. These technologies are not the same, nor are they equivalent. The virtue of the latter type of machines is that they offer voters a "second chance," meaning that if a voter accidentally over-votes or make stray marks on the ballot, the scanning machine "kicks back" the ballot when inserted into the machine for tallying, so the voter gets another opportunity to vote correctly.[18] As Kimball Brace of Election Data Services has noted, precinct-level technology gives approximately 4 percent of voters back their franchise, since the error rate of precinct-level technology compared to central tabulation machines is 4 percent less (0.8 percent vs. 4.8 percent).

But the problem with using two different optical-scanning machines in the same state goes beyond differences in error rate. It raises questions of equity, and fairness. Nowhere is this seen more profoundly than in the racial disparity seen in the distribution of optical-scanning voting machines. Evidence documents that voters in poorer counties, especially those with a substantial African American population, had less access to "second chance" precinct-read optical-scanning machines than whites in wealthier counties. As a result, error rates in heavily black counties were much higher than in those that were overwhelmingly white. The U.S. Commission on Civil Rights, for example, noted that in majority-black Gadsden County, Florida, one of the poorest counties in the nation, the error rate was 12.4 percent; Gadsden County did not use precinct-read optical-scanning machines but instead relied on centrally read scanners. Across the river in adjoining Leon County, a much wealthier and majority-white county, the error rate from the precinct-read optical scanners was a mere 0.18 percent.

Thus, Florida's African American voters had to use less technologically accurate voting equipment than its white voters. The result was that black ballots were thrown out at much higher rates than those of whites. For example, 64 percent of African American voters lived in counties that used unreliable punch-card technology, but only 56 percent of whites did. As a result, black voters had their ballots disqualified because of error at a statewide rate nearly 4 percent greater than whites. In some precincts in Miami-Dade County, the *New York Times* reported, black ballots were invalidated at a rate twice that of ballots in Hispanic precincts, and four times that of ballots cast in overwhelmingly white precincts. One in every eleven ballots in majority-black precincts in Miami-Dade County was thrown out. Of the 100 precincts in the state with the highest rates of disqualified ballots, 83 were majority African American.

The effect of the failure of voting technology in Florida on Election Day and the ensuing debacle over the recount, lasting more than a month, created a national outcry and sensation. Florida became the butt of numerous jokes and acid comments by political pundits and late-night comedians as they watched the election fiasco continue throughout November and into early December. There were even reports that representatives of foreign governments (including authoritarian, nondemocratic rogue states) offered to come to Florida to assist with the counting and recounting and otherwise help the state "get it right."

What was and still is of interest in all of this was the growing realization that, while Florida became the whipping boy of bad electoral practices, in fact the Florida fiasco could have happened elsewhere just as easily.[19] Indeed, breakdowns in voting practices and procedures have been common throughout the voting history of the United States. But this was the first time, at least at the presidential level, where the closeness of the election resulted in two major revelations: how fine the line was between balloting that results in a clear-cut winner and total chaos; and just how creaky and suspect our election machinery really was. Both were true throughout the nation. The Florida fiasco could just as easily have been the California crapshoot or the Massachusetts muddle or the New Jersey nightmare.

What was of even more interest, especially in retrospect, was that criticism of Florida did not address the fundamental problem, namely, that over 100,000 African American voters' ballots had been disqualified, or never even counted (nationally, the figure was over one million[20]). Indeed, issues of racial discrimination were given short shrift by mainstream national media, although to be fair, somewhat greater attention was given at local levels. Issues of racial fairness and inequality played only minor roles in the early criticism of Florida and the soul-searching that began to take place elsewhere in the fiasco's aftermath. Much more attention was paid, instead, to matters of form, and how the election "looked," especially abroad, with racial issues put on the back burner until months later. It was much easier, if less honest, to point to technological failures as the root cause of the problem than to have to own up, to countries around the world, that the heart of the Florida fiasco rested on racial discrimination.

Obviously something had to be done to paper over the problem. And quickly.

What happened was that in every state, and at the national level, cries for "reform" of election practices and procedures became the top priority. Whatever else was at the top of national, state, and local political agendas was swept aside in a tidal wave of ensuring that the Florida fiasco could not happen again and, more especially, could not happen in _____ (fill in the name of your state). At the national level, the Help America Vote Act of 2002 was quickly proposed, and passed.[21] The act provided funds to outlaw and replace antiquated voting systems (including punch cards) and replace them with e-voting technologies (none was favored, but interpretations of HAVA by members of the Bush administration as well as pundits seemed to place more weight on touchscreen technology than on optical scanners, although the latter were permitted). It also established the Election Assistance Commission to work with state and local officials on federal elections. And it established minimum standards for administering elections.[22]

States rushed to make changes as the impetus to reform their voting systems gained momentum. No state wanted to be left behind, and HAVA seemed to guarantee—as the Bush administration sought to do with public school children—that none would be. States vied with one another to adopt substantial, even draconian, reforms. Florida, for example, was one of the first to get on the bandwagon, probably in an effort to save face and repair its sullied reputation. Following a hastily convened governor's commission on voting problems, the state outlawed paper ballots, lever-operated voting machines, and punch cards, and permitted only e-voting technologies.[23] No state wanted to be left with voting mechanisms that appeared old and creaky and unreliable. The politically correct thing was to "do something," and it almost didn't matter what it was, as long as it looked like election reform that included some kind of e-voting technology.

That much of the "reform" was illusory, and perhaps might make things worse, was rarely considered. Critics and naysayers were dismissed as cranks, Neanderthals, Luddites, and troglodytes. Politicians, editorial writers, pundits—everyone loved election reform, and this meant e-voting. An early and prestigious joint study by Caltech and MIT that raised questions about the adequacy and appropriateness of e-voting (even as it criticized older systems) was swept aside.[24] Never mind that the scientists, engineers, and technicians who built and administered e-voting machinery were not nearly as enthusiastic about it as a panacea for America's voting woes as the reformers. Better to get on board the e-voting express while there was still time. No matter that the consequences of buying into e-voting technologies were not even addressed, much less considered. Surely this technology would save America from itself, as technological advances had so often bailed out the nation in the past. Besides, what could go wrong? It had to be better than what it was replacing; after all, it was Progress.

But was e-voting the best solution for the resolution of America's voting woes? No one wanted to ask that question.

Although HAVA was never fully funded, its mandates, along with popular enthusiasm for reform, changed the procedures and technology of American voting practices in just three years. Table 5.1, adapted from Election Data Services (EDS),[25] shows how deeply e-voting had penetrated our election systems by November 2006.

The table documents that on Election Day 2006, 56 percent of counties in the United States, with 49 percent of the nation's registered voters, used some form of optical-scanning voting equipment. Thirty-seven percent of counties, and 38 percent of voters, used some type of touchscreen (digital recording electronic, or DRE) machinery. This means that 93 percent of counties comprising 87 percent of registered voters used e-voting technology when they cast ballots in 2006. Punch cards, the bane of the 2000 Florida fiasco, were used in only 0.4 percent of counties, and by 0.2 percent of registered voters. Lever-operated equipment and hand-counted paper ballots had a larger market share than did punch cards.

What is important, and astonishing, to observe is the speed with which the switch from mechanical to e-voting took place. Table 5.2, also derived from EDS information, indicates the percentage of counties using each of five voting technologies in 2000 and 2006.

Table 5.1

Percentage of Counties and Population Using e-Voting Technology, 2006

Voting Machinery	Percent Counties	Percent Reg. Voters
Punch cards	0.4	0.2
Lever machines	2	7
Paper (hand-counted)	2	0.2
Optical scan	56	49
Electronic (DRE)	37	38
Mixed	3	5

Source: Kimball W. Brace, Election Data Services, "Almost 55 Million, or One Third of the Nation's Voters, Will Face New Voting Equipment in 2006 Election," Washington, DC, Election Data Services, October 2, 2006. Viewed online at http://www.electiondataservices.com/images/File/ve2006_nrpt.pdf, accessed February 8, 2009.

Table 5.2

Percent Change, Types of Voting Equipment Used (U.S.), 2000–2006

	2000	2006	Percent Change
Punch cards	17%	<1%	−98
Lever machines	14%	2%	−86
Paper (hand-counted)	12%	2%	−83
Optical scan	4%	56%	1,300
Electronic (DRE)	9%	37%	311

Source: Kimball W. Brace, Election Data Services, "Almost 55 Million, or One Third of the Nation's Voters, Will Face New Voting Equipment in 2006 Election," Washington, DC, Election Data Services, October 2, 2006. Viewed online athttp://www.electiondataservices.com/images/File/ve2006_nrpt.pdf, accessed February 8, 2009.

The greatest increase, clearly, came in the use of optical-scanning technology. But what is more important than the absolute increases or decreases is the meaning of the numbers. Non-e-voting technologies have virtually disappeared from the United States in a relatively short period of time. The rush to board the e-voting express was overwhelming and irresistible, making winners out of those companies positioned to supply the demand, and placing heavy financial burdens on the backs of state and local governments that were forced to pay for them because of the lack of HAVA funds.

Actually, there is nothing particularly new about e-voting in the United States, if one conceives of the term broadly. Even punch-card voting systems, discussed earlier, became electronically enabled in the mid-1960s. Early sorting and counting of punch cards was done mechanically, but by the mid-1960s IBM had created electronic counters. They eventually became very high-speed, operated by sophisticated programs.

But the electronic side of punch-card technology proved to be unreliable.[26] Although fast, electronic counters are notorious for making mistakes by misreading cards. Even jurisdictions requiring "dry runs" of the machines prior to vote counting discovered that errors not found in practice sessions showed up when the tabulating became real. And of course the counting machines jam and fail to accurately count cards containing one or another form of chad. Thus, votes are lost or mistabulated.[27]

It is well recognized that punch-card technology, including electronic counting of cards, is the most error-prone of any mechanical system used, particularly in its e-version.[28] It is for this reason, along with the terrible black eye the various systems received in Florida 2000, that punch-card technology is barely used any longer in voting, and will likely become extinct in the very near future. The equipment itself has been relegated to storage warehouses, junkyards, and museums such as the Smithsonian. Some machinery has even been offered for sale on eBay, presumably to antique dealers and collectors of historical curios.

Optical-Scanning Devices

More than half of the counties in the United States, and about half of registered voters, use some kind of optical-scanning device for casting ballots. These percentages are likely to increase in the near future. Optical scanning for data collection and analysis has been available since the 1920s, and was first used for standardized testing in educational institutions in the 1950s and 1960s. It was adopted for casting and counting votes in the 1970s.[29]

Optical scanners are at the moment probably the most reliable form of electronic voting. They use a paper ballot, on which the voter marks his/her choice for candidates or issues using a special writing tool. The presence of a paper ballot means a paper trail exists in case a recount is needed. In the event of a disputed ballot, the intent of the voter is generally easier to discern than with punch-card ballots or DRE machines. The use of optical-scanning equipment requires less sophistication on the part of the voter than other forms of e-voting technology, as it is highly intuitive. And virtually anyone who has attended an American high school is already familiar with the technology, having endured batteries of standardized tests. Finally, optical-scanning machines are probably the most cost-effective types of e-voting equipment. While they are not cheap—especially if outfitted with electronic markers allowing disabled voters to use them—fewer of the machines are needed than touchscreens,[30] since voters tend to be able to vote more rapidly with optical-scanning devices than with either punch cards or DRE machines. Whether or not they vote more quickly than with lever-operated devices or simple paper ballots is not known.[31]

But optical-scanning devices also have some serious drawbacks. Unless they are of the precinct-level counting type, they can be notoriously inaccurate. The rates of disqualifying ballots by centrally counting machines are high, thus resulting in unacceptable numbers of lost or uncounted votes; too often, as we have seen, these have been minority votes. Despite the intuitive nature of filling out optically scanned ballots, voters continue to make mistakes that too often cause their votes to be discarded: extraneous marks on the ballot (including coffee stains, lipstick, and mascara) have been regular problems, as is the failure of voters to use the special marker (when available, not always the case) and instead substitute ballpoint pens or pencils that the scanners generally will not read. Power failures—apparently more common than is generally recognized—can not only stop the counting process but erase totals made to the point when the electricity went off. Scanners, like electronic card readers, are also prone to jamming, and if they are not well maintained, they often misread voters' marks. They also will not generally read ballots on which, say, the voter has placed an X beside the name of the preferred candidate, or even over the area to be blackened, even though the intent of the voter is clear.

The major problem with optical scanners, however, is that they can be hacked, and the results manipulated. Several studies indicate that this can be done relatively easily, and with little fear of detection, on Diebold equipment and machines built by some other companies.[32] Thus, it is not a given that the results of elections in which ballots are counted by optical-scanning equipment are fully reliable or valid. Unless and until major safeguards are built in to ensure that voters, and not hackers, determine the outcome of elections, public confidence in optically scanned ballots is assuredly misplaced.

Touchscreen Voting

The most widely used form of touchscreen voting is known technically as direct recording electronic (DRE) technology. In 2006 it was used by 38 percent of all U.S. voters, in 37 percent of all counties. It is a technology well known to anyone who has used an ATM, or checked in for a train ride or airline flight with an e-ticket. It is also likely known to patrons of restaurants where servers create checks using touchscreen technology, and the bill presented sometimes bears little resemblance to what was ordered.

Proponents of DRE machines argue that they have real advantages. Ballots can readily be designed to meet local needs. They can be prepared in any language, and there is never a fear of running out of ballots in case more voters show up at the polls than anticipated. They can readily be adapted for handicapped voters, including those with limited or no eyesight. But the greatest advantage, according to proponents, is that because ballots are tabulated electronically, results can be ascertained almost instantly. And, because there are no paper ballots, turning wheels, or cards to be punched, the likelihood of mechanical failure, jamming, or misreading of the voter's intent is almost nil.[33] But these limited virtues pale in relation to the colossal problems that DRE technology has created. While they are numerous, most of the criticisms can be combined in two categories.[34]

First, most of the DRE technology lacks a paper trail. This means that there is no tangible record of a vote; it is purely digital, purely electronic. If the machines were totally reliable, this might not be a problem, but they are not. As a result, there is no way to verify, independently of the digital count, that the vote recorded by the machine is correct and accurate. In the event of a needed recount, this situation is disastrous. The only way to carry out a recount, in fact, is to re-tabulate the vote using the same program that calculated it in the first place! Whether or not this is done once or an infinite number of times, the result will be the same (assuming there is no electronic failure) in each instance. This is hardly a recipe for building confidence in the totals produced.[35]

The problem of a lack of paper trails has become so widely recognized that paper trails are now being demanded, even mandated, by the public and legislators. Adding paper trails significantly increases the cost of DRE machinery, as well as the possibility of mechanical failure of an otherwise nonmechanical vote-tabulating device. It is of further interest that some of the DRE manufacturers, Diebold most prominent among them, have resisted the inclusion of paper trail capability in their equipment, arguing that it is neither necessary nor desirable.

The second criticism is even more serious: DRE systems are not secure; they can be hacked; and too often the source code (the program created by the manufacturer that enables the machines to read and tally votes) cannot be independently examined and certified. Each of these is a very serious matter. For elections to be credible and legitimate, they have to be transparent. That is to say, at each step of the way, the public must feel assured that its interest is being protected, that everything is done (as they say) fair and square, that independent verification is not only possible but welcomed, and that in fact the results of the election, as constructed by the tabulating machinery, can be considered accurate.

An examination of the literature on DRE machines reveals just how far from transparent voting by touchscreen technology actually is. There are numerous examples of voting tallies making no sense, lost votes, unreasonable numbers of votes for candidates, and the like; the most recent example is the 18,000 "lost" votes in Sarasota County, Florida, in the 2006 race for House District 13.[36] And the work of serious professionals—scientists, engineers, technicians—has raised troubling questions about how easily the DRE machines—especially the most commonly used Diebold model—can be hacked, with virtually no chance of detection.[37] Thus, the possibility exists that the machines can be programmed to ignore votes for some candidates, count only every second (or tenth, or thirtieth) vote, or even direct votes supposedly given to one candidate to a different one, although it must be emphasized that there is no proof that this has yet happened, even though allegations have been made.

But all of this pales in relation to the fact that Diebold, and other manufacturers of DRE machines, have proven reluctant to make their source codes available for independent verification and certification. Aside from the obvious public relations problem this creates for them—"if they didn't have something to hide they wouldn't be so secretive"—they are in fact violating a cardinal rule of American democracy, namely, that the public's business (in this case, an election) has to take place in full view of the public, and must be accountable to the public. In this instance, although no overt wrongdoing has been proven, in fact the attitude of these private sector vendors is to thumb their collective noses at the public as they try to conduct our elections in secret, away from public view, and turn them into private, profit-making ventures without accountability.[38]

The experience of using DRE in other countries is not promising either. Observers of elections in Great Britain, Australia,[39] Venezuela, and Brazil[40] have noted substantial difficulties of the kind found in the United States. In each instance, results of the election have been called into question and their legitimacy undermined.

There are those who say that all of this can be corrected, and perhaps that is true.[41] But the question is, is it worth all the effort and expense when better alternatives are at hand?

Internet Voting

The final e-voting technology to be discussed is Internet voting, or, as it is more formally known, remote electronic voting.[42] Strictly speaking, this kind of voting need not be limited to use of the Internet; it could also be done by telephone (either land line or cellular) or even interactive digital television (the latter was loudly trumpeted by presidential candidate Ross Perot in 1992 as a way of expanding and enhancing democratic governance). For the purposes of this discussion, however, remote electronic voting will be limited to casting digital ballots via the Internet.

Internet voting has been tried in some local elections in the United States (2000) and Great Britain (2002).[43] Its use in local elections in Estonia in 2005 was elaborately discussed in a paper preparatory to voting. In 2007, Estonians employed Internet voting in parliamentary elections; slightly more than 30,000 voters of some 900,000 registered took advantage of the new technology.[44]

It is difficult to assess from a distance the success of the Estonian experiment. News reports at the time described it as a success, but the meaning of that term is unclear. Yet Estonia is clearly in the global vanguard of use of the Internet for all sorts of political, cultural, and commercial purposes, as it is evidently an almost fully "wired" society; observers note that even in rural areas Internet activity infuses itself into the activities of daily life. Thus, the "success" of the Estonian Internet voting experiment may well rest on the ready accessibility of digital life in that country, and the ease and familiarity with which residents enter into it.

During the 2008 Democratic primary season in the United States (January through June), the party for the first time allowed registered Democrats living abroad to vote in the primary by Internet rather than by absentee ballot.[45] Although some analysts were skeptical and at least some called it a "dangerous experiment," largely out of fear of hacking, it appears to have run smoothly. Few problems were reported. Barack Obama won the primary with 66 percent of the vote to Hillary Clinton's 33 percent.[46]

Counterbalancing the Estonian and U.S. Democratic Party experiments was one conducted by the U.S. Department of Defense in 2004. The goal of the so-called SERVE (Secure Electronic Registration and Voting Experiment) effort was to permit U.S. citizens living abroad to participate in the elections of that year. However, a Pentagon report issued in January 2004 raised fundamental questions about the experiment, and it was canceled.[47] The Pentagon tried again in 2006, but only 63 voters cast ballots using its system. (On an investment of over $30 million to date, this amounts to a cost of $476,190.48 per vote!) According to a report published in the *New York Times* in June 2007, serious problems continued to plague the Pentagon's efforts to advance Internet voting.[48]

The major objections to SERVE were exactly the same as those raised against other types of e-voting, primarily security. In this instance, security focused on the ability of the system to ensure that every voter had the capacity to vote, and that the votes would be correctly recorded and stored. Hacking, system invasion, and system failure were among the most frequently mentioned difficulties.[49] In addition, voting via the Internet raises serious issues about protection of the secret ballot, especially in the event of a recount.

Conclusion

The history of American politics can be viewed as an ongoing search for panaceas designed to cure various ills of our democracy. Home rule, nonpartisanship, primary elections—these and many other "reforms" were touted by their advocates as *the* solution that would strengthen our system of governance. And so it has been with electoral systems as well, whether it was the secret ballot, lever-operated machines, or, currently, e-voting. Each one was thought to bring us closer to a "perfect" system of allowing voters to cast ballots. It may well be that many, even most, of our efforts at reform have improved our governance. Yet it is also true, and this is often ignored or overlooked, that at least some of them created more problems than they solved.

In the present instance, it appears that the rush to implement e-voting has substituted one set of election difficulties for another.[50] There is no disputing the fact that punch-card ballots were a recipe for disaster, a train wreck waiting to happen. Nor were lever-operated voting machines necessarily much better; they were subject to frequent breakdowns and could be easily manipulated and the results altered.

The problem, rather, is that in the stampede to adopt e-voting technology without careful consideration of its many liabilities, we have not guaranteed that our current voting systems are necessarily better—more accurate, more legitimate, more credible, more transparent, more public—than they were before. We have, indeed, been looking for answers to our voting ills in all the wrong places.

The question then becomes, can e-voting technology be made to work? The answer depends on the meaning of "work." In a sense, e-voting technology works now: elections have been conducted using various types of e-voting technology, votes cast and counted, and the results publicly disclosed. But the real issue is whether it can be made to meet the standard that states must create for fair, honest, legitimate elections. This standard can be summarized as follows:[51]

- Equal access to polls for all voters;
- Equal access to ballots for all voters;
- Ballots in each voting jurisdiction are identical;
- The technology of voting in each jurisdiction is the same;
- Directions for casting ballots that are clear, unambiguous, and available in a range of languages consonant with a multicultural society;
- Physically disabled voters have equal access to casting ballots as the nondisabled;
- A reliable means of marking a ballot is available to all voters on an equal basis;
- In the event a voter makes an honest mistake, help is readily available and the voter is given a new ballot;
- Equipment recording votes does so impartially, and on an equal basis;
- Equipment tallying votes does so impartially, fairly, and accurately;
- Equipment storing the results is reliable and not subject to post-hoc tampering;
- Mechanics of recounts are clearly and unambiguously spelled out in law, are fully transparent, and not subject to hijacking by outside agents or groups;
- The entire voting process is open to public inspection and investigation at each step, and is fully accountable to the public, before, during, and after the election.

The preceding pages of this chapter have documented the fact that, as presently constituted, e-voting technology does *not* meet the above standards. But could it? The answer is a definite "maybe." A number of important changes and developments would have to take place before rigorous standards can be met.

Changes in Technology Are Needed

This is the most obvious needed change, and without it, hope that e-voting can meet tough state and federal standards for fairness, equity, and transparency is doomed. There is not enough space, nor does the author possess the necessary technical expertise, to discuss all of the technological changes that e-voting equipment needs. But at a minimum, major security issues must be addressed, specifically:

- Assurance that computer programs (source codes) running e-voting technology are unbiased in their design, and vendors can and will publicly so demonstrate;

- Assurance by neutral, impartial agents that source codes can be checked and certified as meeting the manufacturers' claims of accuracy;
- Assurance that equipment is impervious to hacking or manipulation by outside agents;
- Assurance that equipment manufacturers are open to public inspection and testing, regardless of who is the vendor, its ties to centers of political power, or its institutional policies on internal privacy;
- Assurance that recording of votes is done in an unbiased and accurate manner, reflecting the voter's intent;
- Assurance that the secret ballot is protected, even in the event of a recount or other post-hoc investigations, including court action;
- Assurance that tabulation of votes is done accurately and fairly;
- Assurance that examination of results can be carried out openly by public entities, and if this requires a paper trail, it must be part of the system;
- Assurance that all voters—disabled included—have equal access to use of the technology.

Even these steps do not guarantee that a fair and unbiased election will be carried out. For example, it is not at all clear that it is possible to design voting systems of any kind that are completely impervious to hacking. On the other hand, taking these steps will help ensure that the egregious breeches of the public trust that have too often marked e-voting to date will be minimized.

Equity and Fairness

It is all too apparent that quality e-voting technology is not available to all voters on an equal and/or fair basis. In the 2000 election, for example, minority-dominated precincts, especially African American and Hispanic, did not have the same access to more advanced e-voting technology as did white-dominated precincts, with the result that their ballots were disproportionately disqualified because of errors brought on by technical failures and weaknesses. In 2004, African American precincts in Cleveland did not have access to sufficient quantities of voting machines as their numbers warranted, which meant that many were never able to vote. In the 2006 and 2008 elections, issues continued to arise about the accuracy of e-voting equipment, although in the latter case the number of questionable ballots did not influence the outcome of the presidential election. And the public record is strewn with many instances in which language minorities and the disabled were denied access to or use of voting equipment because help was not available, in spite of the insistence of the Voting Rights Act and other legislation that these groups be accommodated.

Even today there is concern among minority groups that e-voting is yet another device used by unsympathetic white politicians to disenfranchise them.[52] Some of this fear may be based on inexperience with the technology. Much of it, however, is based on the very real experience that minority groups, especially African Americans, have had in trying to exercise their franchise. Whatever the cause, the effect is pernicious: it is a sad commentary on American democracy when significant portions of the voting public feel that the means and mechanisms of voting are being used to keep them from casting ballots or from having their votes accurately recorded and tallied.

Back to the Future

What to do in the meantime, while e-voting technology improves to the extent it can meet minimum standards of acceptability? We should go back to hand-counted paper ballots. They are successfully used in many European and other countries[53] whose elections are at least as democratic as our own. They are safe, transparent, fully amenable to public inspection and recount, and inexpensive. The error rate for hand-counted paper ballots is the lowest of any voting technology.[54] They are only what they claim to be, nothing more. They can be used by language minorities and the physically disabled with little besides poll-side assistance needed. If a voter makes a mistake, another ballot can speedily be provided. They can be marked with pens, pencils, markers, paint, food dye, lipstick, ketchup, mustard, shoe polish, mascara, even blood if necessary (or desired). It is almost impossible not to be able to determine the voter's intent using paper ballots; erasures, for example, are much easier to detect, read, and interpret than with optical-scanning equipment. While they can be manipulated, the ease and cost of building relatively simple safeguards (for example, ballots must always be viewed in public settings, with an abundance of witnesses present) is far less than creating safeguards for optical-scanning or DRE equipment.

The author is aware that the media, political parties, candidates, techies, and perhaps even the public at large won't like this idea. He is prepared to accept the criticism of being a Luddite, and antimodern. Americans seem obsessed with time and speed, and paper ballots take too long to count; the fact that citizens in European and other countries often go to bed without knowing definitively who is the election winner probably matters not a whit to most Americans.[55] For Americans who are devoted to gadgetry and gimmicks, paper ballots are too unsexy, too low-tech, too antediluvian. But is it more important that the winner of the presidency or other public office be announced before people go to bed than that the public have confidence that the election was legitimate, the process transparent, and the outcome credible? And is the glitz and glamour and high-tech image of an election more important than its accuracy?

Does anybody want to go back to the nightmare of Florida 2000? Nothing in e-voting as presently constituted guarantees that it will not happen again.

Taking this major step back to the future might help Americans rebuild confidence in our electoral system after its recent debacles, even while strenuous efforts go forward to make e-voting technology all that it might and can and should be.

Notes

1. Douglas W. Jones, "A Brief Illustrated History of Voting," 2003, available at www.cs.uiowa.edu/~jones/voting/pictures, accessed February 7, 2009.

2. Quoted in Richard K. Scher, *Politics in the New South,* 2d ed. (Armonk: M.E. Sharpe, 1997), p. 79.

3. A recent study by the Brennan Center at NYU concluded that the most important causes of voter error are poor ballot design and inadequate, misleading, and/or incomprehensible instructions. See Lawrence Norden, David Kimball, Whitney Quesenbery, and Margaret Chen, "Better Ballots," Brennan Center for Justice, New York University, July 20, 2008, available at www.brennancenter.org/content/resource/better_ballots, accessed February 7, 2009. The report points out that in spite of the fiasco that the "butterfly ballot" caused in 2000, design flaws persist, including for optical-scanning and touchscreen technology. Indeed, the authors detail some thirteen ballot design flaws that continue to plague elections and cause voter error.

4. *Election,* directed by Alexander Payne (1999).

5. Much of the information in the following paragraphs comes from the splendid materials gathered by the Smithsonian Institution in its collection at the Museum of American History. The Smithsonian offers a comprehensive Web site of its collection at http://americanhistory.si.edu/vote/intro.html, accessed February 7, 2009.

6. Jones "A Brief Illustrated History of Voting."

7. Readers are invited to examine the painting by the American landscape artist George Caleb Bingham called *The County Election* (1851–1852), now hanging in the Saint Louis Art Museum in Missouri. It is a Romantic but suggestive depiction of the raucous, rollicking, even rowdy atmosphere in which elections were conducted during the artist's lifetime. A reproduction of Bingham's painting can be seen at www.artchive.com/artchive/B/bingham/bingham_election.jpg.html, accessed February 6, 2009.

8. Smithsonian, http://americanhistory.si.edu/vote/intro.html; Jones "A Brief Illustrated History of Voting."

9. Smithsonian Institution, "Vote," http://americanhistory.si.edu/vote/votingmachine.html, accessed February 7, 2009.

10. Smithsonian, http://americanhistory.si.edu/vote/punchcard.html, accessed February 7, 2009. Anyone over age fifty will remember how common the use of punch cards became during the 1950s and 1960s, with their accompanying warning, "Do Not Fold, Spindle or Mutilate!"

11. Information in this and the following paragraphs comes primarily from Smithsonian, http://americanhistory.si.edu/vote/punchcard.html.

12. In Florida, recounts are conducted at the county level by local canvassing boards. These consist of the supervisor of elections, the chief county judge, and the chair of the county commission. They are required to carry out their recounts in the sunshine (that is, the process is open to public inspection) and representatives of the candidates (or the candidates themselves) and political parties can attend as observers.

13. The literature on the postelection Florida fiasco, including recounts, is enormous. Three readily accessible texts are John Nichols and David Deschamps, *Jews for Buchanan* (New York: New Press, 2001); Julian M. Pleasants, *Hanging Chads* (New York: Palgrave Macmillan, 2004); Lance deHaven-Smith, *The Battle for Florida* (Gainesville: University Presses of Florida, 2005). But the semidocumentary film *Recount,* produced by and aired on HBO (2008), gives a dramatic and helpful overview of what happened after Floridians voted.

14. *Bush v. Gore,* 531 U.S 98 (2000).

15. The phrase comes from Richard K. Scher, "Grasping at Straws, Rushing to Judgment: Election Reforms in Florida, 2001," *Journal of Law and Public Policy* 13 (Fall 2001), pp. 81–102.

16. Douglas Jones, "Chads—From Waste Product to Headlines," 2002, available at www. cs.uiowa.edu/~jones/cards/chad.html, accessed February 7, 2009.

17. Data in this and the following paragraphs come from United States Commission on Civil Rights, *Voting Irregularities in Florida During the 2000 Presidential Election* (June 2001), Chapter 8, "The Machinery of Elections," available at www.usccr.gov/pubs/pubsndx. htm, accessed February 7, 2009.

18. But as with gear-lever machines, there is no warning against under-votes in optical-scanning technology.

19. Problems of a similar kind, although perhaps not to the same degree, occurred in Ohio during the presidential election of 2004.

20. See Greg Palast, "One Million Black Ballots Didn't Count in the 2000 Presidential Election," available at www.gregpalast.com/one-million-black-votes-didnt-count-in-the-2000-presidential-election-rnits-not-too-hard-to-get-your-vote-lost-if-some-politicians-want-it-to-be-lost, accessed February 7, 2009.

21. Help America Vote Act, Public Law 107–252, 2002, available at www.fec.gov/hava/ hava.htm, accessed February 8, 2009.

22. See Smithsonian, http://www.usdoj.gov/crt/voting/hava/hava.html.

23. Scher, "Grasping at Straws."

24. Caltech/MIT Voting Technology Project, updated June 6, 2008, available at www. vote.caltech.edu/media/documents/july01/July01_VTP_Voting_Report_Entire.pdf, accessed February 8, 2009.

25. Available at www.edssurvey.com/images/File/ve2006_nrpt.pdf, accessed February 8, 2009. See also Phil Hirschkorn, "Voting Machine Doubts Linger," August 16, 2008, CBS Evening News, available at www.edssurvey.com/images/File/ve2006_nrpt.pdf, accessed February 8, 2009.

26. As it turns out, the mechanical counters were also problematic. See Frank da Cruz, Columbia University Computing History, updated August 4, 2004, available at www.columbia. edu/acis/history/census-tabulator.html, and Douglas W. Jones, "Punched Cards," n.d., available at www.cs.uiowa.edu/~jones/cards/history.html; both accessed February 8, 2009.

27. See Jones, "Chad—From Waste Product Headline," rev. 2002, www.cs.uiowa. edu/~jones/cards/chad.html.

28. See, for example, the Caltech/MIT Voting Technology Project (updated 2008), available at www.vote.caltech.edu/media/documents/july01/July01_VTP_Voting_Report_Entire. pdf, and Judy Woodruff, "Inside Poltics," CNN, September 15, 2003, available at http:// transcripts.cnn.com/TRANSCRIPTS/0309/15/ip.00.html, accessed February 8, 2009.

29. See Douglas W. Jones, "Counting Mark-Sense Ballots," revised 2003, available at www.cs.uiowa.edu/~jones/voting/optical/. The Smithsonian Institution says the adaptation for voting was available as early as 1968; see http://americanhistory.si.edu/vote/future.html, both accessed February 8, 2009.

30. Suffolk County, New York, Budget Review Office, "Overview of Cost Factors Associated with Electronic Voting Machines and HAVA Compliance," July 26, 2006, available at www.co.suffolk.ny.us/legis/bro/Reports/2006/Voting%20Machines.pdf, accessed February 8, 2009. The study indicates that optical-scanning equipment might replace other voting technologies at a rate approaching 1:4.

31. See Wanda Warren Berry and Bo Lipari, "Scanner and DRE Voting Machine Problems Are Not Equal," September 26, 2006, available at www.nyvv.org/doc/AdvantagesPaper-Ballots.pdf; also Jones, "Counting Mark-Sense Ballots," and Kevin Bonsor and Jonathan Strickland, "How E-voting Works," n.d., available at www.howstuffworks.com/e-voting1. htm; both accessed February 8, 2009.

32. See Black Box Voting.org, "Optical Scan System Hacked," May 27, 2005, available at www.bbvforums.org/forums/messages/1954/5921.html; Voting Technology Research Center, University of Connecticut, Recent Reports, available at http://voter.engr.uconn.

edu/voter/Reports.html; and Jones, "Counting Mark-Sense Ballots"; all accessed February 8, 2009.

33. See Bonsor and Strickland, "How E-voting Works."

34. Criticisms of DRE technology are so numerous that only a few are mentioned here. See, for example, Jones, "Counting Mark-Sense Ballots"; Electronic Frontier Foundation, "E-Voting Rights," n.d., available at www.eff.org/Activism/E-voting/; Philip J. Windley, "eVoting," in *Extreme Democracy,* ed. John Lebkowsky and Mitch Ratcliffe (Lulu.com, 2005), Chapter 13, available at www.extremedemocracy.com/chapters/Chapter%2011-Windley. pdf; John Leyden, "UK e-Voting Pilots Deeply Flawed," *The Register,* July 31, 2003, available at www.theregister.co.uk/2003/07/31/uk_evoting_pilots_deeply_flawed; Verified Voting.org, "Fact: Electronic Voting Machines Have Miscounted Votes," January 7, 2004, available at www.verifiedvoting.org/article.php?id=997; Robert Lemos, "Global Lessons in E-Voting," CNET News, 2004, available at http://news.com.com/Global+lessons+in+e-voting/2009-1008_3-5387540.html; Michael Collins, "New Mexico Law Suite Delves Inside Voting Machines," "Scoop" Independent Media, 2005, viewed online at www.scoop. co.nz/stories/HL0511/S00067.htm; Bruce Schneier, "The Problem with Electronic Voting Machines," Schneier on Security, November 10, 2004, available at www.schneier.com/blog/archives/2004/11/the_problem_wit.html; Jim Lobe, "International Observer Team Urges Reform in U.S. Electoral Process," Common Dreams.org, 2004, available at www. commondreams.org/headlines04/1021-01.htm, Open Voting Foundation, "Open Voting," 2006, viewed online at http://openvotingfoundation.org/tiki-index.php?page_ref_id=1; all accessed February 9, 2009.

35. At this point, readers might wish to remember the famous *aperçu* of Albert Einstein, who once noted, "The definition of insanity is doing the same thing over and over and expecting different results."

36. Rob Mahlburg and Maurice Tamman, "District 13 Race Shows Broad Problem," *Sarasota Herald Tribune,* November 9, 2006, available at www.heraldtribune.com/apps/pbcs.dll/article?AID=/20061109/NEWS/611090343, accessed February 9, 2009.

37. See Ariel J. Feldman, J. Alex Halderman, and Edward W. Felten, "Security Analysis of the Diebold AccuVote-TS Voting Machine," Princeton University Center for Information Technology Policy, 2006, available at http://itpolicy.princeton.edu/voting; and Tadayoshi Kohno, Adam Stubblefield, Aviel D. Rubin, and Dan S. Wallach, "Analysis of an Electronic Voting System," 2004, available at http://avirubin.com/vote/analysis/index.html; both accessed February 9, 2009.

38. See Editorial, "The Unkept Promise on Voting," *New York Times,* May 18, 2007, available at www.nytimes.com/2007/05/16/opinion/16wed1.html?ex=1181966400&en=8a1d7b6d6f189de9&ei=5070, accessed February 9, 2009.

39. For an alternative view on the Australian experience, see Kim Zetter, "The Aussies Do It Right: E-Voting," *Wired,* November 3, 2003, available at www.wired.com/techbiz/media/news/2003/11/61045, accessed February 9, 2009.

40. Leyden, "UK e-Voting Pilots Deeply Flawed"; Stephen Mason, "Is There a Future for Internet Voting?" *Observatorio Voto Electrónico,* May 27, 2005, available at www.votobit. org/lallave/mason.html, accessed February 9, 2009.

41. See, for example, Thomas Green, "E-Voting Security: Getting it Right," July 8, 2004, *The Register,* available at www.theregister.co.uk/2004/07/08/getting_e-voting_security_right. For a differing view see ElectricNews.net, "All Internet Voting Is Insecure: Report," January 23, 2004, *The Register,* available at www.theregister.co.uk/2004/01/23/all_internet_voting_is_insecure; both accessed February 9, 2009.

42. Mason, "Is There a Future for Internet Voting?"

43. Ibid.

44. "Estonian E-Voting System," March 2, 2007, available at www.vm.ee/estonia/kat_340/pea_172/7025.html, accessed February 9, 2009.

45. Oxford Internet Institute, Oxford University, "The 2008 Democratic Global Primary," November 28, 2007, available at www.oii.ox.ac.uk/events/details.cfm?id=167; Associated Press, "Expat Democrats Cast Their Votes in Overseas Primary," *International Herald Tribune,* February 6, 2008, available at www.iht.com/articles/2008/02/06/america/overseas. php; both accessed February 9, 2009.

46. "Expats Around the World Vote in Democratic Primary," *Deutsche Welle,* June 2, 2008, available at www.dw-world.de/dw/article/0,3110918,00.html, accessed February 9, 2009.

47. Mason, "Is There a Future for Internet Voting?"; Andrew Orlowski, "Pentagon Cans Internet Voting System," *The Register,* February 6. 2004, available at www.theregister.co.uk/2004/02/06/pentagon_cans_internet_voting_system; both accessed February 9, 2009.

48. Ian Urbina, "Casting Ballot from Abroad Is No Sure Bet," *New York Times,* June 13, 2007, available at www.nytimes.com/2007/06/13/washington/13overseas. html?hp=&pagewanted=print, accessed February 9, 2009.

49. Mason, "Is There a Future for Internet Voting?"; see also Schneier, "The Problem with Electronic Voting Machines" and ElectricNews.net, "All Internet Voting Is Insecure."

50. Scher, "Grasping at Straws."

51. The legal and political basis for this standard is well established. It can best be summarized by noting that the U.S. Supreme Court states in *Brown v. Board of Education,* 347 U.S. 483 (1954), "Such an opportunity [in our case, the right to vote], where the state has undertaken to provide it, is a right that must be made available to all on equal terms." See www.nationalcenter.org/brown.html, accessed February 9, 2009.

52. See Berry and Lipari, "Scanner and DRE Voting Machine Problems Are Not Equal"; See also Ellen Theisen, "Electronic Voting Machines: New, High-Tech Ways to Disenfranchise African-Americans," Voters Unite.org, available at www.votersunite.org/info/EballotsDisenfranchiseAfricanAmericans.pdf, accessed February 9, 2009.

53. See Bruce Schneier, "Voting Security," July/August 2004, available at www.schneier. com/essay-039.html; Republic of Slovenia, Government Communications Office, "Format of Ballot Paper for European Elections," n.d., available at www.ukom.gov.si/eng/calendar/european-elections/about/ballot; both accessed February 9, 2009.

54. Caltech/MIT Voting Technology Project, 2008.

55. The author was privileged to witness a national election in Turkey in July 2007, conducted solely with paper ballots. While it is true that polls in Turkey close earlier than in the United States, it is also true that at least preliminary results could be reported accurately on the late evening television news, as almost all the ballots had been counted by airtime. The morning papers and TV shows had the complete results.

Part III

Trying to Vote in America

Disenfranchisement
as Public Policy

Chapter 6 investigates how we systemically disenfranchise portions of the population by gaming parts of our electoral system so that votes are essentially rendered meaningless. We can call this "disenfranchisement by other means." The book concludes with a consideration of what we, as Americans, must do if we want to eliminate barriers to the franchise and extend voting rights to all.

6

Gaming the System:
Disenfranchisement by Other Means

Thus far in our survey of voter disenfranchisement we have looked at an array of hurdles that those wishing to cast ballots must overcome in order to do so, as well as having said ballots recorded and counted accurately. We can conclude from these discussions that American policies on voting—consisting of laws, practices, rules, customs, and attitudes—make voting onerous for many people, and impossible for some who should be eligible, rather than easier for all.

But the issue of disenfranchisement extends beyond the machinations of those who want to limit ballot access. There is a deeper, and more pernicious, way to disenfranchise voters: people can be allowed to cast ballots, but by a variety of devices and structures those votes can be rendered meaningless. In other words, it is possible to allow people to cast ballots and to count them accurately, but to ensure that they have little or no effect on the outcome of an election.

When this happens, it qualifies functionally as disenfranchisement every bit as much as do the practices and rules and procedures that we have examined in previous chapters. But it might actually be more insidious, because it is not necessarily obvious to voters, or the public at large, that "the system" has been gamed to prevent their votes from influencing or determining the result. If this is the case, even if only in some circumstances, can we not conclude that the formalism of the election becomes merely a hoax, a charade, or a mirage—a sort of electoral Potemkin village, all front and no substance? If it occurs more than just "occasionally"—as I will try to document here—then can we not say that our democracy has far less meaning than we are taught, indeed that our democracy has serious, even potentially fatal, flaws?

Dr. Martin Luther King, Jr., understood this matter very early in his civil rights career. He recognized, as Southern blacks pursued the right to vote denied them by public officials, that unless and until blacks had the franchise they could not be regarded as full-fledged, first-class citizens.

In this sense, King saw that there was a powerful symbolic element to the franchise. It was a definitive indicator of one's status in the political community. But he also saw that there was an instrumentality to the vote as well, that is, it was a mechanism by which one could influence what happened in the community, state, and nation. Nowhere was this more eloquently stated than in his 1957 "Give Us the Ballot" speech in Washington, D.C.:

> But even more, all types of conniving methods are still being used to prevent Negroes from becoming registered voters. The denial of this sacred right is a tragic betrayal of the highest mandates of our democratic tradition. And so our most urgent request to the president of the United States and every member of Congress is to give us the right to vote.
>
> Give us the ballot, and we will no longer have to worry the federal government about our basic rights.
>
> Give us the ballot, and we will no longer plead to the federal government for passage of an anti-lynching law; we will by the power of our vote write the law on the statute books of the South and bring an end to the dastardly acts of the hooded perpetrators of violence.
>
> Give us the ballot, and we will transform the salient misdeeds of bloodthirsty mobs into the calculated good deeds of orderly citizens.
>
> Give us the ballot, and we will fill our legislative halls with men of goodwill and send to the sacred halls of Congress men who will not sign a "Southern Manifesto" because of their devotion to the manifesto of justice.
>
> Give us the ballot, and we will place judges on the benches of the South who will do justly and love mercy, and we will place at the head of the southern states governors who will, who have felt not only the tang of the human, but the glow of the Divine.
>
> Give us the ballot, and we will quietly and nonviolently, without rancor or bitterness, implement the Supreme Court's decision of May seventeenth, 1954.[1]

What King recognized in this prescient speech was that casting a vote is supposed to make a difference in people's lives at both individual and group levels. They choose this candidate rather than that, or endorse one course of action over another. Thus the vote has meaning beyond its symbolism. It has meaning because it can create change, change that people want, change they prefer; or alternatively, it confirms the status quo by reelecting incumbents or defeating propositions. Either way, the fair election becomes a true expression of popular will. The individual voter is not always on the winning side; the candidate not voted for might win, or the preferred referendum might be defeated. But if the election is a fair one, structured in such a way that the rules allow a true reflection of voters' opinion without prejudicing one side or the other, then that's the nature of democratic elections. Besides, in a true democracy the losing side can lick its wounds and plot its revenge for the next go-around.

We can say, then, that a democratic election gives meaning to the vote regardless of whether or not one's ballot is cast for the winning side. The fairness of the democratic process itself is at stake, regardless of which side emerges as the victor.

Indeed, the fairness of the *process* becomes the measure by which the vote has instrumentality, and therefore meaning.

But what happens when the election system is rigged, or gamed? What happens when it is structured so that it is mathematically impossible for one or more groups of voters to prevail, even though no effort is made to prevent them from voting? What happens when voters cast ballots that are not counted, but instead discarded or ignored? What happens when agents and agencies highjack the election and ignore voter preferences?

Does any of this really happen? Sadly, in America it does, in a variety of ways. We turn now to five different scenarios that illustrate how functional disenfranchisement occurs by gaming the system.

Fraud

Our first scenario is election fraud. Regardless of what form it takes, election fraud prevents the true result of the vote from emerging. That is, it distorts the outcome in favor of the agents perpetrating the fraudulent activity. It undermines the ballots of those who voted in good faith, possibly to the degree that it negates them completely. Fraud renders honest votes meaningless.

Fraud is key in the fundamental questions that King addressed: What value or instrumentality or utility can the vote have if it is washed out or diluted or negated because the results are rigged and voters' preferences don't matter? Why even bother to vote if one knows that the other side is just going to steal the election anyway? To be sure, one might cast a ballot out of principle, even for a candidate that one knows will lose. But at some point the voter has to ask himself if the vote is really important enough to engage in the charade, knowing (or even just suspecting) all the while that the other side already has the result locked up. It is the same as if one baseball team were given more players and more innings than the other; or the pinball machines were tilted in favor of one player rather than another. What kind of contests would these be?

Election fraud is potentially threatening to democracy not just because the results are distorted but, more importantly, because it undermines confidence in the very system itself. The democratic *process* itself is compromised, indeed delegitimized. How are voters to trust the outcome of an election in which fraud has been perpetrated? Indeed, even if fraud is never proven, the mere suspicion that it took place will give voters pause when results are posted. If this happens often enough, and in enough places, voters will begin to doubt that elections are anything but essentially private playgrounds for those controlling election machinery to secure the results they want.

There are actually two different kinds of election fraud. The first is voter fraud, discussed in Chapter 4. Voter fraud refers to individuals who misrepresent themselves at the polls (that is, claim an identity other than their true one), or who seek to vote more than once on Election Day. But as we showed earlier, this kind of election fraud scarcely occurs in the United States any more.[2] Voter fraud exists mainly in the minds of people who want to limit the franchise, to keep "undesirables" (too often, read Democrats or Democratic fellow travelers) away from the polls. Efforts to "eradicate" voter fraud mainly have the effect of disenfranchising otherwise eligible voters.

Voting fraud is another matter entirely. It has been and probably still is endemic in our electoral politics. As Tracy Campbell has shown in his masterful study of election fraud in the United States,[3] it has been with us since before we were a nation. We might even say, to paraphrase H. Rap Brown, that voting fraud is as American as cherry pie.

What is voting fraud? It is deliberate manipulation of election practices to ensure results favorable to those controlling election machinery. How is it done? The techniques are as varied and wide-ranging as human imagination can conceive. The following is a partial but suggestive list of the ways in which voting fraud has been carried out:

- Ignoring the actual results of ballot counts and declaring victory;
- Over-counting ballots favorable to the candidates of those controlling election machinery;
- Under-counting ballots cast for the candidates opposed by those controlling election machinery;
- Stuffing ballot boxes;
- Creating fake ballots for favored candidates (e.g., voting cemeteries, drawing up false lists of registered voters and casting ballots on their behalf, claiming voters in a different state/county are actually registered in the relevant jurisdiction);
- Rigging or jimmying election machinery so that it does not accurately record voters' preferences (this can be done on old-time gear-and-lever voting machines, punch-card systems, optical-scanning devices, and touchscreen equipment);
- Denying that voters registered in a given jurisdiction are in fact qualified, thus denying them access to the ballot;
- Rigging or jimmying vote-counting devices or computer programs so that voters' preferences are not accurately tallied, the rigging done so that ballots for favored candidates are counted correctly but not those for nonfavored ones;
- Manipulating absentee ballots by creating fake ones, ignoring or "losing" others, miscounting those submitted, or changing the rules in mid-election for what constitutes a legitimate absentee ballot;
- "Losing" or misplacing ballots—whole boxes if necessary—before, during, even after vote counting has taken place;
- "Finding" uncounted ballots at the eleventh hour favorable to the candidate(s) of those controlling the election machinery;

- During recounts, disqualifying ballots, especially those for the opposition, whether absentee, early, or Election Day votes, by changing the rules under which they are judged acceptable or unacceptable;
- Ignoring or "losing" ballots from "inconvenient" precincts.

Again, this list is not exhaustive. The question however is not how long is the list of fraudulent election activities, but how and why could these activities be carried out with relative impunity? And how long has this been going on?

The answer lies in several places. For starters, electoral fraud in this country is hard to document or to prove in court if matters get that far. Courts, for the most part, have been reluctant to intervene unless the fraud carried out is so egregious that it cannot be swept under the carpet. As a result, legal redress for those claiming fraud has been highly problematic. And there is the "boy who cried 'wolf'" syndrome: claims of electoral fraud are so commonly heard from losers that their credibility is usually in doubt from the start. Then, too, officials controlling election machinery are rarely held to account, and in some ways have effectively operated in the shadows, away from public scrutiny. Other officials are reluctant to criticize them, as they themselves are obviously successful products of the political machinery in place when they were elected (whether fraudulent or not). As to protests about the conduct of elections, including allegations of fraud, editorial writers, good-government groups, academics, and pundits can largely be ignored, as it is rarely clear that they speak for anyone other than themselves. And too often the evidence they present is scanty, or unconvincing.

Examples of fraud are legion, as Tracy Campbell and other scholars have shown. But a few might be mentioned by way of illustrating how fraudulent electoral practices have worked over time. In the presidential election of 1876, Democrat Samuel Tilden of New York gained a popular vote lead over Republican Rutherford B. Hayes of Ohio, but not a majority in the Electoral College. Returns in three states—Florida (where else?), Louisiana, and South Carolina—were manipulated and traded to throw the election to Hays. In the late nineteenth century, Tammany Hall of New York City was known to boast that the outcome of the election was never in doubt, because Tammany could and did declare the winner(s) while the polls were still open. Tammany was completely indifferent to the actual vote total, even if it were ever revealed/known. In the first decades of the twentieth century, Ed Crump of Memphis established a powerful statewide political machine and ensured the electoral success of his candidates by barging African Americans across the Mississippi River from West Memphis, Arkansas, on Election Day, giving them cash and firewater after instructing them on how to vote. In 1948, Lyndon B. Johnson of Texas gained the moniker "Landslide Lyndon" after the last-minute "discovery" of ballots favorable to him (all conveniently in alphabetical order) in some remote precincts, enabling him to win a U.S. Senate seat by eighty-seven votes out of nearly one million cast. Fraud was suspected but never proven in 1960 when Mayor Richard J. Daley of Chicago held back vote totals from his city until after downstate counties had reported, allegedly so that Chicago would show enough ballots for John F. Kennedy to claim victory in the state of Illinois and thus gain the presidency. In a major case of judicial intervention, in 1998 a federal judge overturned the results of the Miami mayoral contest because of flagrant violations of absentee ballot procedures amounting to fraud, and ordered a new election. In the 2000 presidential election in Florida there were numerous allegations of vote fraud during the recounts and enumeration of both domestic and overseas ballots. In 2006, again in Florida, it was alleged that in a congressional race centered in Sarasota County, some 18,000 votes were "missing," although it was never proven that they truly existed. In Washington State the 2004 governor's race was mired in accusations of fraud and was not decided until months after the election ended, with a total vote differential of 133 between the candidates out of some 2.8 million cast. Following the Minnesota election for U.S. Senate in 2008, months passed as votes were counted and recounted, and tested in courts for fraud, in an effort to find a winner.

What does all of this mean? For one thing, the voter in an election character-ized by fraud knows she has been functionally disenfranchised. Her vote has no impact on the result, because the whole thing was gamed from the outset. Whether this voter ends up on the winning or losing side, she also knows that the outcome lacks legitimacy. What, then, is the vote really worth?

Incumbency Advantage

A second political scenario of rigging the system, in which the value or meaning of the vote is demeaned, is incumbency advantage. It refers to the fact that in Ameri-can electoral politics, incumbents generally have an overwhelming advantage, in many cases to the point that the outcome of the vote is a foregone conclusion well before Election Day.

Readers might well ask at the outset, why is this a structural flaw in the election system? Is it not a reflection of voter preferences, the political skill of the incumbent that allows him or her repeated reelections, luck, or something else? If an office-holder keeps winning, how is it that functional disenfranchisement of voters?

This is an important objection, but let us think of it this way: What is the point of voting if a race is over before it starts? It renders the vote meaningless, effec-tively disenfranchising the voter who casts a ballot for a candidate who cannot possibly win.

Of course, this refers to voters opposing incumbents. Perhaps voters supporting the incumbent view the contest differently. But even in this case, if I vote for a candidate knowing she will win regardless of whether or not I vote, I must recognize that the election is mainly a formality if not a sham, and the meaning of my vote significantly devalued. The marginal utility, and hence, the value, of votes increases as elections become more competitive, and individual ballots become more deter-minative of the outcome. Thus, while a voter supporting a popular incumbent may well vote, it can certainly be said that his or her vote doesn't have much importance, meaning, or utility since the incumbent would win whether or not this particular voter took the trouble to show up at the polls. In a real sense, even voting for the inevitable winner constitutes functional disenfranchisement.

Incumbency advantage is especially evident in the U.S. House of Representatives, and to a slightly lesser extent in the U.S. Senate. We will look at some numbers in a moment, but it is safe to say here that most incumbents for the House have to do something really dreadful, and/or completely lose touch with their constituents, in order to lose either a primary or general election. U.S. Senate seats are a bit more problematic, given that they represent entire states and thus the political dynamics are more complex than for House seats.[4] But, if a first-term U.S. senator survives his initial reelection bid, he is pretty much set for as long as he wishes to occupy his seat.

State and local legislative seats show more fluidity, in part because of term limits, in part because in many areas of the country positions in the state legislature or on city councils or county commissions are not viewed as "career" slots. A goodly proportion of state and local legislators choose to retire after just one or two terms, thus increasing turnover. On the other hand, it is also true that incumbents in local and state legislative seats have a great electoral advantage over opponents, as figures will show. And in large metropolitan areas, especially older ones dominated by ward and machine politics, seats on local legislative bodies are very slow to turn over.

What are we talking about here? How much of an advantage do incumbents have? For U.S. House of Representatives seats, according to the Cato Institute, incumbents won 98 percent of the time in 2004; it was the fourth consecutive election cycle (a total of eight years) in which incumbents had that same level of success.[5] Not only did they win, but their margin of victory increased steadily during that period.[6] Even in the "peculiar" years of 1994 and 2006, when the House changed partisan hands, incumbents still won well over 90 percent of the time. U.S. Senators, as noted, do not do quite as well as their House colleagues, but in a study of all Senate incumbent races between 1914 and 2006, scholars found they still won more than 80 percent of the time.[7]

State legislative races involving incumbents show similar results. According to the 2008 study by the National Institute on Money in State Politics titled "Advantage, Incumbent," of 5,292 state legislative races in 2006, incumbents won 92 percent of the time (87 percent of those by raising the most money).[8] The institute's report showed that over the previous three cycles, 92 percent of the winners were either incumbents or held a financial advantage or both.

But these figures show only part of the story. The institute found that nationwide about one-third of incumbents for state legislative seats had no opponent in the general election, and about one-quarter had none in either primary or general elections. In Oregon, for example, 33 of 75 legislative races (44 percent) were unopposed for the 2008 general election: 8 of 15 U.S. Senate races (53 percent) and 25 of 60

U.S. House races (42 percent).[9] In Florida, 6 of 20 state senate incumbents (30 percent) were unopposed in 2008, and 34 of 120 House incumbents (28 percent) got a free ride. In many of the Florida contests—including those involving U.S. House incumbents, where all had opponents—opposition can most charitably be called "weak," with challengers' chances of winning ranging from slim to none. It is likely that the same is true in other states.

Explaining why incumbents in legislative races have such an extraordinary advantage is beyond the scope of this book. Money, money, and more money accounts for most of the explanation, as incumbents vacuum it up faster and in greater quantities than their challengers. Also important are name recognition, party backing, lobbyist support (in addition to money), easy access to free publicity by the media, casework on behalf of incumbents, favorable legislative districting, and other factors.

Our concern is not to explain this phenomenon, but to consider its impact on the meaning of the vote. It is strongly negative. Surely it is hard to argue that a vote has much meaning in a contest that does not exist because there is no opposition, or where the opposition is so weak as to represent no threat to the incumbent at all. Indeed, in those many legislative contests that are essentially over before they begin, perhaps the wonder is that anyone bothers to vote at all. They are examples of gaming the system, and they represent another way of functionally disenfranchising voters.

Districting

Districting is a mechanism through which all residents of a given jurisdiction—not just citizens, not just voters—are represented in legislative chambers. If we had a fully participatory democracy—the much-mythologized "New England Town Meeting" comes to mind—we would not need districts, because individuals would represent themselves. But we don't, and so we do.

Americans adopted a system of choosing representatives to legislatures by means of districts—discrete geographic entities—before we even became a nation. Voters would choose from a list of candidates the person or persons who would act on their behalf in legislative chambers. There are a host of ways to do this, of course. In single-member districts (now the most common) only one representative per district is chosen, whether to the U.S. House of Representatives, state legislature, or local council or board.[10] But in the past, multimember districts have been used, in which voters selected more than one representative per district. "At-large" districts for local legislative bodies are similar to multimember ones, in that voters choose from a number of candidates for all contested seats; some at-large systems require "residence districts" in which candidates must live within discrete geographic areas, but are voted on by all voters in the jurisdiction.

Drawing district lines is arguably the most complex, controversial, and political act in which legislators are involved. State legislatures draw district lines for the

U.S. House of Representative as well as for their own members;[11] local councils and commissions draw lines for theirs. How the lines are drawn, the technology used, and the political and legal dynamics that go into the process are matters that unfortunately would take us far afield from the scope of this book, important (and interesting) as they are.

But two issues in districting are of such paramount importance to the thrust of this chapter that they require some attention. First, legally, all districts in a given jurisdiction must have equal populations.[12] This is true whether the legislative body is the U.S. House of Representatives or a local council; all the congressional districts in a given state must contain the same number of people, and while courts have allowed state and local legislative bodies slightly more wiggle-room than for congressional seats, most districting plans for these entities attempt to conform closely to the equal-population standard unless there are extenuating circumstances.

Second, political parties will do whatever they can, including engaging in titanic power struggles, to maximize the number of seats that they can win and hold. Individual legislators will also engage in the same kind of behavior and activity to ensure that their seats are as "safe" as possible. The phrase "titanic struggle" actually understates the lengths to which parties and individual legislators will go to maximize their strength and protect themselves. By most accounts, the rancor, acrimony, bitterness, partisan pushing and shoving, and individual battles pitting colleague against colleague (sometimes even within the same party) surpass by far even the most ferocious legislative fights over budgets or policy issues. Districting always leaves blood on the floor of legislative chambers, and especially at the state level (but sometimes at the local as well), the whole matter often ends up in federal courts, as aggrieved parties try to find satisfaction there and winners attempt to defend what they have done as constitutional and legitimate.

These two major districting issues help us see how the whole process affects the meaning of the vote, and potentially functionally disenfranchises some voters. Drawing lines for districts is *not* politically neutral. Lines are deliberately drawn to maximize the number and power—or at least the political inclinations—of some voters while at the same time minimizing those of others. Party leaders want district lines that will ensure that their members are a majority in the legislative chamber, as great a majority as possible, and will stay that way until the next districting cycle. Individual legislators want to make their elections and reelections as safe and predictable as possible, and thus want districts that aggregate the vote of "their" kind of people and minimize that of others.

It is not hard to see what happens next. Architects of districting plans survey the political landscape, finding and harvesting "desirable" voters and drawing lines around them, enough either to create an actual or a functioning majority (the latter is determined by projected turnout rates). "Undesirable" voters—that is, those not likely to support candidates of the architects' party or interests—can be dealt with in several ways. The most common is to "crack" them, that is, to draw lines splitting them into several different districts, thus diluting their voting strength. Another common approach to "undesirable" voters is to "pack" them into a limited number of districts. Plan architects following this procedure concede a few districts to their opponents (as few as possible), but in the meantime "bleed" voters they want into as many as possible, thus creating actual or working majorities.[13] The effect of all this is to create some odd-looking districts, sometimes called "bug-splat" districts, as "tentacles" and "feelers" are created to locate and include sometimes far-flung "desirable" voters, or leave out those who are not.[14] But as long as the districts within a given jurisdiction have equal numbers of people and do not egregiously violate the few remaining districting standards, or successfully explain away why they do not, generally they will be allowed to stand.[15]

The result of all this is that as plan architects divide the population into politically "desirable" and "undesirable" groups of voters[16] for incorporation into districts, those in the latter category are at risk of functionally losing their franchise. If they are cracked and diluted into several districts, their ability to elect their "candidate of choice,"[17] or even to have a serious impact on the outcome of the district's election, will be severely compromised, even reducing it to nil. Numerically, these "undesirable" voters are so divided among various districts that their preferred candidates cannot win. True, if they are packed into one or two districts, they might form an actual or functioning majority and manage to elect their candidate(s) of choice. But in the legislative chamber even these gains might be washed out, as a majority of members from districts composed primarily of "desirable" voters will outvote them every time. Yes, they voted and elected their candidate(s) of choice, but even these successes have no ultimate impact on the instrumentality of the vote, as described by Dr. King.

Has this ever happened? Does it still happen? The answer is "yes" to both questions. In the past, of course, a variety of minority populations—most especially African Americans—were cracked and divided to ensure that they could not elect one of their own to the Congress, state legislature, or local council. The same happened to others, including Hispanics and Asians. Beginning in the 1980s, primarily as a result of the U.S. Supreme Court case *Thornburg v. Gingles* (1986),[18] some protection was offered African Americans and other groups. Jurisdictions were permitted (but not required) to create so-called "majority-minority" districts, which would raise the probability that they could elect their candidate(s) of choice. While a number of these were disallowed by further Supreme Court decisions in the 1990s as unconstitutional racial gerrymanders,[19] it is still possible today to protect racial minorities from the outlandish cracking and splitting that occurred in the not-so-distant past.[20]

But other forms of cracking and packing are very much permitted. Indeed, the so-called practice of gerrymandering, in which districts are drawn, even distorted, for partisan purposes goes back to the early days of this nation.[21] It continues unabated today, with the approval of the U.S. Supreme Court. In another important 1980s voting rights case, *Davis v. Bandemer,*[22] the Court held that there is essentially nothing wrong with drawing district lines for partisan purposes, because that is the way the political game is played. The Court further noted that no one was really injured because of partisan districting, because those elected are still required to represent everybody, not just the people who voted for them, and in any case no one was prevented from voting just because the "other party" won.

Strictly speaking, of course, the Court was right. No one was denied the right to cast a ballot. But functionally, as a result of partisan gerrymandering of districts, certain voters have zero chance, barring something cataclysmic, of electing their candidate(s) of choice.[23] The situation just described is an instance in which one party has such a numerical advantage over the other that the value of the vote for those holding the short end of the stick is reduced to practically nothing. What good is the right to vote when the person holding it knows his candidate cannot possibly win, unless a miracle happens?

Perhaps an example will lock in the point. An examination of voter registration in Florida's twenty-five congressional districts (January 2008) reveals that in seventeen of them the minority party (in this case Democrats) has less than 40 percent of the vote; in ten of these, Democrats have 35 percent or less of the vote. In three districts Republicans comprise fewer than 40 percent of voters (those are the ones the GOP conceded to Democrats); in seventeen they are a clear, even overwhelming majority, with percentages in some cases exceeding 60 percent.[24] Thus, while Democrats constituted 41 percent of Florida's registered voters in early 2008 (and Republicans 37 percent), they have been substantially gerrymandered out of the political picture for congressional districts by the Republican-dominated legislature by being either cracked or packed. Figures for state legislative seats are comparable. Most students of American parties and elections argue that contests do not become competitive until the minority party reaches a minimum threshold of 40 percent; otherwise the results are a foregone conclusion, essentially an empty exercise. Most of the races for Florida's congressional and state legislative seats fall into this latter category.

Is it any wonder that Florida's Democrats have been such a dispirited bunch since the early 1990s, when they lost control of the reapportionment process?[25] It is next to impossible for them to win in any but a few congressional (and state legislative) districts, and there is almost no hope of increasing their numbers unless and until a fairer system of districting is created. In many other states the situation is comparable, if not so extreme. Gerrymandering that virtually guarantees one party a victory with legislative seats, and prevents competitive elections from occurring, cheapens the vote. It is an easy way to game the system to make sure that certain population groups are functionally disenfranchised, perpetual electoral losers.

Disenfranchising Voters After the Election: Recounts and Courts

We naturally think that once an election is over, it's over. Those who wanted to vote, and were allowed to, did so. The votes were recorded and tallied, accurately and fairly or not, and results announced. Eventually, appropriate officials certify them, and the election goes into the record books. Matters quiet down, and people turn their attention elsewhere.

But the truth is different from this scenario of "normalcy." It is still possible to disenfranchise voters even after the polls have closed and all the ballots have been cast and counted. It can be done through recounts, and by action of courts. It is another way of gaming the system, in this case not just to disenfranchise voters but potentially to determine the outcome of an election, even to the point of overturning the results of the popular vote.

States provide for recounts of ballots following their initial tabulation. The standards vary, but generally recounts are automatic if the results are so close as to fall within a very narrow range. In the 2000 presidential election in Florida, for example, the standard was 0.5 percent of the vote—in other words, if candidates' vote totals were within a half percent of one another, a recount was mandated, at public expense.[26] Other states have comparable thresholds and parameters requiring recounts if results are close, although the numbers may vary.

It is also possible for candidates to demand recounts even if the results fall outside of the specified range. Losing candidates often make such demands and requests, particularly if they allege voting fraud, although in most states they have to pay for the recounts from campaign funds if the spread of voting returns exceeds the percentage differential for which the state will pay.

Why are recounts allowed? We already alluded to one reason: the possibility of electoral fraud. If there is suspicion that ballot boxes have been stuffed; if ballots are missing; if there are more returns from one precinct than there are registered voters; if there is reason to think ballots have been mismanaged or tallied inaccurately; if there is suspicion about the way in which election officials have acted; if there are serious doubts about the accuracy and adequacy of the technology (software or hardware) involved in e-voting—the list is endless. All of these can give rise to recounts, sometimes by court order.

But another reason for recounts is technical. If the results of an election are so close as to fall within the margin of error of the tabulating equipment or computer programs, then it is impossible to say what the true results are. Only a manual recount can reveal voter preference. This, of course, is exactly what occurred in the 2000 Florida presidential election. The margin of error of the punch-card devices so widely used exceeded 3 percent, and the error rate of some of the optical-scanning equipment (especially the atavistic kind used in African American precincts) was not much better. These machines could not count accurately at the nano-level required by the closeness of the election. Only manual recounts could reveal the true results. Minnesota ran into a similar problem in its 2008 U.S. Senate election. Although it used a sophisticated optical-scanning system for voting, the results were so close (at most a few hundred votes) that lengthy manual recounts were required before there was even a glimmer of discerning who actually won, and even then the ballots ended up in court for further consideration.

It is for this reason that recounts should automatically be mandated when the margin between the candidates, in percentage terms, falls below the error rate of the technology used for voting. As noted in Chapter 5, results of vote tabulations should always be seen as probability statements. When the candidates' final margin is greater than the error rate, the totals will tell with some degree of certainty (the greater the margin, the greater the certainty) who won. But if the margin is below the error rate, there is no way to tell. The announced results are just a guess, or a political gambit, and a manual recount becomes essential.

But therein lies the rub, and the politics, of recounts. Which ballots are to be recounted? All of them, across the whole jurisdiction? Only in some counties? Which counties? Why? All the precincts in the county, or just a sampling? How is the sample to be drawn? As we have seen so often before in this book, the devil is in the details. How these and other questions are answered will determine whether or not every vote will count, or whether some get shoved aside, with the result that some voters will be disenfranchised even though they cast ballots.

And then there is the question of how recounts are to be carried out. Every state has its own procedure, and if Florida is not the modal example it is at least illustrative of how the process generally works. State law provides that in the event of a recount, the county convenes an election canvassing board consisting of three officials: the supervisor of elections, the chair of the county commission, and a county judge. These individuals are authorized to examine each and every ballot and make a determination of how it was cast. The process is to be carried out in public, in the presence of representatives of the candidates (or the candidates themselves), observers sent by the political parties if it is a partisan election, and open to the media, indeed, the public generally.

The process is intensely political, not mechanical. In the year 2000, there were major differences and arguments on canvassing boards as to how ballots were to be recounted (the same was true during the 2008 Minnesota recount). Readers will recall photos plastered all over the electronic and print media (this was in the days before YouTube and Facebook!) with members of canvassing boards squinting at chads, trying to determine how individual ballots were to be tallied. In some cases—Miami-Dade County is the prime example—extraordinary political pressures were brought to bear on canvassing board members to "tilt" the recount one way or the other; there was even a mini-riot outside the offices of the Miami-Dade Supervisor of Elections where the recount was being conducted, interfering with the proceedings and intimidating board members to such an extent that the recount was shut down. While this degree of fervor is not the norm, candidates, the parties, their lawyers, and the media—who desperately want a winner—do bring pressure to determine and indeed influence the outcome. The rush to judgment, then, speeds up the process, which greatly increases the chances of carelessness and error.

And there is no agreed-upon set of standards to be used in determining how a ballot is to be counted. Standards can vary from county to county, across the whole state, and from one state to another. The general standard by which the boards operate is to determine the "intent" of the voter. While seemingly simple, in practice it can be very complicated. A major issue, for example, can arise when a voter failed to follow instructions. For instance, on an optical-scanning sheet a voter may have marked an X in the circle next to the candidate of his or her choice instead of darkening it in using the marking device provided; robust, time-consuming arguments arose in Florida over whether or not such a ballot should be counted at all since the voter "didn't do it right," even though the intent was clear. In other cases, the voter made extra markings on the optical scan ballot; were these random dots, an effort to vote for two candidates (in the event a mark was near another candidate's name), or something else? And endless arguments over the intent of the voter arose from punch-card devices, depending on the kind of chad that confronted canvassing board members. While a visitor from outer space might think all of this was much ado about nothing, in fact, the outcome was too close and the stakes too high to concede even a single ballot without a struggle.

Other examples could be given, but the point should be abundantly clear. The recount process is not politically neutral, but in fact is politically volatile, highly charged, and sometimes quixotic. Other political forces and issues can intrude on recounts even though they would seem to be side issues—for example, race. Indeed, the Florida 2000 vote some 170,000 ballots were never counted at all, either during the first tallying or the recount period; about 130,000 of them came from primarily black precincts. Subsequent studies of that election revealed that black ballots were far more likely to be disqualified and discarded than white ballots, whether during the initial tally or the recount period. Clearly the racial dimension of how ballots were counted and recounted influenced, indeed determined, the results.

Recounts are perhaps the best support for Marshal Stalin's alleged assertion that "voters don't count, it's the people who count the ballots who count." There are vast oceans of uncertainty, unknown unknowns, black holes really, involved in the recount process. And where there is uncertainty, the political preferences and discretionary decisions of recount officials quickly rush in to fill the void, buttressed by demands from candidates, lawyers, political parties, and the media to resolve the matter, each pushing for one side or another.

One further observation about recounts is in order: no matter how careful, systematic, and thorough is the recount process—the one for the 2008 Minnesota Senate race comes to mind—there is always a cloud hanging over the final result. If there is the slightest suspicion that "politics" influenced the outcome—and of course it has to—then portions of the public will claim that the results smell like a week-old fish. If the politics become heavy-handed, partisan, brutal—the Florida 2000 vote is the obvious example—then major portions of the population will regard the final outcome as illegitimate. The consequence is that confidence in the electoral process—indeed, democracy itself—is significantly eroded. In fact, one can say with certainty that the only real winners in a long, drawn-out recount, especially one that culminates in a range of court battles, are the lawyers. They can collect huge fees and, as always, they get to go home, win, lose or draw.

Thus, recounts are a major way of gaming the system after the fact, after the election is over. They are an exquisite way of favoring some voters over others, counting some ballots but disallowing others. They are indeed a way of disenfranchising otherwise legitimate voters who took the trouble to vote. And, to conclude with the point continually stressed in this chapter, recounts are a way of diminishing the meaning of the vote. If a voter suspects that her ballot was thrown out during a recount, why would she even want to vote next time?

But recounts are not the only post hoc way of disenfranchising voters. Courts potentially can do the same thing when they intervene in the results of an election after it has concluded. The most famous example of this happening was in December 2000, in the case of *Bush v. Gore,*[27] when the United States Supreme Court intervened in the Florida dispute, stopped the recounting of ballots, and essentially handed the election, and the presidency, to George W. Bush. Courts in Minnesota took months to determine the winner of the 2008 U.S. Senate race (Al Franken was the eventual winner), by examining county returns and in some cases individual ballots. Thus, courts are still very much in the business of deciding whose ballots get counted and whose do not.

All states allow voters to contest the results of elections if they have reason to believe that there were sufficient irregularities as to affect the outcome. While the rules and criteria for filing contests vary across the states, those for Washington State are instructive.[28] The complainant must be a registered voter, and must demonstrate that one or more conditions specified in state statutes existed, and affected the outcome. The conditions include but are not limited to: misconduct by election officials, casting of illegal ballots, and/or the ineligibility of the winning candidate to hold office. Washington law specifies the time frame within which the contest must be filed. The court has a number of options, including throwing out the complaint, throwing out the election, declaring a winner, ordering a new election, or handing the whole matter over to the state legislature.[29]

Does this ever happen? The answer is yes, although contested elections seem to occur more frequently for local rather than statewide races. When they do happen, they tend to attract substantial media attention. Again, *Bush v. Gore,* the highly contested 2004 governor's race in Washington, and the aftermath of the 2008 Minnesota elections for U.S. Senate are the best examples. But contested races for Congress also draw serious attention; the 2006 disputed election in Sarasota, Florida, also was a major focus of national attention as it wound its way through a host of courts, trying to determine if some 18,000 votes were in fact missing because of poor ballot design and/or technological failures, and whether election officials had acted in improper ways.[30] I previously noted that in the late twentieth century a federal court threw out the results of a mayoral race in Miami because of irregularities with absentee ballots.

In truth, contesting elections in court is not always successful. The cost of a contest is high, and the burden of proof on the complainant to show that something was seriously awry is substantial. Courts, whether at the state or federal level, intervene only reluctantly unless there are serious mitigating factors and circumstances.

And for the most part, courts, when they do intervene, are hesitant to overturn even disputed election results, arguing that it is not their place to disregard or displace the will of the people unless egregious mistakes or misbehavior can be incontrovertibly documented.

There is a host of literature written by legal scholars and jurists addressing the question of whether or not courts should get involved in elections after the fact. For example, after the 2000 decision of *Bush v. Gore,* an avalanche of books, law review articles, and more general literature appeared, and a considerable number of scholarly symposia were held, in an attempt to address the question of whether court intervention in election results was a good idea or not.[31] As one might expect, the range of opinion was staggering.

Our concern in this chapter is not with the question of whether or not judicial intervention is good or bad, desirable or undesirable. Instead, it is what happens to the individual vote, and voter, when intervention does occur, especially if votes are thrown out and/or results overturned? One of the more shocking developments in the run-up to *Bush v. Gore* was the manner in which courts—state and federal—ran roughshod over election results. Indeed, courts—goaded by lawyers, candidates, parties, and the media—never allowed the Florida recount process to work. Instead, courts insisted on deciding which recounts were permissible and which not (and thus which votes were to be counted and which thrown out).[32] A host of decisions from a variety of courts resulted in mass confusion, uncertainty, and a general sense that not only had Florida's county electoral canvassing boards been preempted, but individual voters were thrust aside, their ballots mere grist for legal and political mills, cannon fodder for the enormous legal and political forces at work that were on display nightly on the national news. Florida's statutes, legal procedures for contesting elections, its constitution, even the very federal system itself, were ignored, wrenched apart, and trampled on as court after court, climaxing with the highest court in the land, issued verdict after verdict and finally a decision that had painfully little to do with voters' preferences or the ballots they cast.[33]

In truth, court activity following the 2008 Minnesota U.S. Senate election has been much more low-key, and the courts involved appear to have moved more slowly and with greater concern for the integrity of the electoral and recount process than was the case in Florida. Of course, Minnesota courts did not have the time pressures that faced those in Florida, as the constitutionally mandated meeting of the Electoral College helped force the rush to judgment. But even in Minnesota, courts were in the position of having to determine which ballots were to be counted, and which not.

Indeed, this is exactly the problem with court intervention in the electoral process, at least as far as this chapter is concerned. Americans like to believe that the results of elections reflect the will of the people. But when courts disregard votes in the pursuit of other interests, they undermine both their legitimacy and that of the election itself.[34] When votes are ignored or set aside, those whose ballots are no longer counted are deeply affected: Why theirs? Why not count everybody's vote equally? Who decides which votes to accept and which to discard? Why? To deny the vote of some individuals or groups and not others cheapens the meaning of all votes. Why should anyone bother to vote if the courts are just going to pay no attention?

We can say with certainty that once lawyers and courts get involved in determining the results of elections, voters get thrown out, along with the democratic process. No longer do those casting ballots decide who won and who lost. Indeed, to the extent that courts determine the winner, voters—on the losing side—are functionally disenfranchised. The system has been gamed so that their votes no longer matter.

True, some elections are flawed, and it has happened that results are tampered with. Courts, especially lower courts, exist to investigate facts and make determinations of whether such things happen, and how serious are the allegations. No one disputes that courts are the proper forum for resolving disputed elections involving fraud or improper behavior by election officials. But this in no way is a license to disenfranchise some individuals and groups. When this happens, the legitimacy of the whole electoral process is called into question, and the meaning and value of the individual vote significantly compromised.

Intimidation

Our final scenario of gaming the system to render votes meaningless is voter intimidation. Some readers might question why the discussion of intimidation has been left for the end of this chapter, and not placed earlier in the book. The reason it belongs here is that voter intimidation, along with voter fraud, are ultimate examples of politics by other means, in terms of violating voting rights. They are immoral, unconstitutional, and illegal. Thus they form a useful set of "bookends" for this chapter, as they are among the worst possible offenses against voting rights. But their perpetrators are seldom held to account for their actions. Too often they have been, and are, carried out with impunity.

There is a certain irony associated with voter intimidation. Like a number of other hurdles and barriers placed in front of voters, it does not deny citizens the right to vote. It denies them the ability to cast ballots, just as so many of the procedures and rules discussed in Chapters 4 and 5 do. But unlike the other four scenarios in this chapter, including fraud, intimidation does not represent a structural effort to render votes meaningless. Far from it. Intimidation occurs precisely when actors in the electoral system fully understand how important the votes of some individuals and groups are, and they thus seek extra- and illegal means to ensure that that importance is never realized. Using tactics that range from terror to fear-mongering to harassment to propagation of lies and misinformation, intimidators will do whatever it takes to ensure that key segments of the voting population—segments whose votes they fear—never get to cast ballots.

Intimidation has a long, nasty, and sordid history in the United States, and unfortunately continues to this day. The first large group to arrive in the United States against whom voter intimidation took place on a regular basis, was probably the Irish, although certainly the practice was well established before their arrival. The Irish, whose immigration to the United States largely resulted from the potato famines of the 1840s, were frequent targets of intimidation and other forms of discrimination designed to keep them from the polls. On the West Coast, as we saw in Chapter 2, the Chinese faced similar kinds of intimidation and harassment, mostly successful, to keep them from voting.

But no population group in the United States has been as targeted for intimidation, over such a long period of time and by such disgusting methods, as African Americans. Intimidation of former slaves started as Reconstruction in the South was coming to an end. By the 1890s, the institution of Jim Crow laws, sanctioned by the U.S. Supreme Court in *Plessy v. Ferguson* (1896),[35] opened the door for a variety of tactics to be used against blacks, intimidation among them. It could take a variety of forms, from economic sanctions to social ostracism to outright violence, with the Ku Klux Klan and other agents of terror committing murder, injury to individuals and property, and general mayhem designed to keep blacks "in their place" and away from the polls.

Violence, terrorism, and other forms of intimidation against black voters continued, in the South at least, well into the twentieth century. The lengths to which some Southerners would go to intimidate blacks from voting have been extensively documented. The atmosphere of fear and terror in which Southern blacks lived was constant and palpable.

But the Irish, Chinese, and African Americans have by no means been the only groups subjected to voter intimidation. Catholics of a variety of nationalities and ethnicities, Jews, Native Americans, and central, eastern, and southern Europeans (including Italians) have at some times and places been excluded from exercising the franchise due to intimidation. In recent times, Hispanic and Asian immigrants have as well, and there are reports of homophobes intimidating gays from voting.[36]

What is extraordinary is that intimidation of voters continues into the twenty-first century. True, the violence and lynchings and beatings are a thing of the past (although in recent years gays have been attacked and beaten). But other forms of voter intimidation and harassment continue, and plague even recent election cycles. The United States Commission on Civil Rights, People for the American Way, NAACP, Common Dreams, and other sources continue to document major instances in which a variety of forms of voter intimidation have occurred.[37]

There is no need to review such comprehensively tilled ground, but a few examples will document the ongoing presence of voter intimidation and harassment. Voter "caging," or the challenging of registration status, while perhaps more of a technique for purging voters than intimidating them, nonetheless has been used to frighten mainly African American voters away from the polls for decades, even though the practice was allegedly stopped in the mid-1980s; it surfaced again in 2004 and possibly 2008. In the 2000 presidential election in Florida, African American voters in some precincts were required to produce two forms of identification before they could vote, even though at that time only one form was legally required. In at least two Florida counties, official law enforcement automobiles were prominently parked immediately in front of polling stations in primarily black areas, presumably to discourage black voters from approaching the polls. In 2003 and 2008, African American voters in a Philadelphia mayoral race were challenged by individuals wearing suits and dark glasses, carrying clipboards, and driving cars with fake official-looking insignias, who demanded identification as they approached the polls. Black voters in Louisiana were targeted with flyers telling them the date on which they were allowed to vote, which turned out to be the day after the actual election was held. In Maryland and Georgia, blacks were sent flyers stating that if they tried to vote without having paid their rent or utility bills or settled outstanding parking tickets, they would be arrested. In Orlando, state law enforcement officers were sent to the homes of elderly black voters ostensibly to investigate voter fraud, but the effect was to significantly intimidate those interviewed, who remembered the not-too-distant past when police and sheriff's deputies actively harassed black voters trying to cast ballots. During the 2008 election, Democracy Now reported that newly registered voters in Ohio were subject to harassment and lawsuits filed against them by the state GOP, which questioned their qualifications. There were reports from North Carolina, Detroit, and other places of voter intimidation on Election Day designed to bring some voters' eligibility into question. Numerous other instances have been documented.[38] As we noted in Chapter 2, Frances Fox Piven and her colleagues have documented that efforts to suppress the black vote, including by intimidation, are ongoing in this country.[39]

Some might object that this is pretty thin stuff, that the number and range of voters being harassed or intimidated are small. Sifting through the full documentation, however, reveals that the number is not small at all; one need only think about the Jim Crow period in the South, the civil rights movement of the 1950s and 1960s, the Irish, the Chinese, and other groups, to realize just how many voters in our history have been victimized by intimidation and harassment.

But in any case, the number of voters involved is not the point. One intimidated/harassed voter is one too many. To say it is unconscionable that at this point in our nation's history there are voters who are the targets of intimidation is a gross understatement. According to Alexander Keyssar, the history of voting rights in the twentieth (and presumably twenty-first) centuries is primarily that of expansion in constitutional, legal, and practical senses; but documented evidence of repeated and ongoing voter intimidation calls this thesis into question.[40] Intimidation of voters then represents regressive, rather than progressive, public policy. If allowed to increase, or just remain unchecked, it threatens to take us back to a past from which it has been extraordinarily difficult to emerge. This is not a desirable version of "back to the future."

Where does all of this come from? Who is doing the intimidating? The answer, both historically and contemporarily, is always the same: those who fear the voting power of groups and individuals different from them. It does not matter whether the differences are racial, religious, ethnic, national, economic, linguistic, sexual, or something else. The goal of the intimidators is to ensure that the groups, however marginalized, are prevented from voting because of the potential, or at least perceived, threat they and their votes represent to the status quo.

Matters go deeper than this, of course. Preventing a group or an individual from voting by intimidation is a means of denying their legitimacy as citizens. It is not simply that they become marginalized. Their very acceptance into the heart of American society as bona fide, full-fledged members is, through intimidation, called into question. Far from underscoring the values of a democracy, intimidation of voters cuts them to shreds. The fact that so few intimidators are ever held to account, or are prosecuted, but instead engage in their practices with relative impunity, simply compounds the socially destructive forces that intimidation creates.

Who is responsible for voter intimidation? In the late nineteenth and early twentieth century South it was largely the Democratic Party, local voting and other public officials, the Ku Klux Klan, and its fellow travelers who were the perpetrators. Know-nothings, anti-Communists, nativists and xenophobes, religious bigots, homophobes, and the like have also been involved at one time or another in voter intimidation throughout the nation's history. In more recent times, evidence suggests that fellow travelers of the Republican Party, if not always the party itself, have taken steps to intimidate and harass marginalized groups of voters, especially those whose citizenship/patriotism they question, or at least those whom they fear might vote Democratic.

In a real sense, though, it is we the people, the public at large, who are responsible for voter intimidation. The reason is that we continue to tolerate it. The public outcry is less than deafening when instances of voter intimidation are brought to light. Especially lacking have been the voices of the parties, both of which at one time or another have either engaged in voter intimidation, fostered or sponsored it, or allowed it to go forward with a wink and a nod. When the parties take the lead in bringing voter intimidation to a halt, public officials at all levels and the public at large will follow close behind. Until that happens, however, voter intimidation will likely continue, and will increase if the election at hand is seen as especially competitive and/or critical.

Conclusion

Much of this book has focused on the way in which election procedures and techniques can be used to disenfranchise voters. But in this chapter the argument shifted to much broader concerns. Is the systemic problem solely that election rules and procedures can be structured to cause individual voters and groups to lose their vote, as we saw in Chapters 3, 4, and 5? Or can the system be gamed or rigged so that not all votes count, or so that the votes of some segments of the population become meaningless because they are ignored or are so diluted as not to figure in the outcome at all, not just in one election but repeatedly? In other words, a voter can have the franchise, but if he can't use it, as in the case of voter intimidation, or it doesn't mean anything, as with instances of disenfranchisement by other means, what good is it? Under these circumstances, does it make sense to cast a ballot? Does not the value of the vote decline to virtually nothing?

Perhaps what is astounding is that voters continue to cast ballots even when they realize their side is lost from the outset, that the outcome of the election is decided even before the election season begins. Clearly the impulse to vote is a powerful one among some, perhaps many, voters; like people who marry multiple times, voting under the circumstances outlined in our five scenarios in this chapter represents the triumph of hope over experience.

This chapter also documents that voting rights demonstrate important instances of "politics by other means." In two cases—election fraud and intimidation—those instances involve activities that are illegal and unethical, even immoral. But in the other three—districting, the effects of incumbency, and recounts/court action—they are totally legal, but not always ethical, moral, or fair. These latter three are especially pernicious, because it might not always be obvious to citizens that their votes are being diluted into virtual oblivion, rendered meaningless, or thrown out after they have been cast. These scenarios exist as a shadowy, dimly recognized political reality, but their effect can be devastating. We shall leave to others the question of whether "politics by other means" as discussed here represents a conspiracy of the powerful against those they wish to marginalize, ignore, or reduce to second-class status. But there is no doubt that this is the effect of "politics by other means" in the voting rights scenarios this chapter discusses.

Can we do better? Can we provide a more level playing field so that every voter has a fair chance to cast votes that count equally? Can we, in fact, game the system in favor of fairness, instead of rigging it so that some voters are perpetually disenfranchised? It is to these and similar questions that I turn in the concluding chapter.

Notes

1. Dr. Martin Luther King, Jr., "'Give Us the Ballot' Address at the Prayer Pilgrimage for Freedom," Washington, D.C., May 17, 1957, available at www.stanford.edu/group/King/publications/speeches/Give_us_the_ballot.html, accessed July 9, 2008.

2. Justin Levitt "The Truth About Voter Fraud," Brennan Center for Justice, New York University, 2007. Viewed online at http://brennan.3cdn.net/e20e4210db075b482b_wcm6ib-0hl.pdf, Saturday, March 14, 2009. See also Levitt, "The Truth About Voter Fraud," press release, November 9, 2007, viewed online at http://www.brennancenter.org/content/resource/truthaboutvoterfraud, Saturday, March 14, 2009. See also Lorraine C. Minnite, "The Politics of Voter Fraud," Washington, ProjectVote, n.d., www.projectvote.org. Viewed online at http://www.projectvote.org/fileadmin/ProjectVote/Publications/Politics_of_Voter_Fraud_Final.pdf, Saturday, March 14, 2009.

3. Tracy Campbell, *Deliver the Vote* (New York: Basic Books, 2006).

4. In states that have only one representative but two senators (Delaware, Montana, North and South Dakota, Vermont, Wyoming), the reverse would be true.

5. Another study shows that between 1982 and 2004, House incumbents won at a rate exceeding 95 percent. See Russell D. Renka, "The Incumbency Advantage in the U.S.

Congress," November 6, 2007, available at http://cstl-cla.semo.edu/renka/ps103/Fall2007/
congressional_incumbency.htm, accessed March 14, 2009.

6. Eric O'Keefe and Aaron Steelman, "The End of Representation: How Congress Stifles
Electoral Competition," Washington, D.C., Cato Institute Policy Analysis No. 279, August 20,
1997, available at www.cato.org/pub_display.php?pub_id=2889, accessed March 14, 2009;
and John Samples and Patrick Basham, "Once Again Incumbents Are the Big Winners,"
Washington, D.C., Cato Institute, November 21, 2004, available at www.cato.org/pub_display.
php?pub_id=2889, accessed March 14, 2009. Project FairVote reported the same phenomenon
for 2008 House races, in spite of the "change" atmosphere of the election. See Rob Ritchie, "Ten
Surprises About Election 2008," Project FairVote blog, November 6, 2008, available at www.
fairvote.org/blog/2008/11/ten-surprises-about-election-2008, accessed February 23, 2009.

7. Gautam Gowrisankaran, Matthew F. Mitchell, and Andrea Moro, "The Effects of
Incumbency Advantage in the U.S. Senate on the Choice of Electoral Design," available at
www.andreamoro.net/perm/papers/why_do_incumbent_senators_win.pdf, accessed March
14, 2009. See also Renka, "The Incumbency Advantage in the U.S. Congress." As a result
of the Seventeenth Amendment to the U.S. Constitution, ratified in 1913, U.S. senators were
first elected by popular vote (instead of state legislatures) in 1914.

8. Scott Jordan, "Advantage, Incumbent," Helena, Montana, National Institute of
Money in State Politics, May 7, 2008, available at www.followthemoney.org/press/Reports/
MoneyIncumbency2006_Final.pdf?PHPSESSID=82e9f3c14645b3d4cc4270b018c58d23,
accessed March 14, 2009. See also "Money Talks, Incumbents Run Unopposed, Democracy
Suffers," *Oregon Independent,* June 11, 2008, available at www.oregonindependent.com/
node/270, accessed March 14, 2009.

9. "Money Talks, Incumbents Run Unopposed, Democracy Suffers," *Oregon Independent.*

10. All states are entitled to two senators, and thus no districting is involved.

11. All states are entitled to at least one seat in the U.S. House of Representatives,
regardless of population size. Currently seven states—Alaska, Delaware, Montana, North
and South Dakota, Vermont, and Wyoming—have only one representative each, and thus
no districting is involved.

12. *Baker v. Carr,* 369 U.S. 182 (1962) and *Wesberry v. Sanders,* 376 U.S. 1 (1964).

13. "Packing" voters, especially minority voters, creates waste; indeed votes in this situation
are referred to as "wasted votes." The reason is that packing often creates very large majorities
in those districts (percentages can rise to 60 percent or more), far more than would be needed
for them to elect their candidate(s) of choice. The "extra" voters could be spread into other,
nearby districts, thereby making them more competitive. Hence, these votes are "wasted." But
this, of course, is exactly what the party in control of the district machinery wants.

14. If all jurisdictions were perfectly square or rectangular, and more importantly if the
population were equally spread throughout them (in other words, population density were a
constant), odd-shaped districts would not have to be drawn. They would all be rectangular
or square. In practice, of course, this does not happen.

15. Contiguity—defined as the ability to go from one part of a district to any other without
crossing a district boundary—must also always be respected. Compactness—which generally means smooth-sidedness, although there are technical, mathematical measures for it—is
frequently ignored. So are respect for political boundaries, attention to topographical features,
and cognizance of "communities of interest." Continuity of representation—a vague standard
at best—is respected, however, because it is justification for incumbency protection.

16. Nonregistrants and other politically inert groups are essentially ignored, except as
grist for the equal-population mill.

17. The term comes from the Senate report of the 1982 amendments for the Voting
Rights Act. In *Thornburg v. Gingles,* 478 U.S. 30 (1986) the Supreme Court used the term
"preferred representatives."

18. *Thornburg* (1986).

19. *Shaw v. Reno*, 509 U.S. 630 (1993) and *Miller v. Johnson*, 515 U.S. 900 (1995).

20. On March 9, 2009, the U.S. Supreme Court significantly limited the extent to which districts could be drawn to protect racial minorities. See *Barnett et al. v. Strickland et al.*, no. 07–689, available at www.supremecourtus.gov/opinions/08pdf/07–689.pdf. See also Christian Smith-Socaris, "Supreme Court Limits Districting Provision of Voting Rights Act," *Facing South*, Institute for Southern Studies, n.d., available at www.southernstudies.org/2009/03/supreme-court-limits-redistricting-provision-of-voting-rights-act.html. Both accessed March 13, 2009.

21. While governor of Massachusetts, Eldridge Gerry became famous, or infamous, for helping to draw an outrageous-looking district resembling a salamander for purely partisan purposes. The practice has been known since then as "gerrymandering."

22. *Davis v. Bandemer,* 478 U.S. 109 (1986).

23. During state legislative redistricting in Texas early in the twenty-first century, Democrats boycotted proceedings—in some cases fleeing the state in an effort to prevent a quorum—in order to keep the Republicans from imposing a plan under which it would have been virtually impossible for a Democrat to win in any but a relatively small number of districts.

24. Calculated from data provided by the Florida Division of Elections, registration figures by congressional district, January 2008. Available at http://election.dos.state.fl.us/voter-registration/statistics/elections.shtml#08presPrim, accessed July 9, 2008.

25. In November 2008, a majority of Florida voters chose Barack Obama in the presidential contest, offering hope to at least some state Democratic leaders. But until congressional and state legislative lines are redrawn in a less partisan manner, the GOP will continue its overwhelming majorities in the congressional delegation and legislature.

26. Florida subsequently tightened the threshold to 0.25 percent. This was done to decrease the state's responsibility to pay for recounts.

27. *Bush v. Gore,* 531 U.S. 98 (2000).

28. See Washington Secretary of State, "Frequently Asked Questions, General Election Recount Procedures," November 15, 2004, available at www.secstate.wa.gov/office/osos_news.aspx?i=SPlmpeBt1xLxpksVqw%2Ft9w%3D%3D; Daniel Kirkdorffer, "Let the Vote Recounting Commence," December 3, 2004, available at www.kirkdorffer.com/ontheroadt02008/2004/12/let-vote-recounting-commence.shtml; and Lewis Kamb, "Contesting the Election: How It Would Likely Work," Seattlepi.com, December 31, 2004, available at http://seattlepi.nwsource.com/local/206025_contest31.html. All accessed March 15, 2009.

29. See also "How to Contest Election Results," n.d., available at www.ehow.com/how_2061788_contest-election-results.html, accessed March 15, 2009.

30. Bob Mahlburg and Maurice Tamman, "District 13 Race Shows Broad Problem," *Sarasota Herald Tribune,* November 9, 2006, available at www.heraldtribune.com/apps/pbcs.dll/article?AID=/20061109/NEWS/61109033; Kim Zetter, "Docs Point to E-Bug in Contested Election," *Wired,* April 17, 2007, available at www.wired.com/politics/onlinerights/news/2007/04/evotinganalysis; David Jefferson, "What Happened in Sarasota County?" National Academy of Engineering, Summer 2007, available at www.nae.edu/nae/bridgecom.nsf/weblinks/MKEZ-744KWK?OpenDocument. All accessed March 15, 2009.

31. See, for example, Richard L. Hasen, *The Supreme Court and Election Law* (New York: NYU Press, 2003), and Samuel Issacharoff, Pamela S. Karlan, and Richard H. Pildes, *When Elections Go Bad: The Law of Democracy and the Presidential Election of 2000* (Foundation Press, 2001). See also Richard L. Hasen, "The Mayoral Election: Off to Court We Likely Go," *San Diego Union Tribune,* December 17, 2004, available at www.signonsandiego.com/uniontrib/20041217/news_lz1e17hasen.html; and Daniel P. Tokaji, "Leave It to the Lower Courts," *Ohio State Law Journal,* 68 (2007), available at http://papers.ssrn.com/s013/papers.cfm?abstract_id=978290. All accessed March 15, 2009.

32. For helpful overviews of the "Florida fiasco," see Julian Pleasants, *Hanging Chads* (New York: Palgrave Macmillan, 2004), and Lance deHaven-Smith, ed., *The Battle for Florida* (Gainesville: University Press of Florida, 2005).

33. It was, for example, very apparent, as recounts proceeded, that Mr. Gore was the winner in Florida. The results of Election Day in Florida, and of all of the permitted recounts, showed that Mr. Gore was the winner with 2,911,417 to Mr. Bush's 2,911,215. This information was known to those involved in the recounts, but not to the general public. It is generally thought that further recounts would have enhanced Mr. Gore's totals, and may well have been a major factor in the Court's decision to shut them down. See Florida Division of Elections, General Election 2000, viewed online at http://election.dos.state.fl.us/elections/resultsarchive/Index.a sp?ElectionDate=11/7/2000&DATAMODE=, accessed March 15, 2009.

34. Tokaji, "Leave It to the Lower Courts."

35. *Plessy v. Ferguson,* 163 U.S. 537 (1896).

36. The best example of intimidation of gays came in Kalamazoo, Michigan, in the fall, 2009. See, for example, Mark Thompson, "Anti-gay Rights Flyer Circulates K'zoo," WoodTV.com, October 20, 2009, http://www.woodtv.com/dpp/news/local/kalamazoo_and_battle_creek/Anti_gay_rights_flyer_circulates_K'zoo, viewed online July 25, 2009. There are many other reported, albeit anecdotal, instances of harassment of gays seeking to vote.

37. See, for example, United States Commission on Civil Rights, *Voting Irregularities in Florida,* 2001, available at www.usccr.gov/pubs/pubsndx.htm; People for the American Way (PFAW), "The Long Shadow of Jim Crow," 2004, available at http://site.pfaw.org/site/PageServer?pagename=report_the_long_shadow_of_jim_crow; Bob Herbert, "Voting While Black," *New York Times,* August 20, 2004, available at www.nytimes.com/2004/08/20/opinion/20herbert.html?ex=1250740800&en=2e315e6b726b38d0&ei=5090&partner=r ssuserland%20; Associated Press, "Kerry Says Trickery Foiled Many Voters," *New York Times,* November 11, 2005, available at www.nytimes.com/2005/04/11/politics/11kerry.html?adxnnl=1&adxnnlx=1218650597-xyJrxCsjV9wQKet8Hv8Vow; Farhad Manjoo, "Voter Terrorism," Salon.com, September 21, 2004, available at http://dir.salon.com/story/news/feature/2004/09/21/intimidation/index.html; Judd Legum, "FBI Investigating Voter Intimidation in Virginia," *Think Progress,* November 7, 2006, available at http://thinkprogress.org/2006/11/07/voter-intimidation-virginia; Jo Becker, "Groups Say GOP Moves to Stifle Vote," *Washington Post,* August 26, 2004, available at www.washingtonpost.com/wp-dyn/articles/A33798-2004Aug25.html; Alan Elsner, "Millions Blocked from Voting in U.S. Election," *Common Dreams,* September 22, 2004, available at www.commondreams.org/headlines04/0922-03.htm; Dahlia Lithwick, "Raging Caging," Slate.com, May 31, 2007, available at www.slate.com/id/2167284; Editorial, "Sorry, I Can't Find Your Name," *New York Times,* October 22, 2008, available at www.nytimes.com/2008/10/23/opinion/23thu1.html; Andrew Burmon, "Where the GOP Could Get Dirty," Salon.com, October 22, 2008, available at www.salon.com/news/feature/2008/10/22/voter_supression_guidehttp; Democracy Now!, "Early Voting Sees Reports of Voter Intimidation, Machine Malfunctions," October 22, 2008, available at www.democracynow.org/2008/10/22/votes; Momie Tullotes, "Presidential Election: 2008 Voter Intimidation Incidents," *Associated Content,* November 4, 2008, available at www.associatedcontent.com/article/1179703/presidential_election_2008_voter_intimidation.html?cat=8.

38. See, especially, the comprehensive survey of voter intimidation in 2008 carried out by the Brennan Center for Justice at New York University. Wendy Weiser and Margaret Chen, "Recent Voter Suppression Incidents," November 3, 2008, available at http://brennan.3cdn.net/e827230204c5668706_p0m6b54jk.pdf, accessed March 13, 2009. See also Weiser and Chan, "Voter Suppression Incidents 2008," the Brennan Center, November 11, 2008, available at www.brennancenter.org/content/resource/voter_suppression_incidents, accessed March 13, 2009.

39. Frances Fox Piven, Lorraine C. Minnite, and Margaret Groarke, *Keeping Down the Black Vote: Race and the Demobilization of American Voters* (New York: The New Press, 2009).

40. Alexander Keyssar, *The Right to Vote* (New York: Basic Books, 2000).

7

Conclusion: Do We Want to Do Better?

During the aftermath of the 2000 presidential election in Florida, a frequently heard line from those wanting to limit or shut down the recounts and cast aside questionable ballots was that those voters who "didn't do it right" deserved to have their votes disqualified. Indeed, the phrase "didn't do it right" became something of a mantra, repeated endlessly by Republican leaders and their faithful. It was clearly a talking point, designed to influence media coverage and shape public opinion in their favor. It worked.

It worked because of the ongoing belief—which we have often confronted in this book—that voting is a privilege, and with it comes the responsibility to "do it right." If voting is a privilege, it can be revoked: if the voter makes a mistake, then his/her ballot has possibly been invalidated and can be rejected. In other words, if you don't "do it right," then we don't have to count your vote. If the voter *recognizes* while voting that he has made an error, then *perhaps* he might be given a chance to rectify it. But once the ballot is completed and the votes recorded, errors subsequently discovered during the counting or recounting process are grounds for disqualification. The privilege of voting does not extend to post facto correction of the error even if the voter's intent is clear. Voting is a one-shot deal, and if the voter blows the chance, too bad, or so the mantra goes.

Accompanying the "voting is a privilege" school of thought is the "it's the responsibility of the voter to do it right" line of argument. The "do it right" proponents argue that it is the duty of the voter to make sure he understands how voting goes forward. The voter himself forfeits his ballot by not following the "rules," or by making even the smallest of missteps, even if his intent is obvious. He has not risen to the level of his civic responsibility, and thus his ballot is null and void.

In the first chapter of this book we dealt with the question of voting as privilege rather than a right. But what about the business of "doing it right"? What does this mean? Or, rather, what does "doing it wrong" mean? Does it mean making a minor error in registering so that the name at the polling station does not exactly match the state's—too often flawed—list, and the "no match, no vote" rule is applied even though it is obvious that the names belong to one and the same person? Does it mean that the voter has done something wrong because she possesses and brings with her an approved identification card but is denied the right to vote because the local official, using his discretion, refuses to accept it?

Or, what about doing it "right"? Does it mean following directions to the letter even when they are vague, misleading, or opaque, such that the voter's diligence causes her ballot to be disqualified? Does it mean trying to negotiate a complicated ballot and directions that are not clear when the voter's English is weak or nonexistent, no help is available, and mistakes are inevitable? Does it mean expecting a physically disabled person to operate voting machinery that cannot accommodate him, but he tries anyway, undoubtedly raising the possibility of error? Does it mean that the voter, arriving at his polling station on the way to work or dashing over at lunch or rushing to get home in the evening, spilling coffee or a Coke on the ballot or making incidental marks on it because of haste, has disenfranchised himself? Why is it that criticisms of voters who "don't do it right" are so often directed at peoples of color, or the poor and uneducated, or immigrants or non-English speakers, or people who merely live on the "wrong side of the tracks" or on the "wrong" side of town?[1]

The Voter's Responsibility, and the State's

Is there any justification for the view that voters have an obligation to "do it right"? The answer is, yes. All citizens have obligations to the state: to obey the law, to pay taxes, to respect public lands and property. As far as voting is concerned, they have an obligation not to cheat by misrepresenting themselves or trying to vote more than once. They probably have a minor obligation—ethical, not legal, based on the obligations of citizenship—to familiarize themselves with candidates and issues, and to show up on Election Day to cast ballots (or participate in early voting, or use absentee ballots). Beyond this, it is not clear what obligations voters have; as noted in earlier chapters, literacy and character tests have long been outlawed, likewise the poll tax, so the voter has no obligation to meet any of them. And even if voters fail to meet the minimum standards of paying attention to candidates and issues, this is hardly a legitimate or acceptable reason for denying them the franchise. Only the most extreme advocates of the "voters-must-be-informed" school say that such a lack of knowledge should justify denying the franchise—and one does hear this view, even in college classrooms. Such advocates would require reinstitution of literacy tests to implement such barriers. Is that where this country should go? Back to an era even more discriminatory than at present?

Indeed, there are two fundamental flaws with the attacks on voters who "don't do it right" and thus cause their ballots to be discarded, and they both render the issue of citizen obligation irrelevant.

The first is that the criticism puts the onus on the individual voter, who is generally perceived to be at fault if there is something wrong with his qualification, registration, identification, or ballot casting. Why is this? Why is it the responsibility of the voter to show he is worthy and qualified? Why is it not the state's responsibility to prove that he is not? Or to prove a voter is not who she claims to be? The whole problem with questioning who is "qualified" is that it is an infinite regress: local voting officials responsible for registering voters can always find some excuse or reason, at every stage of the voting process, to disqualify a potential voter no matter what credentials the person puts forward. The long history of discrimination by local registrars against African Americans, other peoples of color, and undesirable immigrants reveals that their latitude of administrative authority and discretion has allowed them to find ways to prevent otherwise qualified people from voting. They were as inventive in this effort as the situation warranted, with little or no account-ability for their actions required. But if the state had to prove that the prospective voter is not qualified, rather than the other way around, then the whole notion of "doing it right" evaporates into nothingness. Indeed, the obligation then falls on the state, not the voter, to "do it right."

If we learned anything from the Civil Rights Acts of 1957 and 1960, it is that putting the onus on individual voters to secure their voting rights does not work. In those instances, Southern blacks who were denied the franchise had to come forward and convince a U.S. attorney to sue in federal court to secure their reg-istration. Aside from the obvious time and expense involved, too often Southern blacks put themselves at risk—sometimes literally of life and limb—if they chose to sue. As a result, there was little progress in Southern voting rights under these two pieces of legislation.[2]

It was not until the Voting Rights Act of 1965 and its subsequent amendments that the burden of proof was switched and placed where it should be: on the state, to prove that it had not discriminated against blacks (and later other peoples of color). Only then was the burden of proof of discrimination taken off the shoulders of the individual citizen.

To reiterate, then, arguing that the voter did not "do it right" simply turns the clock back to an earlier, hurtful era. Shifting the burden to the state hence makes sense. The same is true in the case of the voter who made mistakes fill-ing out her ballot. Is it always her fault? We are talking about people who make errors through no fault of their own, because of what we mentioned before: the directions were ambiguous, or the level of English required to decipher them was beyond the voters' competence, or they could not get the help they needed, or the technology of the voting machines eluded them. In these cases—and we know from recounts in Florida, Washington, Minnesota, and elsewhere that there are many—the mistakes were caused by errors of omission or commission by voting officials at state or local levels. The individual voter can hardly be blamed for making them.

This raises the second fundamental flaw in the "they didn't do it right" argu-ment, although it is implied in the previous discussion: the argument ignores the obligation of the state to the citizen wishing to vote. Indeed, in all of the jeremiads and outcries against allegedly unqualified voters and supposedly flawed ballots following the 2000 Florida election, cries heard in every election before and since (including 2008, particularly in Minnesota), this very crucial point has virtually never been aired. It needs to be at the center of discussions of voting rights.

What is the state's obligation? For each voter it is:

- To provide fair and equal access to the franchise;
- To provide fair and equal access to the polls;
- To provide clear and accurate means of casting, recording, and counting ballots;
- And to provide accountable, impartial, publicly verifiable mechanisms and procedures in case of recounts or challenges to ballots.

Perhaps put more simply, the state must provide an even playing field for voters. It must not in any way establish laws and rules and procedures that effectively discriminate against some groups of voters by making it harder for them to qualify, register, or identify themselves than others. It must not deny to any group of voters ready access to polls; indeed, it must provide sufficient numbers of polling places and keep them open long enough to accommodate the maximum number of voters possible; in this connection, same-day registration and early and mail voting are extremely important. It must eliminate draconian—or, rather, ridiculous and absurd and discriminatory—voter ID requirements whose only purpose is to keep people from voting. It must make certain that there are enough ballots on hand to accommodate voters who show up, that language minorities are respected, that help is available for those whose English is not proficient. It must have on-site help for those who do not understand how to use the voting machinery. It must accommodate those whose physical disabilities make voting difficult, yet respect the secrecy of their ballot. And it must record ballots in accordance with the voters' intent, tally them accurately and impartially, and provide machinery to allow for open, transparent, accountable recounts, with standards for disqualification that are clearly spelled out and are nondiscriminatory.

In short, it is the obligation of the state to provide fair, equal, transparent, accountable, and politically neutral election systems.

But as we have seen throughout this book, our election systems fail on virtually every one of these criteria. True, in some jurisdictions they get closer to the mark than in others: Minnesota has probably achieved a higher degree of fairness, equality, transparency, accountability, and political neutrality than other states, as the 2008 U.S. Senate election and recount demonstrated. And there are counties—not enough, it should be emphasized—where voting has proceeded fairly, smoothly, and in a nondiscriminatory manner for decades.

But too often states and counties do not meet their obligations to voters. They tilt the field in favor of some groups of voters, and place unacceptable hardships on others. Too often these are groups of voters of color, language minorities, the poor, the marginalized, the disabled, often the elderly, always the outsiders. Until these groups are brought fully and without qualification into our electoral systems, we have to place dampers on frequently heard boasts that this country provides its citizens with truly democratic elections.

Some will argue that all of this will cost money, a lot of money. It will. The Federal Elections Commission, which does not conduct elections, requested over $63 million in fiscal year 2009 for its oversight and enforcement responsibilities.[3] New York State spent about $40 million for elections in 2009–2010.[4] The Florida elections budget (part of the Florida Department of State) called for expenditures of about $13.5 million in 2009–2010, a nonpresidential election year. In 2005, Americans spent $33.5 billion on pet food, services, and supplies.[5] It is not a stretch to say that Americans could spend more money to provide a fair playing field for elections.

I posit at least three rationales for arguing that the state has an obligation to voters extending well beyond any that the voter has to the state:

- Constitutional obligations
- Political obligations
- Ethical obligations

Constitutional Obligations

The U.S. Supreme Court has already set forth the state's constitutional obligation very clearly in *Brown v. Board of Education* (1954) in speaking of children's right of access to public education regardless of race: "Such an opportunity, where the state has undertaken to provide it, is a right which must be made available to all on equal terms."[6]

In the present instance, if the state provides an opportunity for citizens to participate in elections by voting, it must ensure that this opportunity is fair and equal to everyone just as it is supposed to be for public education.

Both the requirements of *Brown* and the state's obligation to voters rest on the Fourteenth Amendment: "[N]or shall any State . . . deny to any person within its jurisdiction the equal protection of the laws." In *Brown,* the Fourteenth Amendment issue was that segregated schools were "inherently unequal" and had to be abolished.

But the application of the Fourteenth Amendment to voting has a more curious history. In Chapter 2 we saw that during the nineteenth century and for more than half of the twentieth the Supreme Court declined to apply it to voting at all. But beginning in the 1960s and for more than forty years thereafter, the U.S. Supreme Court has held that all votes must be considered equal and be treated equally; this is the fundamental reasoning behind such landmark decisions as *Baker v. Carr* and *Wesberry v. Sanders.*[7] In both legal and popular contexts this idea has become known as the "one person, one vote" standard. In *Bush v. Gore,* the Supreme Court wrote:

> The right to vote is protected in more than the initial allocation of the franchise. Equal protection applies as well to the manner of its exercise. Having once granted the right

to vote on equal terms, the State may not, by later arbitrary and disparate treatment, value one person's vote over that of another.[8]

But it was precisely in *Bush v. Gore* that the Court muddied the issue of the state's Fourteenth Amendment obligation to voters, in this case, the recounting of their ballots. In that decision, seven justices held that the standard that the Florida Supreme Court mandated for recounts was unconstitutional: that standard, written into law by the Florida legislature, was to determine the voter's intent in judging whether the ballot was legal and how it was to be judged. The U.S. Supreme Court's reasoning was that the process of recounting under this standard would vary substantially across the state, from county to county, with the result that individual votes would be treated differently depending on who was doing the recounting, and where.

But as one of the country's leading constitutional scholars, Professor Akhil Reed Amar of the Yale Law School, has pointed out, the standard that the Florida legislature created—voter intent—actually came closer to compliance with the Fourteenth Amendment than the standard it replaced, that is to say, no standard at all.[9] Prior to the adoption of the voter intent standard, Florida had no specified statewide criteria for determining how disputed ballots were to be judged; every county made its own decision about ballots. Thus, in rejecting the state-imposed voter intent standard in favor of the previous, nonexistent standard, the U.S. Supreme Court actually moved the manner of treating ballots further away from Fourteenth Amendment compliance than both the Florida legislature and the Florida Supreme Court wanted.

As if this didn't muddy the waters enough, they were further roiled by another part of the decision, one that divided the Court badly (5–4). In this part of *Bush v. Gore,* the Court held that there was not enough time for Florida to create a new statewide recount procedure that would meet the equal protection standard. Florida's "safe harbor" deadline was December 12, 2000, when the state required that all recounts be completed. *Bush v. Gore* was announced that same day.

What the Court did was to tell Florida that its recount procedure based on determination of voter intent was not in compliance with the Fourteenth Amendment. But it refused to give the state an opportunity to create a process that was in compliance.[10]

Where, then, does that leave the state—any state, not just Florida—in terms of its Fourteenth Amendment obligation to voters? Obviously, voters, and votes, have to be treated equally, and statewide variations in how voting can go forward and recounts conducted have to be examined with reference to equal protection. But on the critical question of how this is to happen—since it rejected the voter intent standard in favor of no specified standard—the Court was silent. Indeed, it went out of its way, seemingly in recognition that it was getting into very deep waters, to state that the present decision was "limited to the present circumstances, for the problem of equal protection in election processes generally presents many complexities."

By bailing out as it did, the Supreme Court left states in limbo. Yes, the Fourteenth Amendment applies to their obligation to voters, but a process that allows voter intent to be determined on a county-by-county basis would seem to fall short of equal protection requirements. But even as the Supreme Court retreated from mandating what might meet the test, it created a 900-pound gorilla that hasn't gone away and must eventually be faced (even as some states, such as Minnesota, have done).

A number of possibilities exist:

1. *Create national standards.* The federal government could impose a set of standards for qualifying, registering, and identifying voters, access to polling stations, the manner of voting and tabulation of ballots, and rules for recounts and contests of elections. Presumably these standards would comply with the Fourteenth Amendment. In some respects we are already moving down this path, with the introduction of the HAVA-created national voter registration form (which states can opt out of, or modify) and increasingly rigorous—indeed, draconian—voter ID requirements imposed by the Supreme Court.[11] Adoption of a national ID card as proposed by the Baker-Carter Commission (see Chapter 4) might regularize the criteria for IDs nationally, eliminate some of the more absurd rules imposed by states (such as requiring proof of citizenship), and lessen the burden on the poor and elderly to acquire the needed documentation. Civil libertarians, however, continue to recoil with horror from the idea of national ID papers, noting correctly that these are generally associated with authoritarian regimes, not democracies, and are seldom used for benign purposes.

But the biggest problem of nationalizing elections is that doing so probably violates the Tenth Amendment, which places the conduct of elections squarely in the hands of states. Indeed, the Tenth Amendment is one of the key pillars of our federal system, one that guarantees to states rights and powers that do not lie with the national government. Nationalizing elections would represent a serious challenge to the Tenth Amendment, one that states' rights advocates would greatly fear. Given the legal and political tradition in this country that states (and counties) run elections, unless and until the U.S. Supreme Court holds that nationally imposed election procedures and standards do not violate the Tenth Amendment, we would have to assume that they would.

But in reality, the politics of nationalized elections might trump constitutional and legal issues and keep them from happening. It is possible to imagine the explosive, vitriolic outcries of opposition from state and county election officials, public officials who have benefited from a decentralized system of elections (essentially the entire universe of elected officials), good government groups for whom local control of elections is paramount, and a host of others.

It is possible, perhaps likely, that over time our election systems will become more national than they are now. If some of the developments already in place continue to move forward (for example, the national voter registration form becomes mandatory, with no variations allowed), then indeed incrementally voting and elections will become more consistent throughout the nation. Another possibility is a voting rights constitutional amendment, which we shall discuss. But whether we will ever achieve the uniformity of many modern democracies in the way people become voters, cast ballots, have their ballots recorded and tallied, and contest the results is highly doubtful.

2. *Impose statewide standards.* Many states have already reduced or eliminated county discretion over registering voters and conducting elections, but there are still a substantial number that have not. Oregon, for example, allows only mailed-in (or dropped-off) ballots; there are no polling places and no absentee ballots. Many states mandate one consistent form of voting technology across the state (different varieties of second-chance optical-scanning equipment have become popular as the luster of touchscreen technology has faded), but some still allow county options. Imposition of statewide standards would seem to address the key issue bothering seven justices in *Bush v. Gore.* Undoubtedly other statewide rules could be imposed that might pass constitutional muster, but it would have to be said emphatically that if the statewide requirements were draconian and had the effect of disenfranchising voters rather than accommodating them (such as is the case with current state voter ID rules), then no good will have come of the effort and they would have to be protested in the strongest possible ways.

But imposition of statewide rules and procedures can also founder on the rocks of county/local politics and local patriotism. Local supervisors of elections are notoriously jealous of their prerogatives (so are other local officials), and to the extent they have discretion they will complain bitterly about infringements on their territory and powers. The fact that at present their levels of discretion sometimes lead to disenfranchisement of potential voters will conveniently be overlooked. Rather, they will voice the usual reactions—ranging from lamentations to outrage to defiance—of local officials who feel they are being stepped on by the state. They don't like it, they will resist state "takeovers," and might even work to subvert statewide rules. If any of these happen, then the state is no closer to complying with Fourteenth Amendment requirements than if it had done nothing.

But there is still the matter of what statewide standards might look like. In the previous paragraphs there were several suggestions that would create greater levels of uniformity in voting for states that do not now have them, and thus bring them in greater compliance with the Fourteenth Amendment. But what about recounts? Seven justices in *Bush v. Gore,* it will be recalled, felt that the way in which Florida's sixty-seven counties implemented the state standard of determining the voter's intent violated the equal protection clause. Two points need to be made about this. First, there is nothing inherently unconstitutional about the standard itself. Determination of voter's intent has long been recognized as the fairest, most reasonable way to count and recount ballots, and to judge disputed ones. In a sense, the Florida standard violated nothing, at least not until efforts were made by local canvassing boards to implement it, and state judges to evaluate it.[12] Moreover, it should be remembered that the voter intent standard replaced a vacuum of no standard at all. Most constitutional and political scholars would recognize that replacing nothing with something that at least can be examined, measured, and tested against the equal protection clause enhances the possibility of compliance with the Fourteenth Amendment.

But this raises the second, and in some ways more important, point. It is very likely that at least some of the justices' negative view of Florida's treatment of the voter intent standard was motivated at least as much by political, indeed partisan, considerations as constitutional ones. If this is true—and there is at least indirect evidence based on the 5–4 decision to shut down the recount, as well as journalistic and anecdotal accounts—then the *Bush v. Gore* holding that the Florida Supreme Court's standard for recounts violated the Fourteenth Amendment was a red herring, an excuse, a rationale by five justices to find a way to shoehorn Candidate Bush into the White House not because of, but in spite of, constitutional principles. Distinguished constitutional scholars, including many of those who signed the statement protesting the decision in *Bush v. Gore,* have made this point repeatedly since the dénouement of the case in December 2000.

Why is this relevant to the present discussion? Because it points up the importance of examining political contexts in discussions of how the Fourteenth Amendment applies to states' obligations to voters. One of the beauties of the Fourteenth Amendment is its flexibility, and applicability in a variety of political and social circumstances. But one of its downsides is exactly the opposite: because of its flexibility, it can be used for purposes that extend far beyond what is constitutionally warranted and move fully into political realms. This can do more harm than good.

3. *Do nothing.* Another option is to do nothing to address the Fourteenth Amendment and its linkage with states' obligation to voters. The effect, of course, would be to continue the current hodgepodge system of elections that we have now. Would this move elections into greater compliance with equal protection requirements? Of course not; the very question points to the absurdity of doing nothing.

Thus we return to where we began this discussion: instead of criticizing voters for not "doing it right" and disenfranchising them when they don't, those who loudly and prominently trumpet the "they have to do it right before they can vote or have their ballot counted" argument need to recognize that the state has an obligation to meet voters on their terms, and to institute rules and procedures (some of which we have mentioned in previous paragraphs) that meet the state's constitutional and other obligations to voters. Following this course of action will bring states and counties into ever-greater compliance with the Fourteenth Amendment.

Political Obligations

Constitutional obligations are not the only obligations that states have to voters. There are political obligations as well. At the most fundamental level, the political obligation of the state is to provide democratic elections. What does this mean?

Individuals, from the most learned scholars to the *habitués* of local bars and barbershops, may argue and disagree about what constitutes democratic elections, but the one aspect on which everyone is likely to agree is that the state must not create barriers to voting. Rather, in democratic elections voting must be accessible to all voters on an equal and fair basis. And in particular, the rules for voting must not differentiate or discriminate against different groups of voters or potential voters.

But unfortunately, too often states fail in their political obligations to voters. Rather than removing stumbling blocks and unnecessary barriers to voting, states impose them. Let us examine just one: voter registration. Readers will recall from Chapter 4 that the greatest inhibitors to voting are archaic, opaque, confusing, and too often arbitrary rules for registration. Without doubt, streamlining registration would do more to promote voting in this country than any other potential change. Indeed, instituting same-day registration throughout the nation would make most of the registration hurdles go away, from lengthy (and ridiculous) time lags to the bizarre questions and oaths that some states require.

But what is of great interest, and concern, to this book is that Americans continue to insist on forcing potential voters to register. It is not necessary. In many other democracies, a person is automatically registered upon reaching the requisite age, unless there are mitigating or special circumstances. The voter receives his or her card in the mail on or around the time of the appropriate birthday; all he or she must then do is show up at the polling station at the next election and present it. All of this could now be done electronically, and in the future probably will be. The effect, by the way, of registering voters when they reach their majority would be to enhance voter turnout substantially in the United States. While undoubtedly there are forces at work besides automatic registration that help augment voter turnout—holding elections on Sundays seems to make a big difference, for example—it should be pointed out that turnout in many modern democracies (excluding the United States) of 90 percent and more is not unusual.

Why do we not take steps to make voting easier in the United States, as other democracies have done? Inertia and tradition account for part of the reason. But the most likely explanations are fear of voter fraud on the one hand, and fear of uncontrolled expansion of the franchise on the other.

We have already dealt extensively with the red herring of voter fraud, and need not delve into it again. But automatic voter registration as described earlier strikes deep into the heart of what many Americans feel about voting. On the one hand, it is counter to the "voting is a privilege" view that is widely held in this country. That view collapses utterly if one automatically becomes a voter upon reaching the age of majority. But there is more. Unrestricted suffrage—because that is what automatic registration amounts to—runs counter to many, many entrenched interests that want to construct and maintain tight boundaries around the acceptable universe of voters. Political parties, for example, strenuously resist vast increases in the franchise because they cannot predict the party allegiance of the newcomers, or how they would vote. In some respects, Republicans may be more honest than

Democrats in this regard; the former are very careful about where and how they recruit new members, and actively seek to prevent potential voters from registering who don't fit the mold (generally not the poor, and those of color). But even the Democratic Party is not as inclusive in its voter recruitment efforts as it claims to be.[13] If it turned out that a substantial number of new voters affiliated with the other party, or, worse, registered as independents,[14] Democratic leaders would be filled with fear and loathing.

Other entrenched interests also oppose dramatic expansion of the franchise. Elected officials at all levels like to know who and where are their voters; an onslaught of newcomers, with no voting history, would make their election and reelection far more problematic. Advocates of particular policy issues—gun ownership, gay rights, abortion rights, solar energy, and the flat tax are just a few examples—as well as nongovernmental organizations (NGOs) and good government groups might face uncertain futures as unknown voters started coming to the polls; some might be helped by the influx, but others might well be hurt, even run out of business. Entrenched economic interests would assuredly feel the wrath of new voters, especially during economic downturns and as revelations of corporate greed and corruption became known; the widespread populist revolt against Wall Street, banks, and corporate bailouts beginning in the fall of 2008 and continuing for months thereafter are examples of how entrenched economic interests might fear vast expansion of the franchise.

Thus, the politics of easing registration requirements or even making registration automatic are complicated. But let us return to the original point: the political obligation of the state to the voter. Seen in this light, the continued existence of stumbling blocks and unnecessary hurdles in the form of burdensome, often nonsensical rules for registering potential voters is inexcusable and counter to the spirit of democratic elections. This point also applies to third-party registration, which, in the absence of automatic or same-day registration, should be encouraged and facilitated, not discouraged or outlawed and penalized as has recently occurred in a number of jurisdictions.

But the political obligation of the state to the voter extends well beyond voter registration. We have seen that even such seemingly mundane matters as the location and hours of polling stations can create barriers to voters. So do now-outdated rules about voters who show up at the wrong location—whether deliberately, inadvertently, or because they were not informed about location changes. These matters can easily be dealt with. Longer periods of early voting, and especially voting by mail, eliminate the question of polling station location and hours completely. And even if states and counties want to maintain polling stations (although it would seem to be unnecessary if they adopted the Oregon model of voting by mail), linking them electronically (the technology already exists) with centralized voting lists combined with instant, same-day registration can readily accommodate the voter who shows up at the wrong place (including providing the appropriate ballot). It is even possible that some of these changes would save money, or at least would not cause extra expenses for county officials.

So why don't we make these changes, except in very limited places? Again, inertia and vested interests in the form of state and local voting officials—always very reluctant to change their modus operandi—act as a strong countervailing force against even sensible reforms. But even more fundamental is the ongoing belief that voting is a privilege. If voting were viewed as a right, there would be no reason whatsoever to create barriers to accessing the ballot.

And so it goes with the other aspects of the state's political obligation to the voter. Purging of voter lists can and should be done without reference to partisanship, race, geographic location, or anything else; robust efforts to contact potential purged voters should be carried out promptly and fairly, with benefit of the doubt given to the voter, not local or state voting officials. Voter ID rules at the polls could be relaxed, replacing the draconian ones now being imposed, because even as the U.S. Supreme Court noted in *Crawford v. Marion County,* there is no evidence that voter fraud is a problem. Instead of relying on dubious but sexy high-tech voting machines, we could do what other democracies do—use simple, readily understood, readily recountable, cheap paper ballots, at least until the technology of e-voting (especially Internet voting) becomes reliable. Recounts could be systematized using the standard of the voter's intent, with the result that the recount process would disenfranchise fewer people than it does now. (With the use of paper ballots this becomes very easy, much more so than with e-voting, which can easily mask or hide voter intent.) And it is essential to stop disenfranchisement by other means. For example, elections could be made more competitive, and cracking and packing of political, racial, ethnic, or religious minorities eliminated, by taking the districting process out of legislative hands and putting it into the hands of more politically neutral ones, such as Bipartisan Election Commissions, or panels of retired federal judges, thus ending political gerrymandering.

Adopting any of these measures, as well as others, would help satisfy the state's political obligation to voters. At a minimum such measures would remove, or at least alleviate, many of the barriers that many voters encounter when they attempt to cast ballots. As barriers and impediments to voting are removed, elections become more democratic. As it stands now, most states do a poor job of meeting this obligation. As a result, when voters don't "do it right" it can hardly be said to be their fault. It is the state that has failed them, not the other way around.

Besides removing structural barriers to voting, the state has another political obligation to voters: to ensure that their votes matter, that is, that they have meaning. This is not merely a matter of accurately tallying votes, an obligation that is self-evident. It is to remove the problems discussed in Chapter 6, namely the functional disenfranchisement of actual voters who cast ballots that are tallied, but are without significance or meaning in helping to determine the election's final outcome.

The two most obvious steps in meeting this obligation are for the state to crack down on voting fraud, and to create zero tolerance for voter intimidation. Both practices are totally unacceptable, and there is no excuse for their existence in the electoral arena. It is the state's responsibility to root them out and eliminate them entirely. Constant vigilance and monitoring are essential to prevent outbreaks of either. Severe penalties for those occasions when either or both occur need to be promptly meted out.

The other forms of functional disenfranchisement may be more problematic to eliminate, because they lie at the heart of how the game of politics is played, but that is no reason for the state to stand passively aside and do nothing. Creating electoral districts that are competitive so that real electoral contests take place (instead of contests decided even before they take place), and ensuring that neither partisan nor racial/ethnic/religious gerrymandering takes place, are fundamental political obligations of the state that are too often ignored. The only way to attack them is to take the job of drawing of legislative districts—congressional, state legislative, and local—away from legislatures. Ways to do this include nonpartisan commissions charged with drawing lines, establishing panels of retired federal judges to create districts, allowing federal judges sitting en banc to draw them, and so forth. None of these solutions is perfect. It is not possible to fully remove partisan and other political pressures from the drawing of district lines. But to allow the present situation to continue—in which legislatures essentially draw their own lines for their own benefit—is simply to perpetuate a condition in which at least some voters will be functionally deprived of their votes.

The final form of functional disenfranchisement that was discussed in Chapter 6—depriving voters of their votes through recounts and court action—also needs to be addressed by states. That recounts need to be carried out fairly and honestly seems self-evident, and yet we know that they are not always conducted in this manner. States need to ensure the political and legal independence of bodies charged with recounting ballots—whether at the state or local level. The consequences of partisan politics invading recounting procedures are too severe to condone, as we saw in Florida 2000. But we also know that they can be politically insulated, and allowed to do their work unfettered and unpressured, as the 2008–2009 Minnesota recounts showed. One of the best ways to ensure that this happens is for the state to lay out, as explicitly as possible, rules for determining voter intent in the case of disputed ballots during recounts (or even for the initial count, for that matter) *and* to ensure that no other public agencies, including courts, preempt these bodies until they have fully completed their work. There is every reason to think, for example, that local canvassing boards in Florida 2000 could have arrived at just and fair conclusions if they had been left alone to consider ballots free of media, public, legal, and political pressures. But they were not, and so could not do their work.

Legislative specificity about the determination of voter intent and requirements for the independence of recounting agencies might also act as a brake on aggressive court intervention into recount procedures. At a minimum, it would allow reasonable assessment of how closely the recount process conforms to Fourteenth Amendment requirements before stopping it and throwing ballots out the window, thus disenfranchising some voters. It would also be helpful if the American Bar Association issued guidelines about the manner in which voter intent is to be determined, when it is appropriate for courts to intervene in recounts, and how the procedures can be assessed against the Fourteenth Amendment. And finally, there were many lessons for state and federal courts from *Bush v. Gore*. But one of the most important was that trampling on state constitutions and recount procedures in a rush to judgment brought the U.S. Supreme Court no credit.

In the end, it is the state's political responsibility to ensure that each and every vote is accurately recorded, accurately counted, and applied toward determining the outcome. There is simply no excuse for functionally disenfranchising any voter who casts a ballot.

Ethical Obligations

Finally, the state has ethical obligations to the voter. There are two major ones: to ensure that elections are public, not private, events, and to grasp, and act on, the principle that it has the responsibility to do whatever it can to help the voter "do it right," rather than the other way around.

What does ensuring that "elections are public, not private, events" mean? Readers will recall from earlier chapters that too often in this country elections become essentially private affairs, limited to a constrained and carefully regulated universe of voters and (perhaps more importantly) run by and for the benefit of special, usually entrenched, interests. As we have seen, rules that constrain or limit the franchise move the electoral process toward privatization instead of securing it firmly in the public square.

But the issue of privatizing elections expands beyond even those who are threatened by more voters. The real question is, who runs the election machinery? By keeping close reins not just on who gets to vote but also where, when, and how, as well as the manner of recording, tallying, and if necessary recounting ballots, the machinery of elections begins to resemble a closed shop or system in which not all can participate, or can even find out who is running the election, or how.

How does this happen? We can start with the two dominant political parties. They have a firm grip, if not a stranglehold, on how elections are carried out; this is true even in the case of nonpartisan elections, which more often than not simply mask active partisanship occurring behind the scenes. The reason is almost too obvious to have to mention: parties want to control election machinery so that they can influence outcomes, stealing victory if necessary or at least preventing the other party from doing so. Indeed, it is not an unreasonable argument to assert that parties actually want to control elections at least as much as they want to elect candidates.

Can we break the grip that the parties have on the electoral process? Probably not, unless we outlaw them. But what we can do is require that party election machinery operate in the sunshine. We can also establish high-level watchdog groups with the authority to examine how parties run elections, and make public reports on how fairly and honestly they do so.

But the closed shop nature of our elections extends beyond the parties. State and local election officials are among the most intransigent opponents of change in how our elections are conducted. Part of this, of course, is bureaucratic inertia: instituting new election practices is time-consuming and difficult. Part of it is money. County elections offices are notoriously underfunded, especially when it is necessary to buy new or additional voting machines, establish more polling places and keep them open longer, and hire more poll workers to run them. Part of it also is partisanship: state and county election officials are generally registered with a party (especially state officials, who are often appointed in a partisan environment, such as the governor's office), and as hard as many of them try to avoid favoritism, it cannot be said that their political leanings and affiliations have no effect on how elections (and especially recounts) are carried out.

Would it help to require that election officials be nonpartisan by, say prohibiting them from registering with one of the parties? Probably not; as noted before, shoving partisan affiliations into the background is simply a mask, a smokescreen, for allowing partisan activity to go forward outside of public view. Again, a better idea is to demand that election officials carry out *all* of their tasks in full public view, and be overseen by public watchdog agencies or groups.

Some may object that all of this is overstated, that the election officials in their state/county are cooperative, responsive public servants. Perhaps so, and in truth many undoubtedly are. But what cannot be gainsaid is the opposition and foot-dragging many election officials have demonstrated toward changes in election rules and procedures, whether they involve new election machinery, early voting, voting by mail, or something else. A general denial of the necessity for change seems to be the basis for this obstinacy.

Too often state and local voting officials work to protect themselves and their interests, and not necessarily those of the public. How many are we talking about? As we have said elsewhere in the book, if it happens once, it is once too many. When administrative decisions of local voting officials disenfranchise someone, the effect is to substitute their discretion for the legal rights of voters, keep at least some voters from casting ballots, potentially influence the outcome of the electoral contest, and thus move toward privatizing the whole activity. None of this is acceptable in a democracy.

There is a third indicator of the privatization of elections in this country, noted in Chapter 5. It is the unwillingness of the vendors of some e-voting machines to release to the public the source codes for the programs that run the machines. Without this information, there is no way for the public to ascertain how votes have been recorded and tabulated. For example, it is impossible for citizens to determine if some votes are skipped, if some votes seemingly cast for one candidate are actually recorded and tabulated for another, if tallying procedures skip every tenth (or ninth, or twenty-fifth) vote, and so forth.

Opponents will argue, correctly, that not one instance of this kind of corruption has been discovered since the introduction of e-voting, especially touchscreen technology. Let us pass over the obvious flaw in their logic: if the source codes are not released, how would errors be discovered, especially since, until recently, paper trails were not required with touchscreen machines? Instead, let us assume they are right, and the machines are fully accurate, reliable, kosher.

None of this matters. What does matter is that in a democracy the public needs to know how its elections are conducted, including the casting and tabulating of votes. The question in determining the degree of democracy is, how open and aboveboard is the *process?* If the source codes are not available, there is no way to be sure the results are legitimate. Accountability and transparency are synonyms for light, sunshine, accessibility, and information. If anything in the voting process is kept hidden from public view—anything—then accountability and transparency have been compromised, perhaps fatally. When this happens, voters and the public instead must *assume* that the machines are accurate; theirs is an act of faith. Democratic elections do not rest on faith; they rest on sunshine peeking into dark corners, revealing whatever is there, giving information to the public. Without transparency, the notion of a democratic election becomes suspect.

There is also the argument that vendors have a commercial interest in protecting their source codes. Some may well be patented. This is not a trivial matter. Vendors have a right to be paid for the use of their equipment, even to make a reasonable profit. And patents need to be protected, and respected.

Of course, if this country were to move in the direction advocated in Chapter 5—namely, go back to the future and use simple paper ballots—the problem of private vendors and source code patents disappears completely. Elections would be much more public than they are now because there would be no opportunity for private vendor involvement, except possibly to sell paper to election officials and contract for the printing of ballots.

But the author is under no illusions that the public will demand a return to simple paper ballots. And it is unlikely that any public officials, including election officials, would support the idea—not after making such huge monetary investments in sophisticated, expensive voting gadgetry.

So the task becomes one of protecting private vendors and their patents while ensuring that they serve the public interest, not their own. This is clearly a balancing act. But too much of the "balance" has favored the private vendor. The public must be equally protected, and respected. This can and should be done during state certification processes, when officials require that the machines and accompanying software demonstrate their accuracy and fairness. But this requires that the certification process be carried out in a rigorous, responsible, publicly visible way. Of course, public officials have also to assure vendors that they will not violate the patents and copyrights with which they have been entrusted. But public officials must do more than this. There are too many reports in which the certification process has been little more than a wink and a wave, with rigorous standards not applied. Failure to apply standards makes the process a charade, and means that the accuracy and fairness of voting machinery will be based on faith, not empirics. Officials must oversee the source codes with rigor and demonstrate that the soft- and hardware are fair and accurate. If this requires the creation of nonpartisan boards to ensure that the public as well as the vendors are protected, then this is a cost we must be willing to pay.

In the end, the state's ethical obligation to voters is to do whatever it can to ensure that elections are firmly grounded in the public square. This is an affirmative duty. State and local election officials—indeed, the public at large—have constantly to monitor elections rules to ensure their fairness and equity, and that they do not discriminate. They have an affirmative duty to root out any elections practices that might allow even the smallest feature of running elections to become the private domain of an interest—even if that interest is a public agency. Convenience, bureaucratic inertia, partisanship, economic clout, tradition—none of this matters. All that matters is that elections be fully and totally public. To the degree they are not, they are not democratic.

Some would say the state has no greater ethical obligation to voters than to implement fair, honest, and open procedures for carrying out elections. But it does. Even more so, it has the obligation to shoulder the *responsibility* of doing them right, that is, in the most democratic way possible. The key word in the previous sentence is responsibility. It is the state's ethical job to do it right, and the onus should be on the state to maximize the voters' chances of doing their part right. The onus should *not* be on the individual voter to hope he or she "did it right." Indeed, central to the argument of this book is that unless and until we get past the idea that it is solely the voters' responsibility to do it right, we will never move closer to fully democratic elections.

What Is to Be Done?

When Vladimir Ilyich Lenin published a pamphlet called "What Is To Be Done?" in 1902, he called for the formation of a revolutionary political party of workers that would replace the czarist regime in Russia. The present work does not call for a new revolutionary political party. But it does call for thinking about voting rights in new, even revolutionary ways.

For Americans, the most revolutionary step would be to stop thinking of voting as a privilege. It has to be conceived as a right, because once it is, most of the blockades that we set up to keep people from voting will, like the walls of Jericho, come tumbling down. Voting, as I have repeatedly noted, already *is* a right. The problem is that because it is not constitutionally guaranteed but rather defined legislatively, too many people don't see it for what it really is. Somehow it doesn't rise to First Amendment status, or to the status of other constitutionally guaranteed rights, and so can be treated differently than, say, the right of assembly or trial by jury.

In truth, the situation is probably worse than this. If voting is not really seen as a right—even a second-rate right—then it can be extended and withdrawn at will, depending on the wishes of those in power. We have seen repeatedly that this is exactly what happens.

How, then, to change this? How to make Americans think of the right to vote as having the same high status, the same gravitas, as the right to freedom of the press, or *habeas corpus?*

Clearly, change is not going to happen overnight. Thinking of voting as a privilege and not as a right, as we saw in Chapter 2, antedates the founding of our nation. Deeply held customs and beliefs such as these are slow to disappear. But I propose two steps that could be taken which, over time (it might take more than one generation) will change people's perceptions of voting as a privilege and help them feel more comfortable with the idea that it is a basic right.

The first is to pass a constitutional amendment that conveys, absolutely and without exception, the right to vote for Americans. Which Americans? As many as possible. This includes the marginalized groups discussed in Chapter 3. The amendment should be designed for inclusion, not exclusion. How to do this without creating a lengthy amendment that, in its wordiness, might make things worse rather than better? By insisting that the language of the amendment apply universally. The assumption behind the amendment would be that everyone sixteen or older could vote. Such an amendment would offer guarantees that even the Voting Rights Act cannot, because state law (including state laws disenfranchising portions of the population) would have to give way before its demand for universality. In the light of such an amendment, states wishing to limit the franchise would have to demonstrate in federal court what compelling state interest forced them to seek to exclude certain categories of potential voters, whether they are felons, noncitizens, the physically challenged and mentally incapacitated, language minorities, those between sixteen and eighteen years of age, the homeless—and to defend that their choices are narrowly tailored.

In other words, the burden of proof would be on states to show why a certain voter, or groups of voters, should not hold the franchise. This is where the burden of proof should rest, unlike the situation today.

What would be the consequences of such an amendment? At the macro level, most of the barriers to voting would disintegrate, as it would be difficult for states to demonstrate to federal judges why some individuals and groups should have the franchise but others not. Equal protection as spelled out in the Fourteenth Amendment would demand exactly that—equal protection. Any deviation would require a rigorous application of the strict scrutiny test, that is, demonstration of a compelling state interest in depriving a voter or bloc of voters of the right to vote, narrowly tailored. This would stand in stark contrast to the situation today, in which the state can broadly disenfranchise virtually any individual or group it so chooses, with virtually no rationale for doing so required.

At the micro level, many of the rules and procedures that cause voters to be disqualified would have to be sharply modified or eliminated. For example, complex or incomprehensible registration practices would disappear, as they would be superseded either by simplified, nationally mandated forms or, better yet, same-day registration. Or no registration at all. Voters showing up at polls would not have to worry that they had been purged and not notified; nor would eleventh-hour changes in polling station locations or hours be tolerated. Perhaps most importantly, individuals would not have to meet rigid, even impossible standards to prove their identity; instead, the state would have to prove that they are phonies or imposters. Lengthy early voting periods or vote-by-mail ballots would lessen the burden on voters still further, and move voting procedures closer to Fourteenth Amendment requirements.

But why is such a proposed amendment necessary? Does not the Voting Rights Act provide the necessary guarantees? The answer is, apparently not. If it did, there would be no need for this book, and no need for a constitutional amendment. The truth, of course, is that an amendment still has to be enforced or it is just empty words. But it is also true that in the public's consciousness an amendment carries greater weight, greater stature, than a law. If nothing else, the presence of a voting rights amendment would loom over state legislators, voting officials, and local voting registrars like a pillar of fire,[15] leading them in the right direction and away from impulses they may have to revert to former practices of placing stumbling blocks in front of voters.

And perhaps among the public at large the presence of a voting rights amendment would serve as a psychological prop, a reminder that the right to vote is serious business. It is not like getting a driver's license or a zoning exemption, but rather it constitutes a major part of our civic obligation and has to be treated as a funda-mental constitutional right in the same way as other such rights. Yes, this change in perception will require time. But it is a necessary step, because it is clear that if we do not take it, we will not change our attitude toward voting rights and will continue instead on our present course, which, judging from the past few years, means limiting, qualifying, and decreasing these rights. This is hardly in the spirit of democratic governance that so many Americans claim they want.

There is, of course, one additional issue that the passage of a voting rights amendment raises: conflict with the Tenth Amendment. The clash between federally mandated voting standards and the traditional states-rights view that voting is the purview of states would have to be resolved by the U.S. Supreme Court. And the Court's interpretation of that conflict might vary from time to time, just as its view of states' rights has been anything but linear and consistent throughout its history. Nonetheless, this is a risk worth taking. It would be a mistake not to put a voting rights amendment on the books and to rely instead either on incremental, tortoise-like imposition of voting rights requirements and standards, or on states to design more flexible and reasonable voting rules. Neither of these is acceptable; the first will still leave too many voters disenfranchised for too long a time, and the latter would essentially deny and ignore the often repressive history of too many states as they created rules for voter qualification, registration, voting, and counting.

A second step that we as a nation might take to reinforce voting as a right would be to demand that our political leaders become advocates for voting rights for all. The most important group of political leaders to whom this applies is political executives: presidents, governors, even mayors. As noted in Chapter 1, political executives have, at particular times and places, strongly influenced the course of voting rights in this country—but not always positively so. But how can this task be accomplished? At present there are many political leaders who would not lift a finger to extend the franchise and make voting easier. Nor is it clear that political winds currently blowing are favorable to increased voting rights.[16]

Without letting governors, mayors, secretaries of state, other state officials involved with voting procedures (including attorneys general), and local supervisors of elections off the hook, it is probably presidents and presidential candidates who will have to do the heavy lifting. The reason is that the presidency is the focal point for all federal issues, including voting rights. No other office has the capacity to mobilize public opinion, to lead and shape and mold it, and to promote changes in policy when needed. And presidents occupy a unique position to remind us of our responsibilities, and our rights.

But presidents rarely push policy changes in areas that have low public visibility and salience. In Chapter 1, we saw that voting rights often is scarcely on the public's radar screen. An examination of post–World War II presidents reveals that few paid the issue any attention. Lyndon Johnson was probably the only president who cared passionately about voting rights and pushed it strongly (in the form of the 1964 Civil Rights Act and 1965 Voting Rights Act). Both Jimmy Carter and Bill Clinton were favorably disposed, but neither pushed voting rights strongly. Even Barack Obama, at least during his campaign and first months in office, did not rank voting rights as a high-priority item. Among Republican presidents, all have been cool at best toward voting rights. Dwight Eisenhower did sign the Civil Rights Acts of 1957 and 1960, both of which had voting rights components, but he was never enthusiastic about either bill. Ronald Reagan had to be persuaded to sign the renewal and extension of the Voting Rights Act in 1982. And as noted in Chapter 1, the forty-third president, George W. Bush, actively sought to undermine voting rights through his Department of Justice.

Thus, the record of presidential leadership on voting rights is at best mixed, and that may be too positive a characterization. But the past is not always prologue, and it is possible that in the future, presidential candidates and occupants of the White House will push voting rights more strongly than in the past. Certain things need to happen if this is to come about:

1. The rise of a "new politics" as advocated by President Obama, in which traditional rhetoric and partisan policies begin to morph into less rigid and ideologically defined positions, would provide room in the political landscape for voting rights, something that has not occurred in more than twenty-five years. New rhetoric, new vocabularies, new forms of political discourse, such as the Obama administration is pushing, would have to replace the void left by the politics of the last twenty-five-plus years and perhaps create opportunities for voting rights to secure a prominent position in the American political agenda.

2. A reaction against recent draconian changes in state voting rights laws sets in. This is especially likely to happen as the public becomes aware of just how much stricter voter ID requirements actually disenfranchise major portions of the population. Public outcry over this would cause politicians at all levels, including presidents, to sit up and take notice.

3. Civil and voting rights advocates and groups regain the central position in political arenas that they had achieved from the late 1950s through the late 1960s. During the heady days of the active phase of the civil rights movement, voting and other civil rights issues occupied prominent positions on national, and even state and local, political agendas. It will not be easy for them to regain this stature. Advocacy groups such as the American Civil Liberties Union, People for the American Way, Lawyers for Justice Under Law, the Brennan Center for Justice, and others will have to ratchet up their efforts to show the extent of voting rights erosion and deterioration in this country. It would be helpful if more moderate, mainstream groups—such as chambers of commerce, labor unions, and religious and civic organizations—would include voting rights on their active political agendas. Even more helpful would be the emergence of another figure of the prestige and gravitas of Dr. Martin Luther King, Jr., who could reframe voting rights in terms of ethical issues and define the high moral ground on which he or she could lead public discussion of them.

4. Presidential candidates and presidents themselves have to be pushed by advocacy groups, journalists, opinion leaders, and other political figures at all levels to define their positions on voting rights and defend them publicly and repeatedly. How often are presidential candidates asked during campaign stops about voting rights? How often in recent decades have presidents, during news conferences, TV and press interviews, town hall meetings, and other public events been asked about—pushed on—civil and voting rights? When will the political parties place in their quadrennial platforms meaningful planks reaffirming voting rights and commitment to their expansion, instead of merely repeating their commitment to the status quo?

There are no guarantees in any of this, of course. Presidents cannot be made to speak about voting rights if they don't want to. And some presidents, like George W. Bush, might actually oppose the expansion of voting rights. And yet it seems clear that unless and until they come forward and discuss their view of voting as a basic right, very little change in the extent of voting rights in this country will occur. In order for real movement in extending voting rights to occur, in order for the voting-as-privilege nostrum to atrophy, presidents have to become energizers, the little engines that could. Otherwise, our past and present paths will be our future, and we will continue our policies of disenfranchisement.

Creating Our Future

In the end, it is the public who will decide what happens to voting rights. The question posed in the title of this chapter was deliberately chosen. It is not enough to ask, Can we do better? Of course we can. The real question is, Do we *want* to do better? Do we want to create a future that improves our election system, makes voting easier and more accessible to more people, makes voting more reliable and accurate, or do we want to just keep stumbling along the way we have? That we can do better is self-evident: this book is full of suggestions on how to improve our elections and make voting better. But the public has to want this to happen. There is nothing inevitable about the progress of voting rights. In spite of quantities of readily available data on the degree of voter disenfranchisement, where is the evidence that the public cares? Of the four scenarios listed above that might lead to improved voting rights, what is the chance of any one of them happening, let alone all of them? Where is the groundswell of public sentiment favoring a constitutional amendment that would guarantee voting as a right, once and for all?

Presidents, as has often been noted, lead from the rear as much as from the front. So do other political figures, whether executive, legislative, or even judicial. Politicians at any level will rarely get out in front of an issue if they do not perceive some benefit for doing so. Unless and until they sense a public desire to enhance voting rights in this country, no change is likely.

And yet the stakes are huge. At the most fundamental level, the question of who gets to vote, and whether the vote has any real meaning, defines the degree to which elections are publicly grounded and democratic or merely bear the trappings and appearance of such. If Americans really believe their own rhetoric, and what they have been taught since elementary school—namely, that voting is a duty and an obligation—then we have to take serious steps, such as have been outlined in this book and summarized in this chapter, to remove hurdles and barriers from those who wish to exercise their franchise. It is time to change our present policy of disenfranchising potential voters, actually and functionally, to one that enfranchises as many potential voters as possible, and to accommodate them in as many ways as the imagination can conjure up in order to expedite their ability to vote. Truly democratic elections demand nothing less.

To return to a point made earlier in the book, there is nothing inevitable about leaving many groups of Americans aside when it is time to vote. As Jonathan Kozol has pointed out about inequalities in education, they exist because of decisions that we, as a nation, make (or don't make) about who gets what kind of schooling. The same is true in voting rights: if we want more people to be able to vote, steps are available to make this happen. We need to take them.

On the other hand, there is nothing inevitable about making the franchise more universal, or making voting easier and more accessible. It will require a serious commitment by all Americans, and especially elected leaders, to bring this about. The question is, do we want to?

Notes

1. We are reminded at this point of the muttered remark of Florida's Governor Jeb Bush in 2002, after new voting technologies introduced into the state were used for the first time, "Why can't Democrats vote right?" The remark was interpreted in the media as referring to African Americans in Miami-Dade and Broward counties, where numerous voting errors took place.

2. Steven F. Lawson, *Black Ballots: Voting Rights in the South 1944–1969* (New York: Columbia University Press, 1976).

3. Federal Elections Commission Budget Request, 2009, available at www.fec.gov/pages/budget/fy2009/FY_2009_OMB_Budget-FA.pdf, accessed July 1, 2009.

4. "2009–2010 All Funds Financial Plan," non-personal service, New York State Budget, 2009–2010 Enacted Budget Financial Plan, p. 115, available at www.budget.state.ny.us/budgetFP/2009–10EnactedBudget-FINAL.pdf, accessed July 1, 2009.

5. Projections of BCC Services, "The Pet Industry," January 2001, available at www.bccresearch.com/report/FOD007G.html, accessed July 1, 2009.

6. *Brown v. Board of Education,* 347 U.S. 483 (1954).

7. *Baker v. Carr,* 369 U.S.186 (1962); *Wesberry v. Sanders,* 376 U.S. 1 (1964).

8. *Bush v. Gore,* 538 U.S. 98 (2000).

9. A summary and discussion of Professor Amar's analysis of *Bush v. Gore* given at the Levin College of Law, University of Florida, can be found at Florida Law Online, March 20, 2009, available at www.law.ufl.edu/flalawonline/2009/03302009/dunwody.shtml, accessed July 13, 2009.

10. The 5–4 decision that shut down the recounts and handed the White House to Governor Bush unleashed a firestorm of legal outrage. More than 670 law professors signed a statement indicating that they believed the Court had decided the case incorrectly, in some cases suggesting that politics rather than legal reasoning pushed the Court to decide as it did.

11. *Crawford et al. v. Marion County Election Board et al.* (2008).

12. As any number of legal scholars have noted, it is not completely clear that any of the ways Florida's sixty-seven counties implemented the voter intent standard actually violated the Fourteenth Amendment. The Court said they did, but presented no real proof that they had; asserting the point does not make it so.

13. It is of interest that in 2007–2008, as the Obama campaign actively registered droves of new voters (particularly young voters, college students, and various minority groups), not only did Republicans complain and often raise challenges once the primaries were over, but so did many old-guard Democrats (some of whom were Obama's opponents) because they did not know who they were getting or what impact these new voters would have on the party.

14. In recent years, the most rapid growth in voter registration has been among unaffiliateds and independents.

15. The metaphor, of course, comes from Taylor Branch's magisterial *Parting the Waters,* in which he compares the late Dr. Martin Luther King, Jr., to a pillar of fire as he led all Americans—not just African Americans—toward more and deeper civil rights, including voting rights. There is every reason to think that Dr. King would have favored a voting rights amendment such as the one proposed here.

16. To cite but one example, in its regular legislative session during the spring, 2009, the Florida House of Representatives considered a truly draconian bill, one that would have, among other things, sharply limited the types of voter ID documents acceptable at polling stations. For example, many community centers serving elders and retirement communities provide members and residents with an ID that they can use for accessing facilities. In the past, these have been acceptable forms of ID at the polls. Under the proposed legislation, these would no longer have been valid, which would have made voting for many seniors highly problematic if not impossible. The Senate was cool to the bill, civil and voting rights groups strongly opposed it, Republican Governor Charlie Crist said he would veto if it passed, and House leaders eventually withdrew it, but indicated they would put it forward again next year.

Index

Italic page references indicate tables.

Estonia, 129–130
Ethical responsibilities in voting,
    178–181
Eulau, Heinz, 6
European Convention on Human
    Rights, 54
European Union, 57
Evers, Medgar, 39

Failure to recognize voting rights,
    10–11
Fairness issue, 132–133, 168
Felons, alleged and convicted, 19,
    52–56
Fifteenth Amendment, 7, 34–37,
    41–42, 81
50 foot rule, 14
First Amendment, 10, 56
Florida
  absentee ballots in, 101
  African American and voting system
      in, 88, 122
  butterfly vote in, 115
  Democratic Party in, 151
  Duval County, 115
  early voting in, 98
  election of 1876 and, 35, 145
  election of 2000 and, 88, 120–124,
      146, 154–156, 172–173, 177
  election of 2006 and, 128
  election of 2008 and, 13–14, 22–23
  felon voters in, 53
  ID cards and, 104
  intimidation practices and, 159
  language minority voters in, 69
  Palm Beach County, 115
  physically impaired voters in, 62
  presidential election of 2000 and, 22
  purging voters in, 102–103
  recounts and, 153–154
  reform in voting system of, 124
  registration of voters in, 82, 85–86,
      88, 151

Florida *(continued)*
  residency requirement and, 89
  third-party registration in, 93
  "Florida syndrome," 88
Foner, Eric, 32
Force bill, 35–36
Fourteenth Amendment
  Breedlove v. Suttles and, 37
  Brown v. Board of Education and,
      169
  Bush v. Gore and, 6, 173
  constitutional obligations in voting
      and, 169–170
  equal rights struggle and, 7–8
  noncitizens and, 56
  poll taxes and, 37
  qualifying for voting and, 81
  ratification of, 34
  Reconstruction era and, 34, 41
  recounts and, 177–178
  U.S. v Cruikshank and, 36
  voting and, 6, 169–170
  women's suffrage movement and,
      41–42
France, 54
Franken, Al, 22, 155
Fraud, voter, 8–9, 93, 101, 104,
    143–146, 176
"Freedom Summer," 39

Gaming the system
  courts, 151–157
  districting, 148–151
  fraud, 8–9, 93, 101, 104, 143–146,
      176
  incumbency advantage, 146–148
  intimidation practices, 157–160,
      176
  overview, 139, 141–143, 160–161
  recounts, 151–157
GAO, 62
Gender restrictions on voting, 30–32,
    40–45

About the Author

Richard K. Scher received his Ph.D. from Columbia University. He has been a member of the department of political science, University of Florida, since 1979. He served as a Visiting Fulbright Scholar, John Marshall Distinguished Chair of American Government, Hungary, from 2002 to 2003. He has also been a Visiting Professor of Political Science at the Central European University, Budapest (2006), and Bogazici University, Istanbul (2007). He has lectured at universities in Leipzig, Chemnitz, and Dresden in Germany, and Sarajevo (Bosnia). Professor Scher is a specialist in voting and civil rights, and the politics of political campaigns. He also is frequently consulted by print and electronic media on political issues, and has served as an expert witness in several voting rights trials in federal court, always on the side of the angels.